AF349107

ALEKSANDAR DENIĆ

Exposition Coloniale

Beograd | Belgrade, 2024

If from great nature's or our own abyss
Of thought we could but snatch a certainty,
Perhaps mankind might find the path they miss—
But then 't would spoil much good philosophy.
One system eats another up, and this
Much as old Saturn ate his progeny;
For when his pious consort gave him stones
In lieu of sons, of these he made no bones

(George Gordon Byron – Don Juan)

The exhibition title *Exposition Coloniale* instantly sheds light on the ramifications of the colonial era. This historical context sets the stage for Denić's exploration of colonialist legacy and the persisting impact of cultural and ethnic stratification. His theatrical artistic conceptions use the power of visual storytelling through symbolic and semantic constructs to tackle complex and delicate issues and themes. By employing Brecht's distancing effect (V-effect) to create a picture of reality rather than reality itself, he challenges viewers to think critically about power dynamics, consumerism, and the multiplied bitter realities of history. Instead of simply criticizing and provoking thought, he also demands empathy and attentiveness. In today's society, notions of alienation, division and control remain relevant, not just in politics and power accumulation, but also in the realm of fundamental human values and principles.

The show is staged at the Serbian national pavilion, which features a monumental inscription *Jugoslavia* on the façade, a territory that geopolitically disintegrated as a result of hostilities that swept the region in the 1990s. The Pavilion, located in the right corner of the Giardini on the island of Sant 'Elena, was originally designed by Brenno Del Guidice in 1938 and exemplifies the refinement of Italian Novecento architecture. Architecture is, in this case, an emotional statement, demonstrating that it is more than just form and function, since it testifies to the social and cultural context in which it exists. As a result, the exhibition space becomes not only a representative structure, but also a living monument to a fractured country and a shattered identity. When entering the Serbian pavilion, one is immediately struck by the ambiguous identity of the space itself. In this zone of discomfiting meditative encounter, Denić intervenes as a foreigner himself – being an artist who is professionally integrated into Germany and German-speaking areas.

WILD
TURKEY
BOURBON
WHISKEY
BANANIA
CINEBANA
West
BP
Coca-Cola

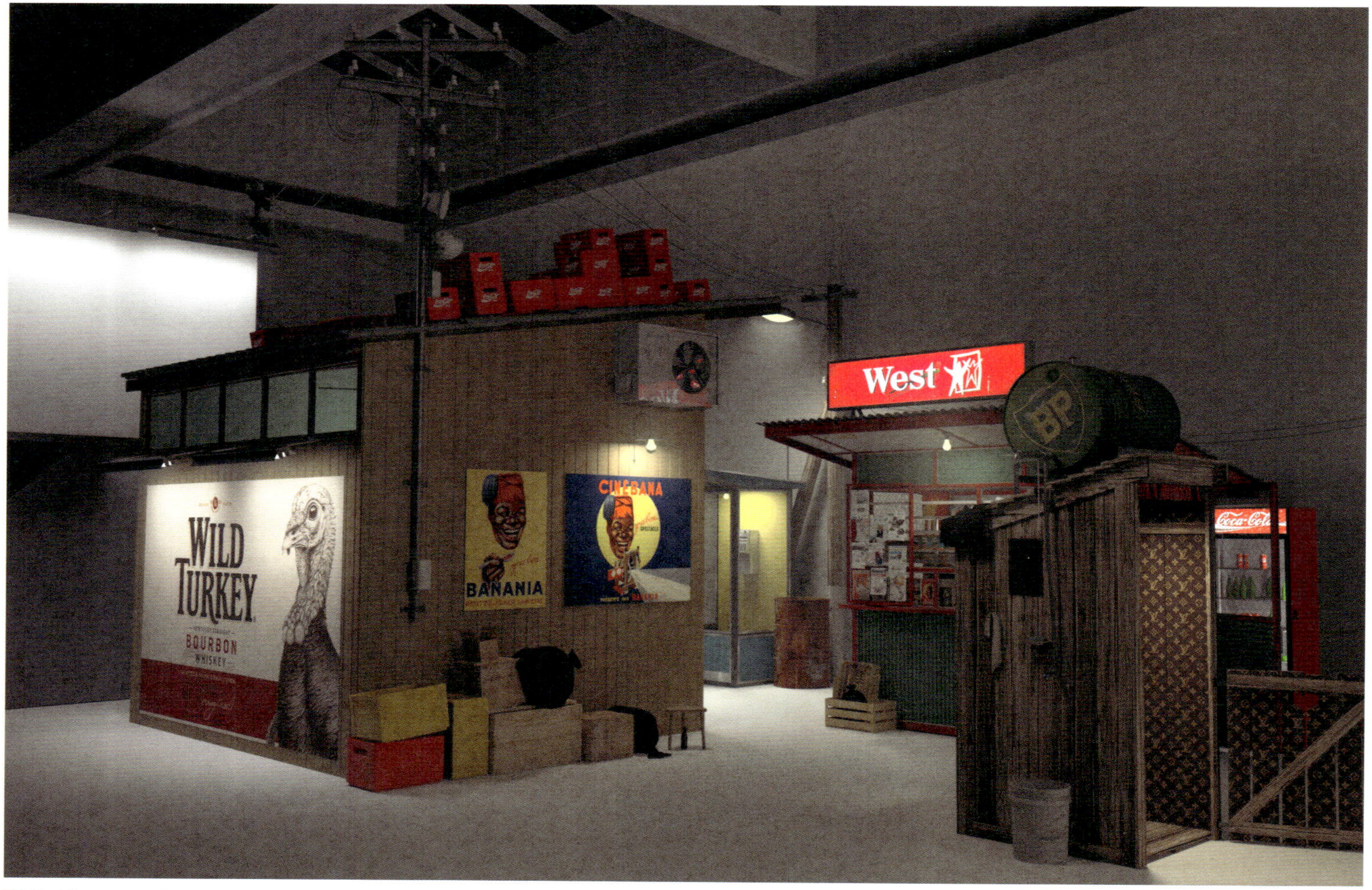

3D Model

Ksenija Samardžija

In any case, along with the official history of memory, there exists the official history of remembrance as its complement and its criticism. Because history is more than just what happened to states, nations, and their institutions; it is also how these events have been reflected and expressed in the souls and spirits of individuals: from being something external, history becomes internal, events become experiences, and history becomes biography

Đuro Šušnjić

Denić's arrangements allow for a complex dialogue between elements-symbols resulting in a visually appealing and conceptually challenging architectural situation. The inclination to manipulate spatial aspects generates tension not only from physical presence, but also from the interaction between the spectator and the manifold narrative, while music from various sources, sound, light, heating systems and other sensory elements add to the complexity and further blur and disrupt the boundaries between the physical and the emotional. The result is a vibrant and appealing spatial experience that relies on realistic components, which have been either originally constructed or completely reinterpreted. In his work, Denić uses conventional patterns to convey familiar locations, rather than depicting particular places or periods. His ability to create a dialogue between what is, the real and the surreal, monumental yet fragile and intimate in

detail, gives us an unsettling feeling, similar to déjà vu (memory anomaly) or a powerful vivid memory that haunts us. Creating an experience through discomfort or tension is closely tied to Heiner Müller's theory about the constant need to question the system of thought and values through art's capacity to make reality impossible.

By linearly moving through time in both directions, merging historical facts with current, recognizable elements, Denić deprives the moment of any meaning. The present is the fission of the past, which perpetually decomposes, dissolves and never leaves us. By accumulating time, he creates a distinctive intensity of a timeless content and place. He is, in fact, a tyrant of space. It is the mercy and cruelty of earthquakes that break the wings of butterflies, shaping in time a radically different vision of the world. The arena of life strives for orderliness, but in this case this privilege is used as a "dangerous situation" that grants access to the realm of accumulated objects, which by entering the zone of artwork, Denić manipulates transforming the space into a dynamic eerie being. This reversal is monopolistic, but it is justified and premeditated as a precondition to put up "props" which are, in fact, the artist's weapons. This is precisely what Paul

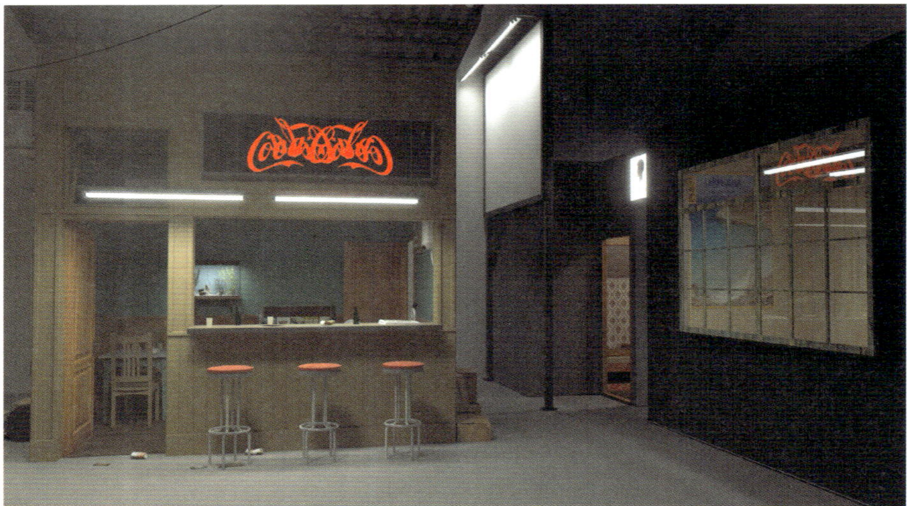

3D Model

Valéry spoke of: communicating emotions without becoming bored with the process. The author's driving idea throughout the project is to use "place" in such a way that the Pavilion becomes a heterotopia, as described by Michel Foucault, so that the associativity of the space packed with evocative materials alters the boundaries of viewers' expectations.

Aesthetic phenomena, an amalgam of images, gather experiences through numerous segments, becoming a vortex – a stage in which perceptual patterns are erased to the point where the senses are completely overwhelmed. What unfolds before the visitor is a postmodern cabinet of curiosities (Wunderkammer) in which one is enthralled by the abundance and diversity of content (video, sound, installation). Within these monumental structures borrowed from the repertoire of real circumstances and transit locations, such as a restaurant/kiosk, public bath, hotel room, phone booth, street photo booth, the uncertainty of drama evolves. Denić deconstructs the arena of life into a potential labyrinth of desires; he acts like a painter of space, who neither prevents nor abuses any of its substances, while building a sort of anarchistic "timeless" contemporaneity.

As always in such situations, the observer might expect too much, but in this case, that's exactly what is in front of his eyes: an arrangement that is not only replete with accumulation of objects and situations, but they also attain their higher form within the space. His spatial sets are easily relatable to Patrice Pavis' definition of the stage space, which has the property of a sign because it constantly oscillates between the concretely visible space of the signifier and the exterior space of the signified to which the viewer must abstractly relate in order for it to function. All these objects, are infused with the anxiety of the society in which they exist. They act as social memorabilia, capturing the essence of human habitation while reflecting the lost sensibility and intimacy of our interactions with them. The artist, with a lengthy gaze, delves into undesired situations and the solitude of abandonment.

Aesthetic integrity is constituted from meaningfully related elements forming a semiotic system that decodes consumer society and the values it generates. Concerned with representation rather than the actual image of reality, Denić insists on its undeniable physical endurance. Similarly, W.J.T. Mitchell in *What Do*

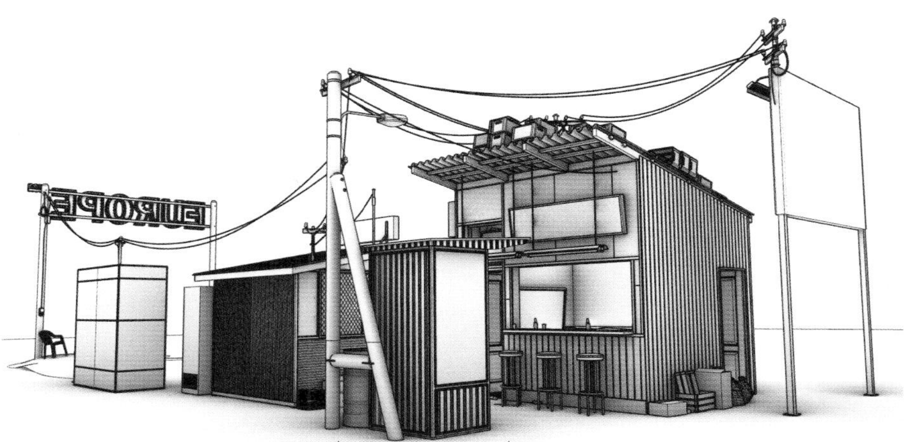

Sketch | Skica

Pictures Want? points out that the symmetry between iconoclasm and idolatry explains how it is possible for acts of 'creative destruction' (spectacular annihilation or disfigurement) to create 'secondary images' that are in their way forms of idolatry just as potent as the primary idols they seek to replace. Without doubt, Denić can be perceived as more than just a painter and sculptor, and possibly, least of all a set designer. Driven by Philip Gaston's axiom, I paint what I want to see, and with the spatial wisdom of Piero della Francesca and transformation of Goethe's thoughts, he acts as the creator of love and hate – Eros and Thanatos— shaping the content not only to trigger emotional reaction, but also to materialize the experience into a monumental heritage of horror, sadness, and nothingness. Yet, at times, he grants us a more beautiful, better world that unfolds and flickers before our eyes. When we examine the spatial condition we encounter, we see how it is disrupted by human presence/absence; it is an environment akin to a "wabet" (pure place, place of purification) in which a situation similar to building a collage occurs. The tavern is messy, the kitchen area full of dishes. The presence of a large mirror over the table covered with a plastic tablecloth adds to the discomfort, which is only heightened by the mirror's repeated use as a motif in each subsequent room. The uniqueness of the fact does not prevent the universality of the lesson learned from it, as Tzvetan Todorov puts it in his *The use of memory.* An aquarium is placed on a wall-mounted shelf: the absence of life in it intensifies the sense of emptiness or despair. The landscape is enhanced by the presence of a diver next to an open treasure chest painted blue with yellow star-shaped rivets. The air conditioner runs continuously, infusing the area with a persistent, mechanical presence while simultaneously cooling the interior of the space and heating it on the outside. The jukebox offers a selection of hits such as Toto Cutugno's "Insieme" from 1992, Kraftwerk's "Trans Europe Express", R.E.M.'s "Radio Free Europe", Suede's "Europe is Our Playground", or Roxy Music's "A Song for Europe". On the tavern's right external wall, there is a billboard advertising a chocolate drink for children called Banania. The back wall of the tavern features an advertisement for Wild Turkey whiskey. In this case, enumerations are not merely an inventory list, though they may resemble it, but rather baits or masterfully woven capillary network of everyday spaces-desires

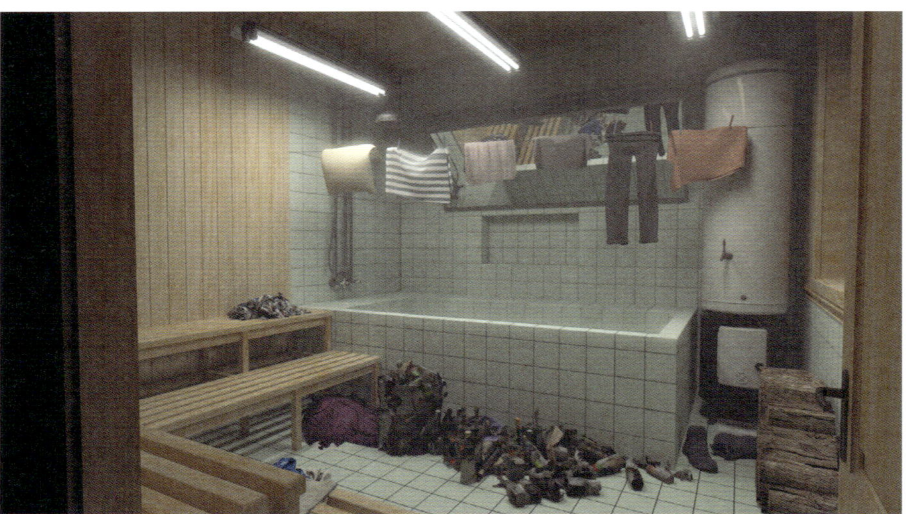

3D Model

or pleasures-discomforts-fantasies-wishes.
We see a public bathroom with a large pool — a
bathtub. Water flows continually from the shower.
The floor, benches and bathtub are littered with
discarded everyday "usefully useless" objects
such as shirts, tracksuits and sneakers. Steam
and smoke are billowing. A big poster resembling
an iconostasis hangs on the wall, recommending
a family holiday that includes riding a rubber
banana on Mediterranean beaches. The backyard
toilet is made of wooden boards in a coffin-like
design. On the roof, an old British Petroleum
oil barrel acts as a toilet tank, connected like a
catheter to the floor. The scene transitions from
a funeral to a wedding and back. The inside of
the toilet is covered with Louis Vuitton pattern
wallpaper. The hotel room is neglected, like an
attic filled with whispers (genre-scene-noir).
The color brown, like the mud of anti-secession,
dominates the scene. Rain rumbles ceaselessly
but impotently. Coca-Cola adverts are displayed
on the wall-mounted television, celebrating
false reasons for fulfilled life and happiness. A
metal kiosk serving as a little grocery shop is
a compact area with two bunk beds, secluded
from life. The mattresses have worn out like an
arabesque of an old wall. Instead of bedding,

there are newspaper pages with yellowed urine
patina (promoting special price items and prize
contests) reeking of hopelessness. Several
boxes of moist cigarettes lay on the shelves in
the window display and along the back wall. The
kiosk roof features an illuminated advertising
sign for the cigarette brand WEST that reads:
No choice! A telephone booth leans against a
street lamppost. The receiver has been ripped
out, but the phone continues to ring. Porn ads are
plastered all over — memento mori. Only a few
photographs of footballers (the most expensive
transfers) are haphazardly glued on the front door,
like an illness or insult. All of this is shrouded in
a single sound: the white noise of a screen that
rustles ceaselessly. The aforementioned objects
are primarily concentrated on the pavilion's left
side. On the opposite side, mounted on two pillars,
an illuminated sign/advertisement "EUROPE™"
faces the wall, acting as a warning. As the light
reflects off the wall, their characters are reversed
so that their shadow reads backward. Below
the sign are two Chinese-made white plastic
chairs that symbolize abandoned affluence.
After taking in the whole scene, it is impossible
to avoid the impression that we are faced with
something that could be defined as a delicate

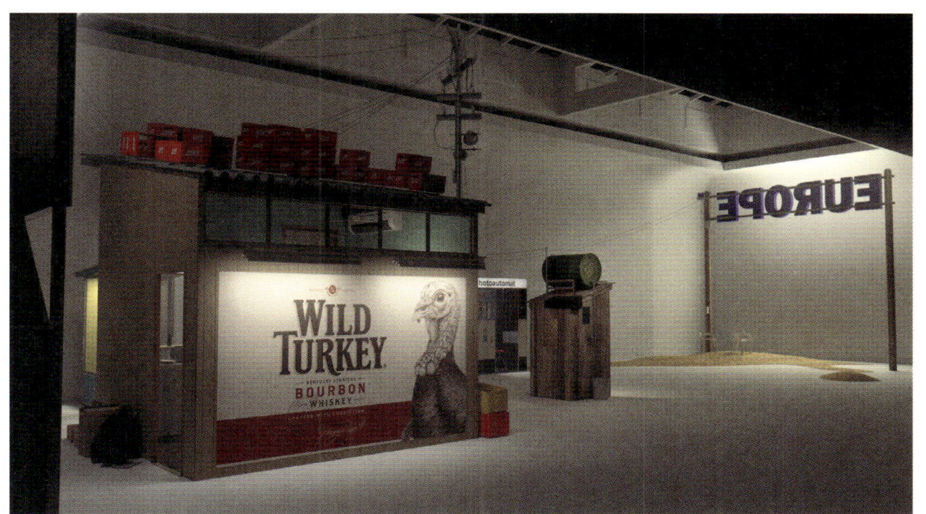

3D Model

situation of an actual life, that not only captures the attention of the sensory world it is exiled to, but also addresses us directly in the language of contemporary thought and aesthetics. On the edge of contemporaneity, we are pushed to read the installation's wise articulation and observe the process expressed by the author's meta-language, masterfully used in his super-narrative manipulation of space. If we were to consciously misuse Benjamin's criticism that "there is no document of culture which is not at the same time a document of barbarism" and consider it as a warning a logical question emerges over a personal interpretation of these spaces' transition into a pseudo-catastrophe. Invoking Alessandro Baricco's "new barbarians", these spaces with temporary residence in a temporary paradise of cynicism and the autoimmune survival of "trade paradise" stare at the abyss of their own healing. One of the re-evaluations of the edge of contemporaneity, or a possible imaginarium within the pavilion, is mutation of objects and their deconstruction. Drawing on ritual, social, cultural-political and philosophical totems, the artist creates and incorporates a living organism and its menagerie into the space. The process is precisely what renders this project complete: in

addition to the sensory shaping of voices, their torsions through emotional receptors and a sense of belonging in this overwhelming scenery, this work is a temple of phantoms and hallucinations, an intuitive miracle that engages the viewer to the point where one is completely dislocated, exorcised to the last atom, to the last detail of the whole, placed in an order serving as reality's analogy, as opposed to its exact replica.

Sketch | Skica

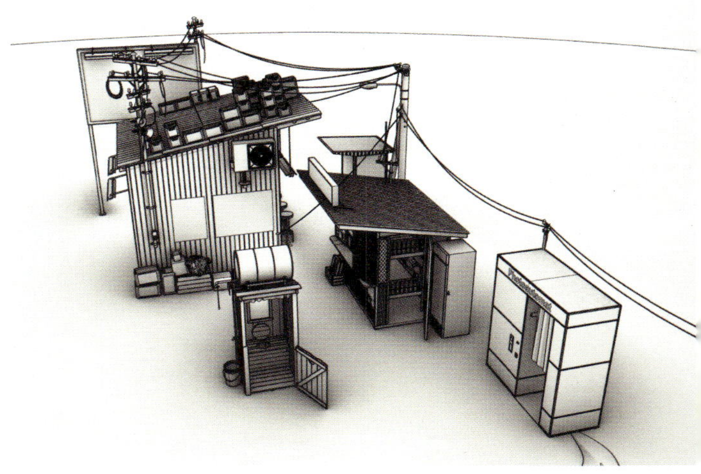

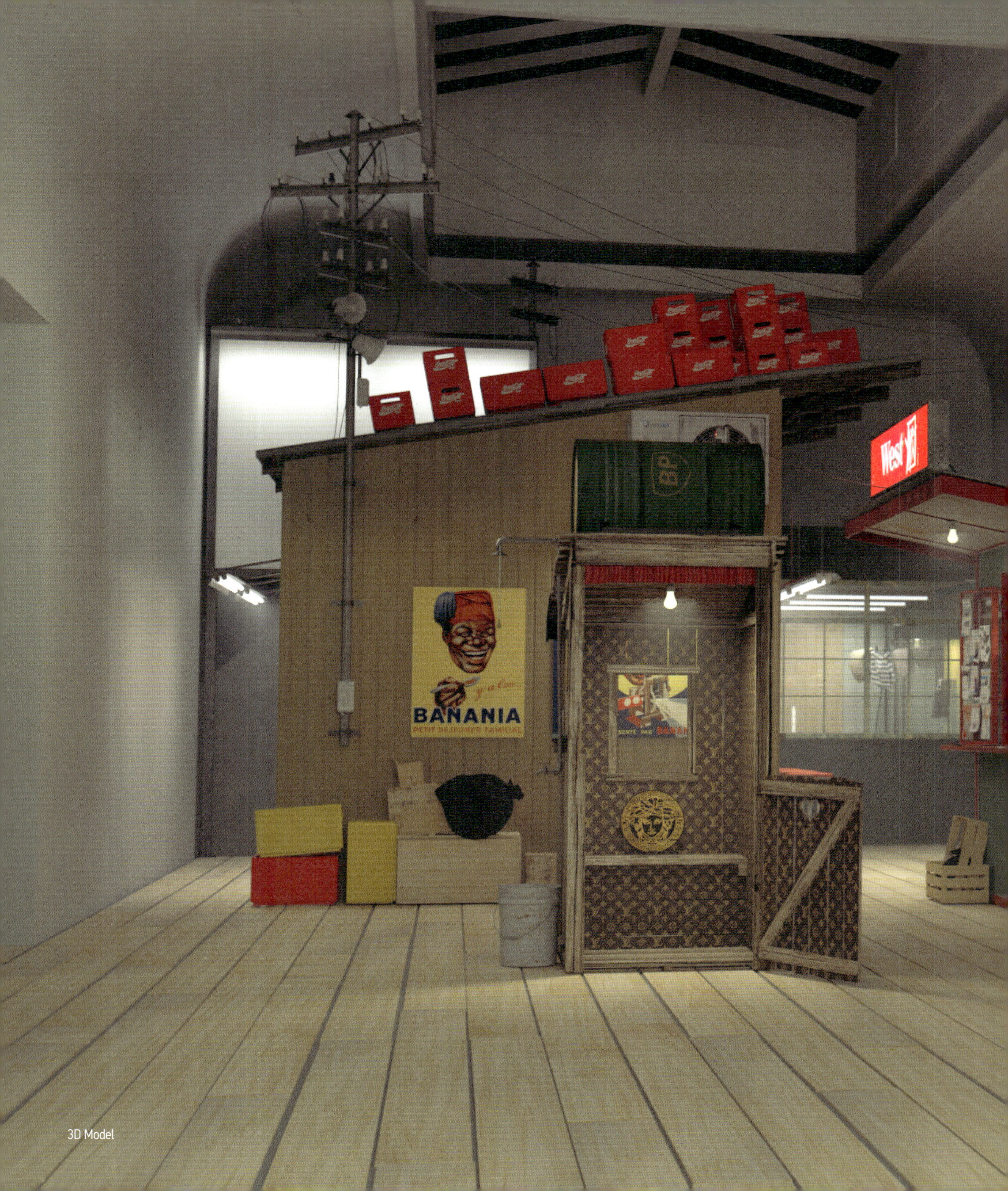

BANANIA
PETIT DÉJEUNER FAMILIAL
y'a bon
BP
West

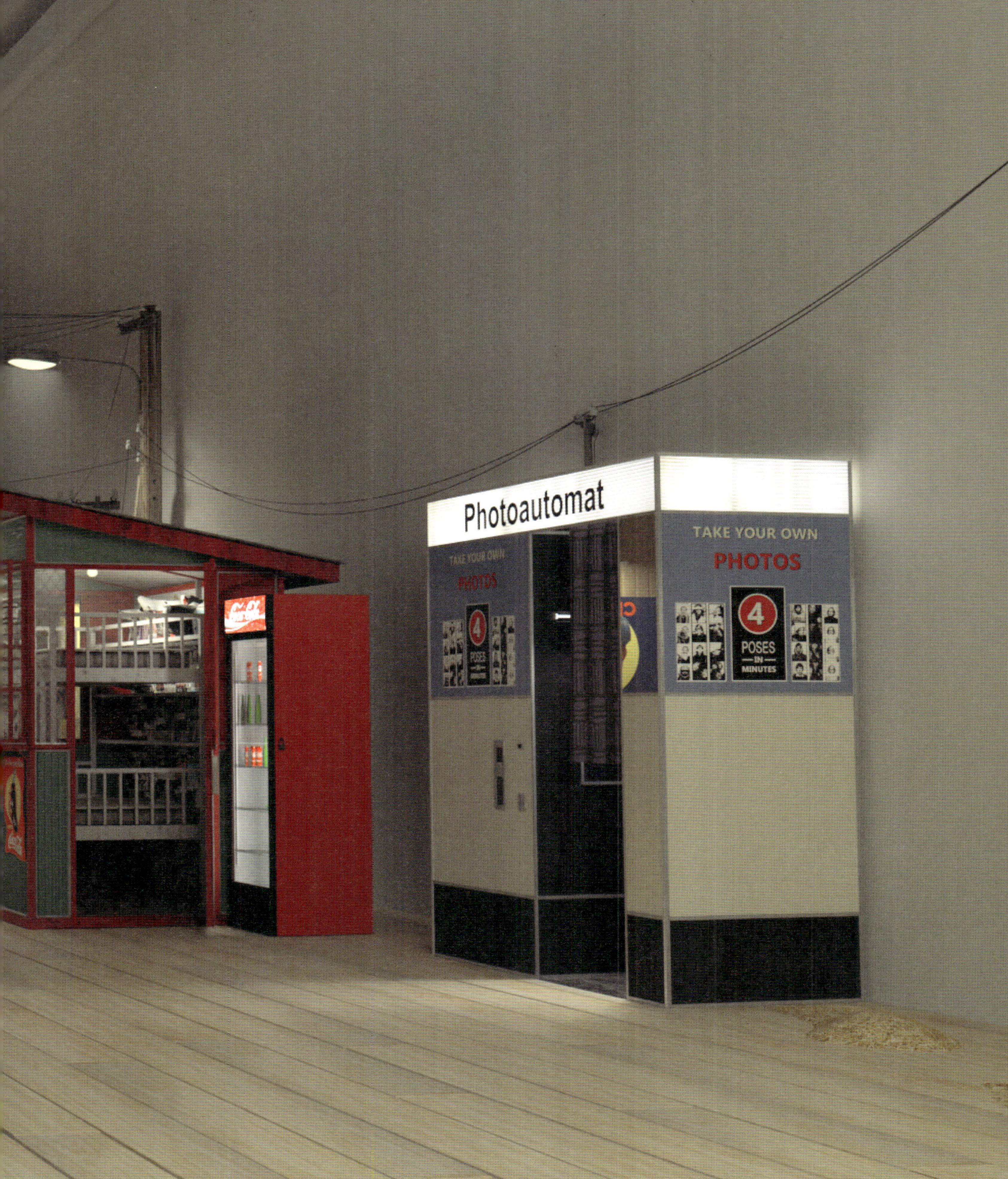

Photoautomat
TAKE YOUR OWN
PHOTOS
4
POSES
IN
MINUTES
TAKE YOUR OWN
PHOTOS
4
POSES
IN
MINUTES

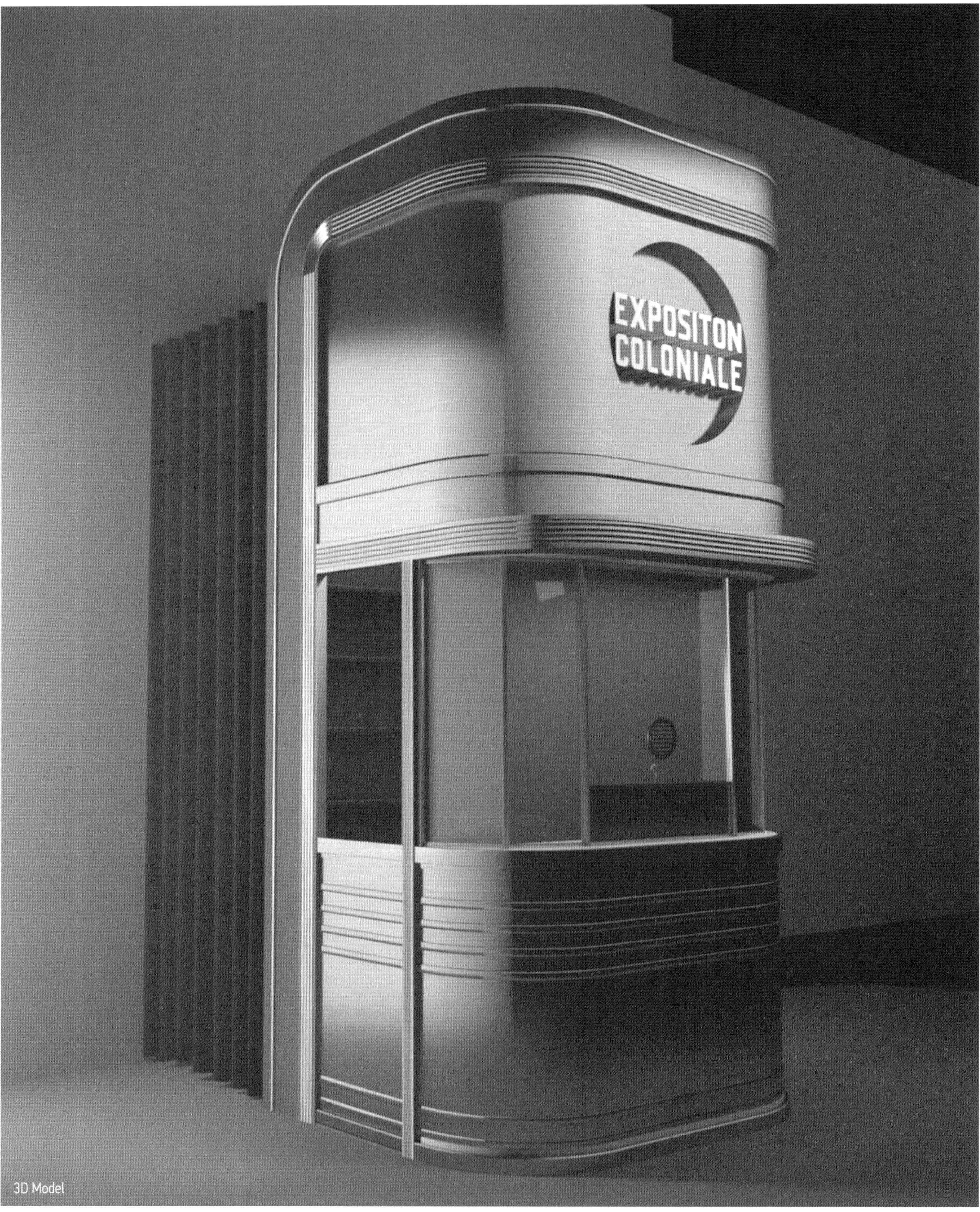

3D Model

zložba Exposition Coloniale ukazuje na posledice kolonijalne ere i ovaj istorijski kontekst predstavlja polaznu tačku za Denićevo istraživanje njenih tekovina i njihovog trajnog uticaja na kulturne podele i društvena raslojavanja. Kroz svoja umetnička iskustva u pozorištu, Denić koristi sposobnost da upotrebom vizuelne naracije kroz strukture simbola dopre do kompleksnih i neuralgičnih pitanja. Koristeći se Brehtovim efektom distanciranja (V efekat), on nudi *sliku* realnosti, a ne realnost kakva zapravo jeste. On izaziva posmatrače, stavljajući ih u položaj da preispitaju svoje razumevanje dinamika moći, konzumerizma i mnoštva gorkih stvarnosti, ne uslovljavajući ih da samo kritički promišljaju, već izazivajući empatiju i osećajnost. U današnjem svetu, teme otuđenja, podele i kontrole i dalje su relevantne, ne samo u oblasti politike i akumulacije moći već i u sferi osnovnih ljudskih vrednosti i principa.

Izložba se realizuje u nacionalnom paviljonu Srbije na čijoj se fasadi i dan danas nalazi monumentalni natpis *Jugoslavia*, prizivajući sećanje na teritoriju koja se geopolitički dezintegrisala kao posledica sukoba tokom devedesetih godina prošlog veka. Ova struktura, koja je otkupljena 1938. godine, zauzima desni ugao Đardina na ostrvu Sant'Elena, a originalno je delo arhitekte Brena Del Đudice i epitomizacija sofisticiranosti italijanske arhitekture Novećenta. U slučaju Paviljona, arhitektura postaje i emotivni iskaz, potvrđujući da nije reč samo o formi i funkciji, već i o društvenom i kulturnom kontekstu u kom opstaje. Na ovaj način, izložbeni prostor prevazilazi okvire reprezentativnog zdanja, i preuzima ulogu živog spomenika ukinute zemlje. Ušavši u paviljon Srbije, neminovno osećate nesigurnost identiteta ovog prostora. Kao umetnik profesionalno integrisan u Nemačku i nemačka govorna područja, u ovakvoj zoni reflektivnog i neprijatnog susreta, Denić i sam interveniše kao stranac.

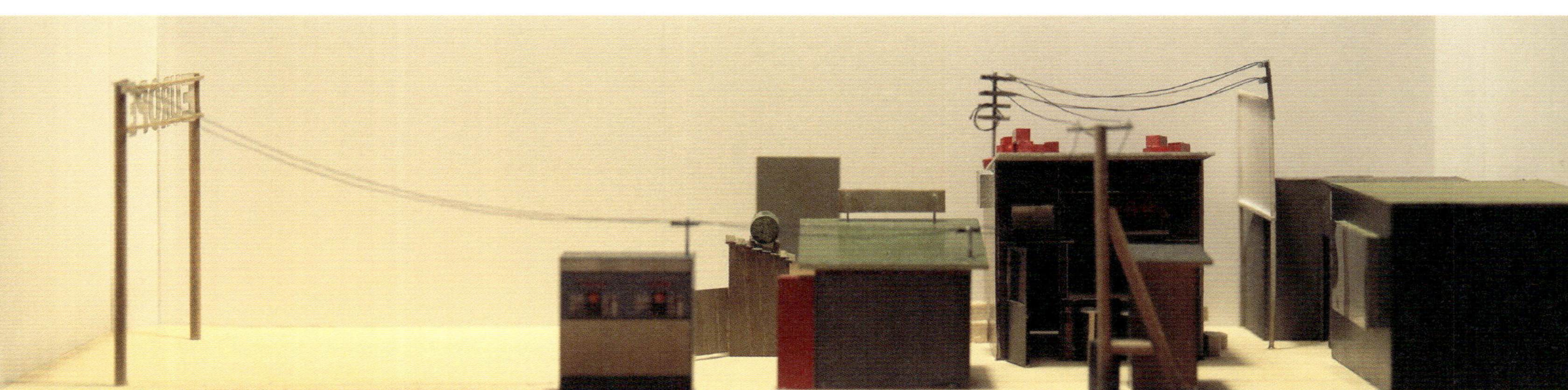

Maquette | Maketa

U svakom slučaju, pored zvanične istorije pamćenja postoji nezvanična istorija sećanja, kao dopuna ove prve i njena kritika. Jer istorija nije samo ono što se dogodilo državama, nacijama i njihovim ustanovama, nego i ono kako su se ti događaji prelomili i izrazili u dušama i duhu pojedinaca: od spoljašnje, istorija postaje unutrašnja, događaj se pretvara u doživljaj, istorija u biografiju.

* Đuro Šušnjić

* Šušnjić D. „Lično i zvanično sećanje i zaboravljanje"; *Sećanje i zaborav*; zbornik radova, CEIR i Filozofski fakultet Novi Sad; 2016.

Denić posmatrača uvlači u manipulaciju prostorom koristeći se elementi-ma-simbolima postavljenim u različite dijalektičke okvire što rezultira vizuelno privlačnom i konceptualno izazovnom arhitekton-skom situacijom. Posledica ovakve upotrebe prostornih elemenata je napetost koja ne pro-izilazi isključivo z njihovog fizičkog prisustva, već i same interakcije između posmatrača i višeslojne naracije. Uvođenje muzike i različitih izvora zvuka i svetlosti, grejnih sistema i drugih senzornih elemenata doprinosi kompleksnosti i dodatno zamagljuje i remeti granice između fizičkog i osećajnog. Rezultat je dinamično i privlačno prostorno iskustvo koje se oslanja na realistične komponente u potpunoj reinter-pretaciji i originalnoj izvedbi. Denićeve postavke se ne odnose na konkretne lokacije i vreme, već učitavaju poznate obrasce koji asociraju na opšta mesta bez obzira na geografski prosede. Njegova sposobnost da stvori dijalog između onoga što jeste, stvarnog i nadreal-

nog, monumentalnog ali krhkog i intimnog u detaljima, ostavlja nam neugodan osećaj poput deža vi (déjà-vu – anomalija pamćenja) ili snažno proživljenog sećanja koje nas uznemi-rava i remeti. Stvaranje iskustva kroz nemir ili napetost direktno je povezano sa Milerovom (Heiner Müller) tezom o stalnoj potrebi da se dovede u pitanje sistem mišljenja i vrednosti putem funkcije umetnosti da učini stvarnost nemogućom.

Kretanjem kroz vreme, linearno u oba pravca, kombinovanjem istorijskih fakata sa aktuelnim i prepoznatljivim elementima, Denić uskraćuje značenje trenutka. Sadašnjost je fisija (fissio) prošlosti, koja se neprestano razlaže, deli i koja nas ne napušta. U datoj akumulaciji vremena Denić stvara sebi svojstven intenzitet sadrža-ja i mesta (zonu van vremena). On je tiranin prostora. Dešava se milost i nemilost potresa koji izazivaju slomljena krila leptira, vajajući u vremenu jednu sasvim drugačiju sliku sveta. Prostor života podstiče potrebu za uređivanjem, ali u ovom slučaju, ta privilegija postaje *opasna situacija* koja omogućava pristup prostoru nagomilanih predmeta u zoni umetničkog rada. Preuzimanje prostora odigrava se kroz njegovu

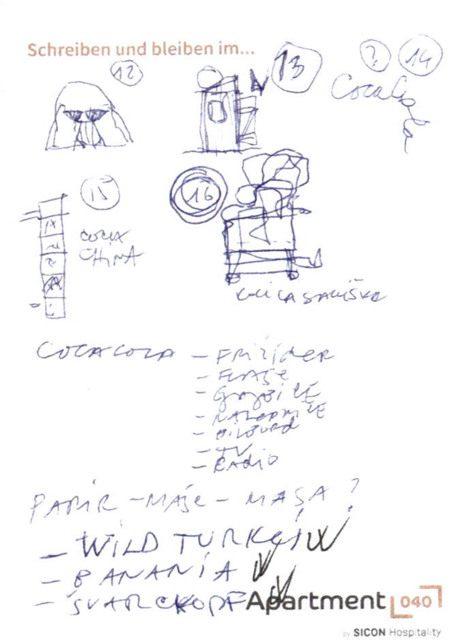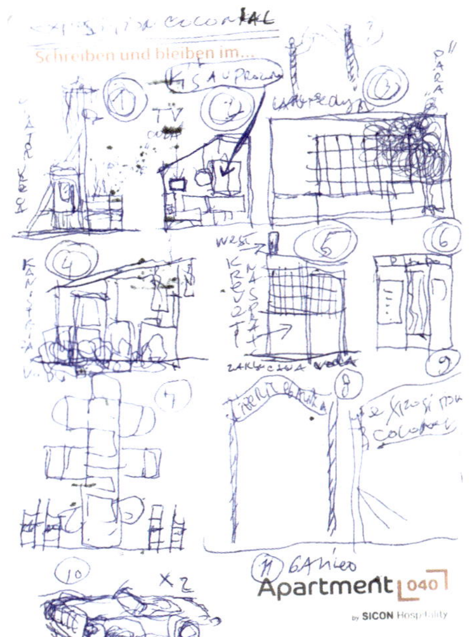

Sketches | Skice

transformaciju u aktivno, dinamično, sablasno biće. Takav preokret je možda monopolistički, no on je opravdan i osmišljen kao pripremanje terena u potrazi za mestom postavljanja "rekvizita", koji su zapravo oružje umetnika. Upravo ono o čemu je govorio Valeri (Paul Valéry): preneti osećanja izbegavši dosadu prenošenja. Ideja vodilja autora kroz projekat je upotreba "mesta" tako da izložbeni paviljon postaje heterotopija—onako kako je definiše Fuko (Michel Foucault)—prostor čija asocijativnost akumuliranih evokativnih elemenata pomera granica očekivanja. Estetski fenomeni, konglomerat slika, kroz različite segmente gomilanjem iskustva, stvaraju vrtlog—scenu u kojoj se brišu planovi sagledavanja do nivoa zaslepljenosti svakog čula. Razvija se postmodernistički kabinet čuda (Wunderkammer) u kome ste u potpunosti zaneseni unutar sadržaja, koji sa svih strana neprestano deluju (video, zvuk, instalacija). Kretanjem unutar monumentalno izvedenih struktura, preuzetih iz repertoara realnih okolnosti i tranzitnih prostora, poput restorana/kiosk, javnog kupatila, hotelske sobe, govornice, uličnog foto-automata, razvija se neizvesnost drame. Denić dekonstruiše životni milje i oblikuje ga u mogući lavirint želja. On deluje kao slikar prostora, ali bez prevencije i zloupotrebe svake supstance istog, formirajući jednu vrstu anarhistične savremenosti koja je razvila sopstvenu rezistentnost. Kao i uvek u ovakvim situacijama, posmatrač sam po sebi očekuje previše, no u ovom slučaju upravo to i stoji pred njegovim očima, postavka koja ne samo da nosi nagomilanost već generiše viši oblik svakog od zatečenih predmeta ili situacija u prostoru. Njegovo scensko delovanje pronalazi se u definiciji Patrisa Pejvisa (Patrice Pavis) prema kojoj scenski prostor sam po sebi poseduje svojstvo znaka, jer stalno oscilira između konkretno vidljivog prostora označitelja i vanjskog prostora označenog na koji se gledalac mora apstraktno pozvati da bi ušao u funkciju. Svi ovi objekti, prostorni skupovi, prožeti su anksioznošću društva u kojem opstaju. Deluju kao društvena memorabilija, beleže suštinu ljudskog boravka i reflektuju izgubljenu osećajnost i intimnost naših interakcija unutar njih. Umetnik dugim pogledom zadire u nepoželjna stanja i privatnost napuštenog.

Estetska celovitost organizovana je iz delova koji su objedinjeni u značenju i tako postavljaju semiotički sistem koji dekodira potrošačko

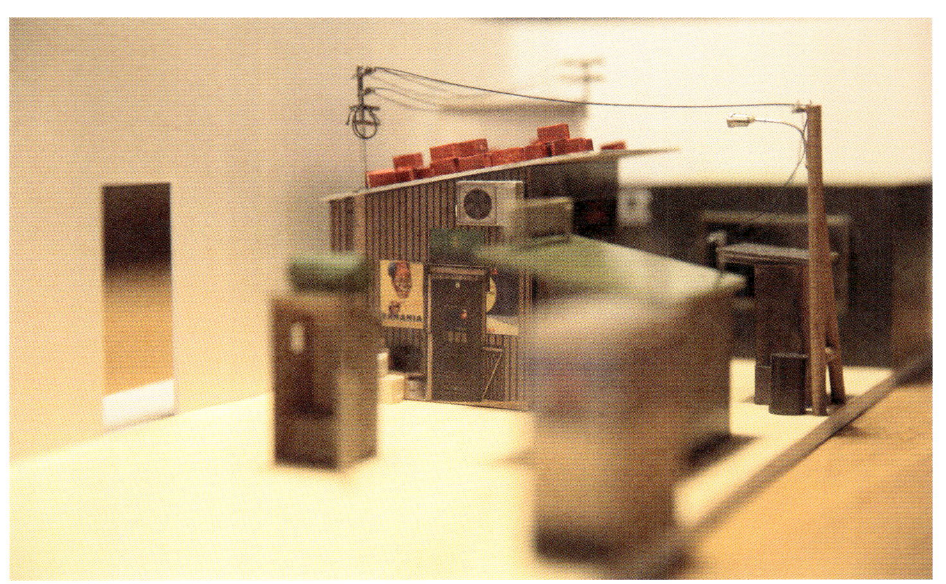

Maquette | Maketa

društvo i vrednosti koje ono generiše. Okupiran reprezentacijom pre nego samom slikom realnog, Denić insistira na fizičkom, konkretnom trajanju i stabilnosti stvarnog sa činjenicama van svake sumnje. Kako V.Dž.T. Mičel u *Šta slike žele?* obrazlaže: Simetrija između ikonoklazma i idolopoklonstva objašnjava kako je moguće da čini 'kreativnog uništenja' (spektakularno uništenje ili izobličavanje) stvaraju 'sekundarne slike' koje su na neki način oblici idolopoklonstva jednako moćni kao i primarni idoli koje pokušavaju zameniti. Zato je opravdano tvrditi da je Denić ne samo slikar i skulptor, već i nešto sasvim više od toga, a ponajmanje scenograf. Vođen aksiomom Filipa Gastona (Philip Gaston) „ja slikam, ono što želim da vidim", uz prostornu mudrost Pjera dela Frančeska (Piero della Francesca) i transformaciju Geteovih misli, on delujući kao tvorac ljubavi i mržnje—Erosa i Tanasosa—modeluje sadržaj koji nam se, ne samo spušta u cipele u obliku osećanja, već se i samo iskustvo materijalizuje u strukturu spomeničkog nasleđa užasa, tuge i ništavila, a opet tako da na trenutke nudi lepši, bolji svet koji se emituje i treperi pred našim očima.

Prilikom istraživanja prostornog stanja koje zatičemo, a koje je narušeno ljudskim prisustvom/odsustvom, u ambijentu poput „vabeta" (čisto mesto, mesto pročišćenja), odvija se situacija poput građenja kolaža: kafana je neuredna, kuhinjski deo pun posuđa. Veliko ogledalo iznad stola koji je pokriven plastičnim stoljnjakom doprinosi nelagodi koja se intenzivira činjenicom da se u svakoj sledećoj prostoriji motiv ogledala ponavlja. Rečima Cvetana Todorova: Jedinstvenost činjenice ne sprečava univerzalnost pouke koja se na osnovu nje izvlači. Na zidu je polica sa akvarijumom. Nedostatak života u akvarijumu pojačava utisak praznine ili pustoši. Pejzaž je dopunjen prisustvom ronioca pored otvorenog kovčega plave boje sa zakivcima u obliku žutih zvezda. Klima uređaj neprestano radi, ispunjavajući prostor stalnim, mehaničkim prisustvom istovremeno hladeći unutrašnjost, dok sa spoljne strane dodatno zagreva prostor. Džuboks po izboru nudi hitove: Toto Kutunjo „Insieme" iz 1992, Kraftwerk „Trans Europe Express", R.E.M. „Radio Free Europe", Suede „Europe is Our Playground", Roxy Music „A Song for Europe". Na desnom spoljnjem zidu kafane je bilbord za čokoladni napitak za decu

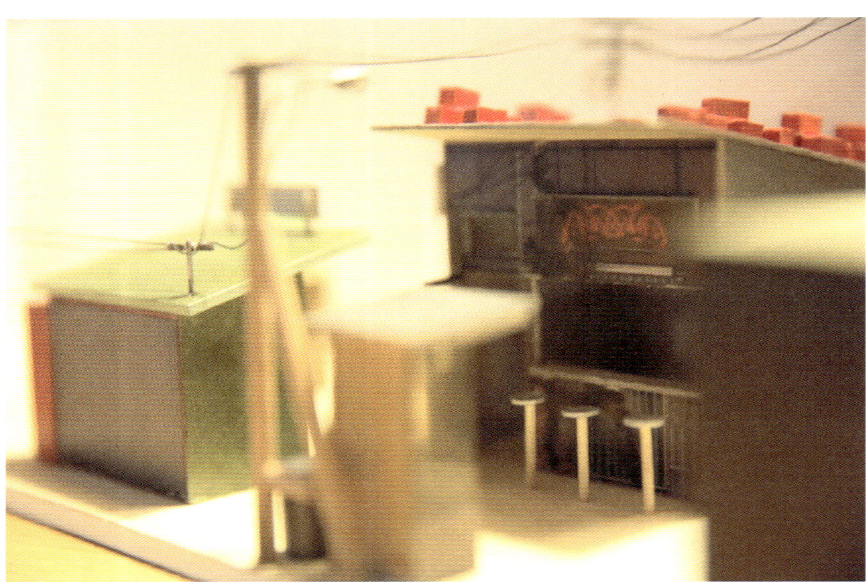

Maquette | Maketa

Banania. Na zadnjem zidu kafane je reklama viskija Wild Turkey. Nabrajanja u ovom slučaju nisu popisi inventara, mada na to liče, već mnoštvo bačenih udica ili vešto tkan kapilarni krvotok prostora-želja, ili prijatnosti-neprijatnosti-maštanja-želja. U javnom kupatilu nalazi se veliki bazen, kada. Iz tuša voda neprekidno teče. Po podu, klupama i u kadi su pobacani delovi odeće, trenerke, patike—odbačene stvari svakodnevnice, beskorisno korisne. Para i dim kuljaju. Na zidu je veliki poster poput ikonostasa: preporuka za porodični odmor—vožnja gumenom bananom po mediteranskim plažama. Dvorišni WC je napravljen od čamovih dasaka u stilu pogrebnog sanduka. Na krovu se nazire staro bure za naftu kompanije Britiš Petroleum koje ima ulogu vodokotlića i poput katetera gravitira ka podu. Prostor migrira sa pogreba u svatove i nazad. Unutrašnja strana WC-a je obložena tapetima satkanim po dizajnu kuće Luj Viton (Louis Vuitton). Hotelska soba je zapuštena potkrovna prostorija u kojoj se šapuće (žanr-scena-noar). Braon boja utkana je u blato antisecesije, kao dominanta na sceni. Preko prozora, kiša rominja beskonačno ali impotentno. Na televizoru pričvršćenom na zid emituju se reklame Koka Kole koje slave pogrešne razloge života i sreće. Limeni kiosk/bakalnica je skučen prostor sa dva metalna kreveta na sprat, izolovan od života. Dušeci su pohabani poput arabeske starog zida. Umesto posteljine su novinske stranice požutele mokraćne patine (posebna ponuda artikala po sniženim cenama, nagradne igre…). Na policama u izlogu i na zadnjem zidu je nekoliko kutija vlažnih cigareta. Na krovu kioska je svetleća reklama cigara marke WEST i slogan –Bez izbora! Telefonska govornica je naslonjena na uličnu banderu. Slušalica je iščupana ali telefon ne prestaje da zvoni. Oko telefona su izlepljeni oglasi pornografskog sadržaja—memento mori. Na ulaznim vratima samo nekoliko sličica fudbalera (najskupljih transfera) razbacanih poput pošasti ili uvrede. Sve ovo je upakovano u specifični zvuk, beli šum, ekrana koji beskrajno šušti! Do sada navedeni objekti se nalaze koncentrisani na levoj strani paviljona. Na suprotnoj strani u blizini zida je svetleći natpis/reklama, poput opomene, „EUROPE™" podignut na dva stuba. Natpis je okrenut ka zidu. Svetlo se odbija od zida tako da su slova u kontra svetlu, senci i čitaju se unazad. Ispod natpisa na stubovima su dve plastične stolice bele boje kineske proizvodnje koje asociraju na napušteno

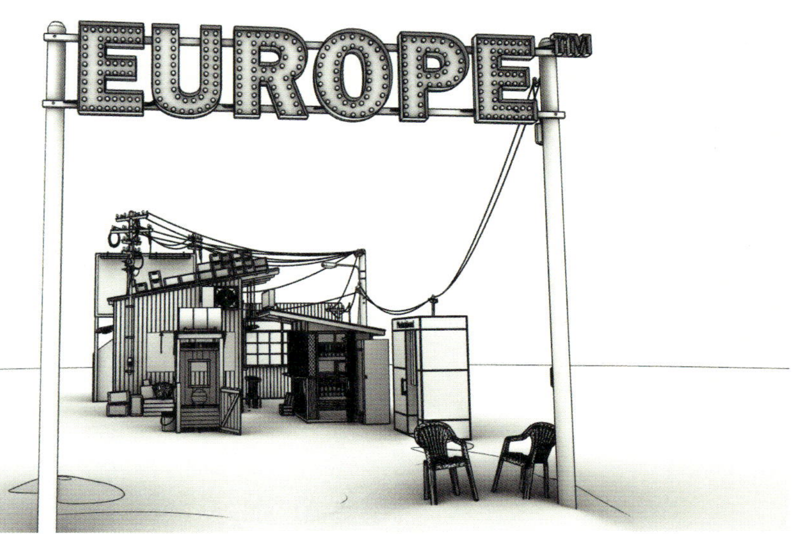

Sketch | Skica

izobilje. Nakon predočenih popisa osećanja uz
opis postavke, nemoguće je otrgnuti se utisku
da je pred nama nešto sto je najbliže definisati
delikatnoj situaciji jednog od postojećih života,
koji ne samo da podstiče pažnju čulnog sveta
u koji je izgnan, već se obraća na direktan
način jezikom savremenog mišljenja i estetike.
Ukoliko bi svesno zloupotrebili Benjaminov
pokušaj prekora kroz upozorenje, poput puto-
kaza, da nema ni jednog dokumenta kulture
koji istovremeno nije i dokument varvarstva,
logično je pitanje ličnog tumačenja tranzicije
ovih prostora u pseudo-katastrofu. Pozivajući
se na „novo-varvarstvo" kako ga posmatra
Bariko, ovi prostori sa privremenim boravkom
u privremenom raju cinizma i autoimuni opsta-
nak „raja trgovine" zagledani su u ambis svog
sopstvenog isceljenja. Na tom mestu umetnik
utemeljen u tradiciji ritualnog, socijalnog, kul-
turpolitičkog uz toteme filozofije ne nudi pogled
ka platnu ili skulpturi, objektu ili instalaciji već
živi organizam integrisan u prostor i njegov
zverinjak.

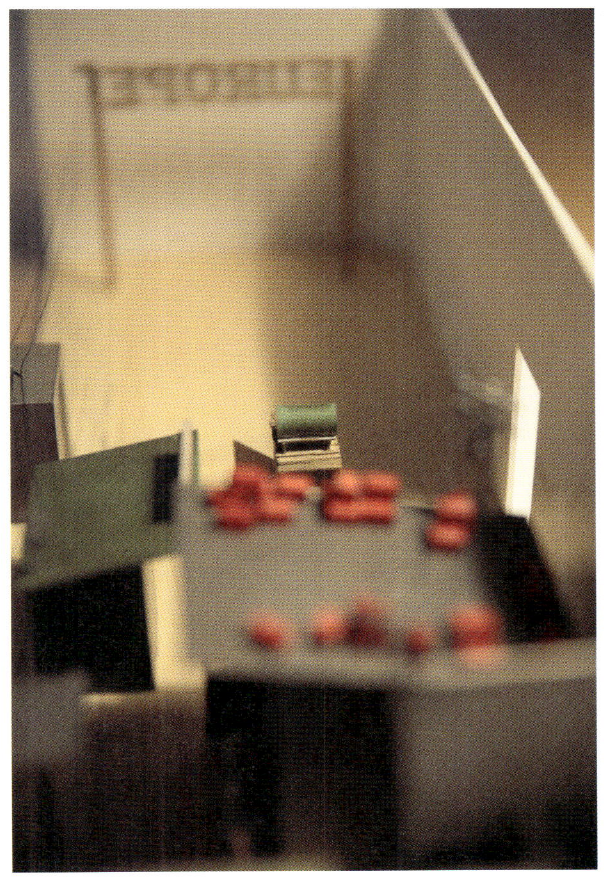

Maquette | Maketa

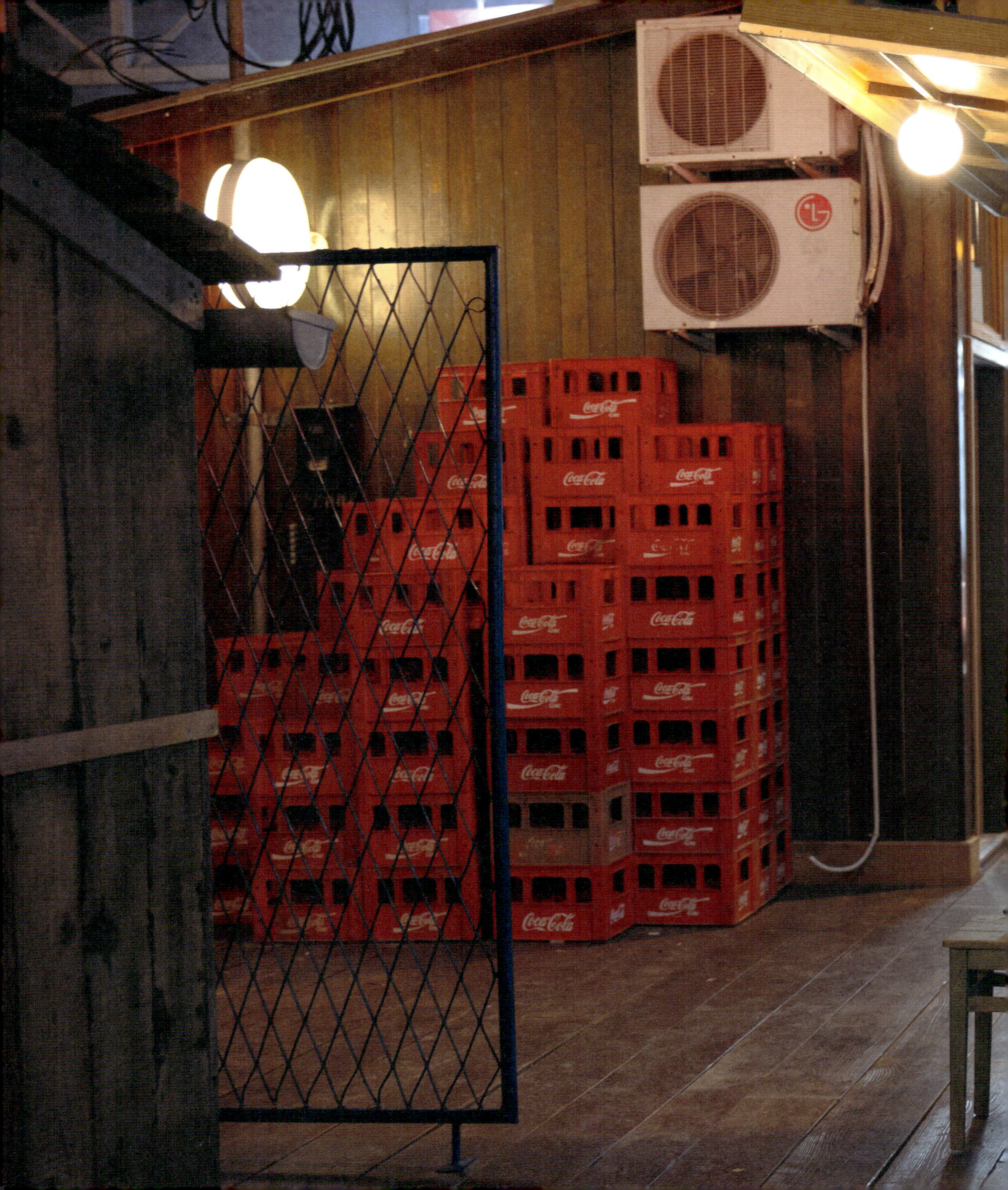

Coca-Cola

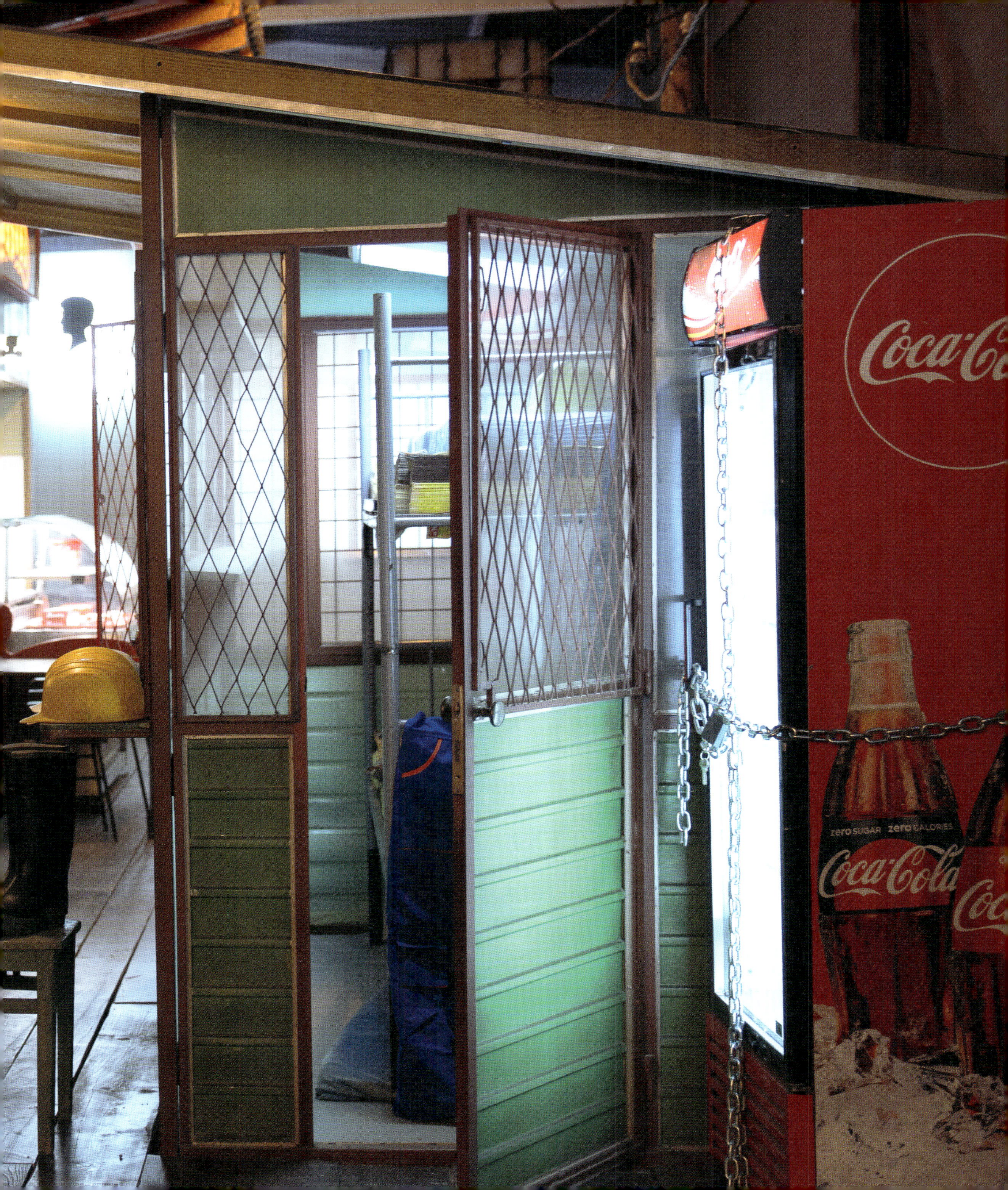

Coca-Cola
zero SUGAR zero CALORIES
Coca-Cola

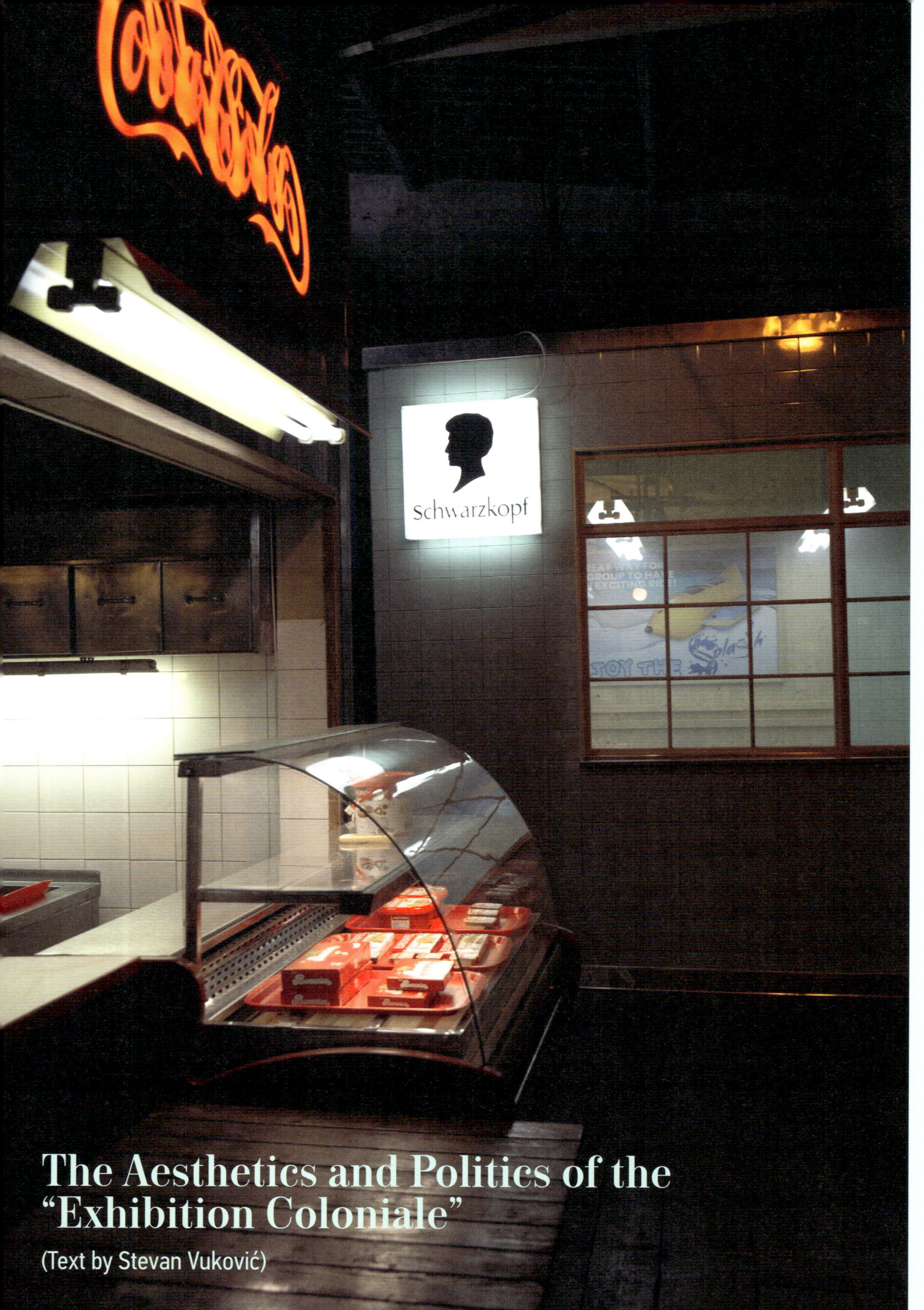

The Aesthetics and Politics of the "Exhibition Coloniale"

(Text by Stevan Vuković)

"Critical art is an art that aims to produce a new perception of the world, and therefore to create a commitment to its transformation. This schema, very simple in appearance, is actually the conjunction of three processes: first, the production of a sensory form of 'strangeness'; second, the development of an awareness of the reason for that strangeness; and third, a mobilization of individuals as a result of that awareness."

(Rancière 2010, 142)

"*In a strange land within my own country*"

As I walked into the total installation by Aleksandar Denić, entitled "Exposition Coloniale", which was, for the first time, mounted in a former warehouse on the outskirts of Belgrade, as a quickly test before being dismantled and transported to the Serbian Pavilion at the 60th Venice Biennial, words from the title of the Louis Aragon's book came to my mind, those that were used as one of the mottos of Julia Kristeva's book "Strangers to Ourselves". Specifically, I felt as if I was "in a strange land within my own country". Knowing that I would enter an art installation, derived from Denić's experiences as a set designer for theater performances, I was prepared for something in a completely different visual code, much more remote from the one I could actually encounter when getting lost during strolls in some metropolitan suburbia.

The setting was quite similar to some of the self-regulated and self-built spontaneous peri-urban fringe settlements that are common in the country where I currently reside, and many others that I have visited, but it was reduced to the absolute minimum of utilities and amenities, and it appeared as dismal, dreary and desolate. On the other hand, it was fully colonized by brand representations, ranging from Coca-Cola, Schwarzkopf, West and Wild Turkey, to Texaco, British Petroleum and Rosneft, Versace and Louis Vuitton, some of them on recycled objects, such as a barrel which is commonly used for collecting rainwater for an improvised public shower. Even the lighted letter sign "Europe", turned towards the wall, was written as "Europe[tm] "- not as the name of the territory one belongs to, but as a trademark in a franchise business.

This set of para-architectural objects and installations wasn't produced only for the gaze of the visitors, to fascinate or seduce them, or to represent or to illustrate an idea. The work was obviously formatted as a total installation - a "completely reprocessed space" (Kabakov 1995, 127), whose features, according to the interpretations of the late Russian philosopher Valery Podoroga "cannot be comprehended, only recognized", and that is " nearly always instantaneous" (Podoroga 2003, 351). It was made in order to "make the visitor active" as Lissitzky expected regarding his installations (Küppers-Lissitzky 1967, 362), or as Allan Kaprow regarding his environments. In a brochure titled "Notes on the Creation of a Total Art," in 1958 Kaprow even gave instructions to the visitors, writing that "in the present exhibition we do not come to look at things", but "are surrounded, and become part of what surrounds us" (Kaprow, 2003: 10-11.)

Close to the logic of the environments, this work does not rely on a set of predefined actions the visitors are to perform, as in most of the works of relational art, which use existing "social forms", as Bourriaud has called them (Bourriaud, 1998: 13), inviting visitors to a set of actions limited to, say, sliding, floating or cooking. Even more, this work is made keeping in mind to avoid two types of mistakes Claire Doherty attributes to relational art. One is related to the already described "gap between the rhetoric of engagement and the actual experience of the work", which "may make for impotent participation rather than dynamic experience" (Doherty, 2004: 6). The other is in that exhibitions of that kind "may operate as novelty participatory experiences, rather than on their own terms."(Ibid.) Claire Bishop has clarified further that second mistake, writing that, in relational art," the artist should renounce authorial presence in favor of allowing participants to speak through him or her", following the idea that art "should extract itself from the 'useless' domain of the aesthetic and be fused with some social praxis." (Bishop, 2006: 183)

Authorial presence is quite clear in this display named "Exposition Coloniale", even though it invites the audience to get into physical interaction with every item in the setting, without scripting in advance what one might do. As in Denić's scenographic work, that is a completely self-sufficient world, in which whoever may be performing has just to inhabit and the narrative to be performed in it will find its place. In this specific case, it consists of a small room (with no toilet and bathroom), a kiosk, a pub, an outhouse, a public bathroom with sauna, and a public photobooth; enough for a simple working person to rest between the shifts of hardship somewhere where one does not belong (regardless of the fact of, perhaps, being of that place). The difference to his scenographic work for theater is only in the fact that in this display there is neither a stage to be viewed from a distance, nor a script, actors or directors involved.

During his collaborations with theater director Frank Kastorf, it was always clear that the procedures for their collaboration were derived from Bertold Brecht's principles, explained in his "Mahagonny notes", by which, according to Douglas Kellner he "distinguished his separation of words, music and scene from the Wagnerian Gesamtkunstwerk, which fused the elements into one seductive and overpowering whole in which word, music and scene work together to engulf the spectator in the aesthetic totality." (Kellner 1980, 33). In that case, "each aesthetic medium (involved into the production of the play) retains its separate identity, and the product is an 'aggregate of independent arts' in provocative tension" (Ibid.). Brecht has derived that theory from Karl Korsch's model for the workers' councils, but it worked in the case of Brecht directing his plays on stage for decades, and for Kastorf and his collaborators as well.

In the case of the "Exposition Coloniale", instead of a stage there is a total installation, whose elements will all appear as quite familiar to most of the visitors of the Pavillion, but the atmosphere which they jointly build adds a kind of strangeness to that familiarity. It has most of the generic features of a temporary lodging for one or more (since the kiosk is already converted to a collective lodging place) persons in need, but it does not really induce a 'being at home', nor even 'being at someone's home' feeling. There are also no clear indications of the presence of anyone who would consider it a home for at the moment. Even though everything around seems to have been well used (the kitchen to the bathroom, the benches, the phone booth) there are no signs of their use by a particular person, or specific group of people, and there are no items to be found around that would be of personal value to someone.

So, there is only one logical solution to the question "Who are to be the users of that space?" – the visitors of the Pavillion themselves. Whoever enters the installation is the right person in the right place, or the one for whom this place was made. That stranger, or "foreigner, immigrant, expatriate, diasporic, émigré, exiled, or refugee" about whom Adriano Pedrosa wrote defining the title and the main topic of the 60th Biennale, resides in each particular visitor. According to Julia Kristeva's words, somewhere deep inside "we know that we are foreigners to ourselves, and it is with the help of that sole support that we can attempt to live with others". (Kristeva 1991, 170) Only when we find that stranger in ourselves can we really think about the conditions that brought many people around us into the situation of being seen as a stranger, as well as to experience the complete loss of public interest about the condi-

tions in which such a stranger is to live. "Ghettos and slums are by no means new components of urban structure", wrote Paul Knox decades ago, even though his words are actual today, "landscapes of the excluded are unprecedented in the intensity of combined poverty, violence, despair and isolation. (Knox, 1993b, 231)

So, as Annaleen Masschelein already wrote, referring to Freud's interpretation of the uncanny (Das Unheimliche) phenomenon, on which Julia Kristeva has built her own, "the basic Freudian definition of 'the familiar that has become strange' cannot be disconnected from one of the most important concepts in many discourses of the twentieth century: alienation as an economic, political, psychological, and existential condition." (Masschelein 2011, 136) How can someone who was the victim of forced migration, and/or forced labor - trafficking for the purpose of labor exploitation, feel anything else but alienated in the place where some company, governmental institution or international humanitarian organization has provided them with a place to temporarily reside?

In a bathroom of the "Exposition Coloniale" installation, there is a poster of Lampedusa island, on the 35th Parallel, which became a symbol of the senseless deaths of African migrants striving to get to Europe by any means available. Namely, on the night of 3 October 2013, a wooden boat with a stated capacity of 35 passengers was filled with around 500 asylum-seekers from Eritrea, Somalia and Ghana. It was wrecked very close to the shore of the Italian island, and 368 people drowned. Even before that tragic event, Joseph Pugliese, taking into consideration also the history of Lampedusa as a detention island in some previous times, has defined it as an uncanny space of holiday isle/penal colony, in which, next to the tourists enjoying their holidays, migrants live their lives "remaining invisible to First-World subjects, despite being directly in their line of sight". (Pugliese 2009, 664) After the tragic event, Federica Mazzara has extended his text, writing that "in an attempt to keep the two spatial dimensions separate yet coexistent, Lampedusa has gradually transformed itself into a 'third space', a combination of real and imagined space, where the migrants alternatively occupy spaces of 'invisibility' and 'visibility', depending on who is looking and from which perspective". (Mazzara 2015, 452)

This combination of "real and imagined space" takes us back to Julia Kristeva's statement, according to which "uncanniness occurs when the boundaries between imagination and reality are erased". (Kristeva 1991, 188) That is why it is important to stress that in the installation of "Exposition Coloniale" there are no ready-made objects. Everything was designed by the artist, and

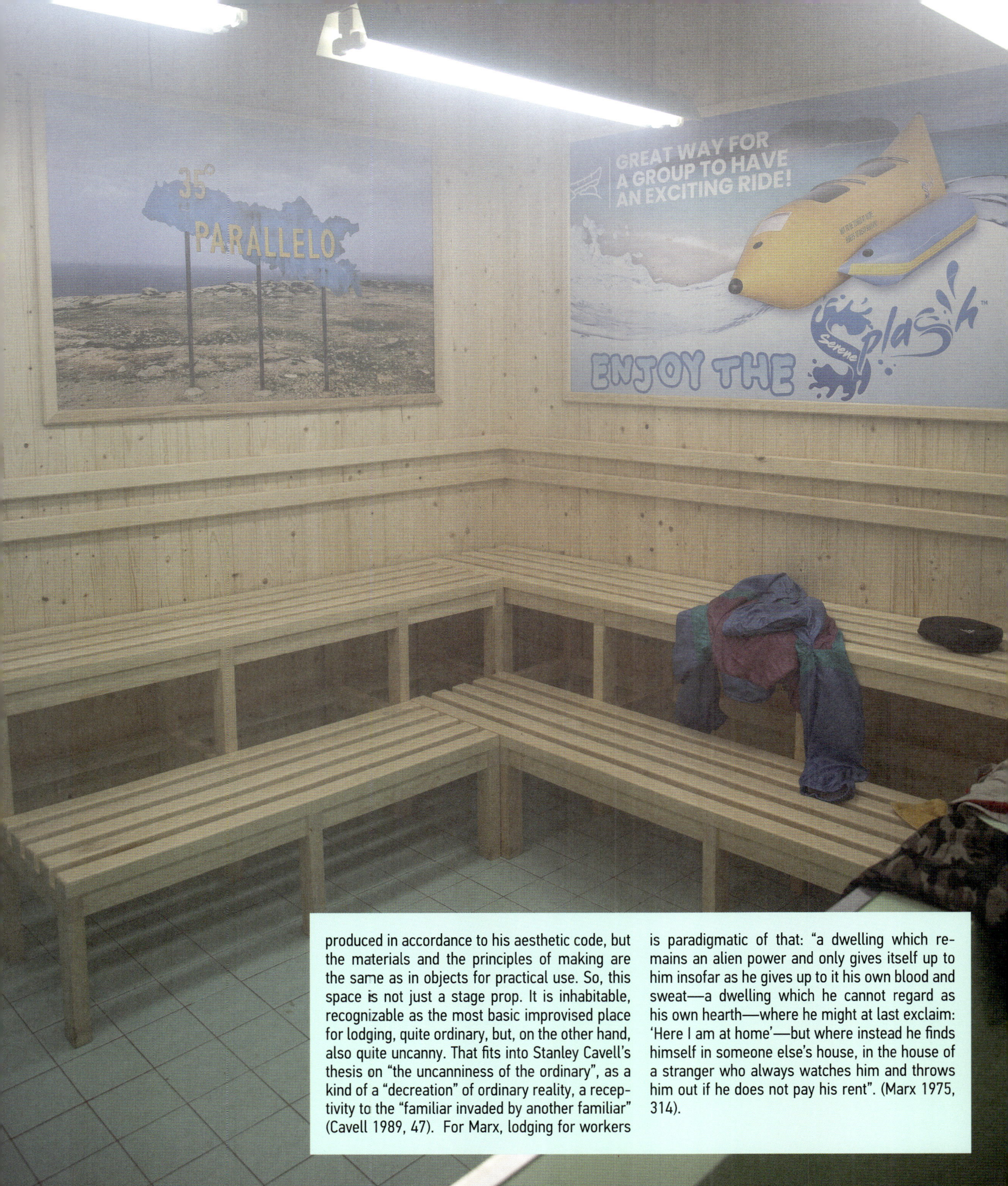

produced in accordance to his aesthetic code, but the materials and the principles of making are the same as in objects for practical use. So, this space is not just a stage prop. It is inhabitable, recognizable as the most basic improvised place for lodging, quite ordinary, but, on the other hand, also quite uncanny. That fits into Stanley Cavell's thesis on "the uncanniness of the ordinary", as a kind of a "decreation" of ordinary reality, a receptivity to the "familiar invaded by another familiar" (Cavell 1989, 47). For Marx, lodging for workers is paradigmatic of that: "a dwelling which remains an alien power and only gives itself up to him insofar as he gives up to it his own blood and sweat—a dwelling which he cannot regard as his own hearth—where he might at last exclaim: 'Here I am at home'—but where instead he finds himself in someone else's house, in the house of a stranger who always watches him and throws him out if he does not pay his rent". (Marx 1975, 314).

The Extraction Zone Exhibited

As Karl Marx observed back in his days, the capitalist system "squanders human beings … more readily than any other mode of production, squandering not only flesh and blood, but nerves and brains as well" (Marx 1992, 182). Capitalism dispossesses people and subjects them to different modalities of violence, suffering, and neglect that produce "the bodily debris that [capitalist] conquest leaves on space" (Gordillo 2013, 246). In more precise terms, "colonial capitalism has been the main catastrophic event that has gobbled up the planet's resources, discursively constructing racialized bodies within geographies of difference, systematically destroying through dispossession, enslavement, and then producing the planet as a corporate bio-territory" (Gómez-Barris 2017, 4) It maps the whole globe, in order to identify and demarcate potential extractive zones, in order to exploit them to their outermost limits, regardless of the histories they may be witnesses of, or legal and customary regulations related to the ways of their use.

The earliest maps of that corporate bio-territory were presented at the Colonial exhibitions, whose highest peak was a century ago. Their major predecessor was the exhibition held in 1851 at the Crystal Palace in London (The Great Exhibition of the Works of Industry of All Nations), followed by the 1853 Crystal Palace Fair in New York, Expositions Universelles of 1889 and 1900, in Paris, and by several others. Their economic, social and political role was to foster "production, trade and consumption, in addition to socio-cultural aspects". (van Wesemael, 2001: 21). As Hoffenberg wrote, "exhibitions were at the heart of imperial and national social and commercial enterprises during the Victorian and Edwardian Eras" (Hoffenberg, 2001:20) in the manner that "Imperial, colonial, and national inventories were linked at the exhibitions by official tests and jury reports, consumption, tourism, and historical pageants" (Ibid, XV).

During the economic crises of the 1930s the exhibition format was used by the main imperialist states to "promote the idea of the empire and imperialism, which they considered essential for modernity and progress" and to "show the supposed benefits of colonialism for the colonizers" (Ferraz de Matos at all 2022, 3). Furthermore, "museums expressly founded for the purpose of promoting colonialism eventually took pride of place in showing off the colonies", so that "their builders, backers and curators intended them to proclaim the merits of empire, to win over a not always enthusiastic public about the benefits of colonial adventures, that cost many lives and much money, to advance the mission to civilize the 'savages' and develop the resources over which colonial flags flew, and to educate the public about the obscure corners of greater Britain *or la plus grande France*, to stimulate imperial vocations" (Aldrich, 2009: 138).

Between 1889. and 1914, even those exhibitions that were not named Colonial started including human groups from the colonies, in a kind of hu-

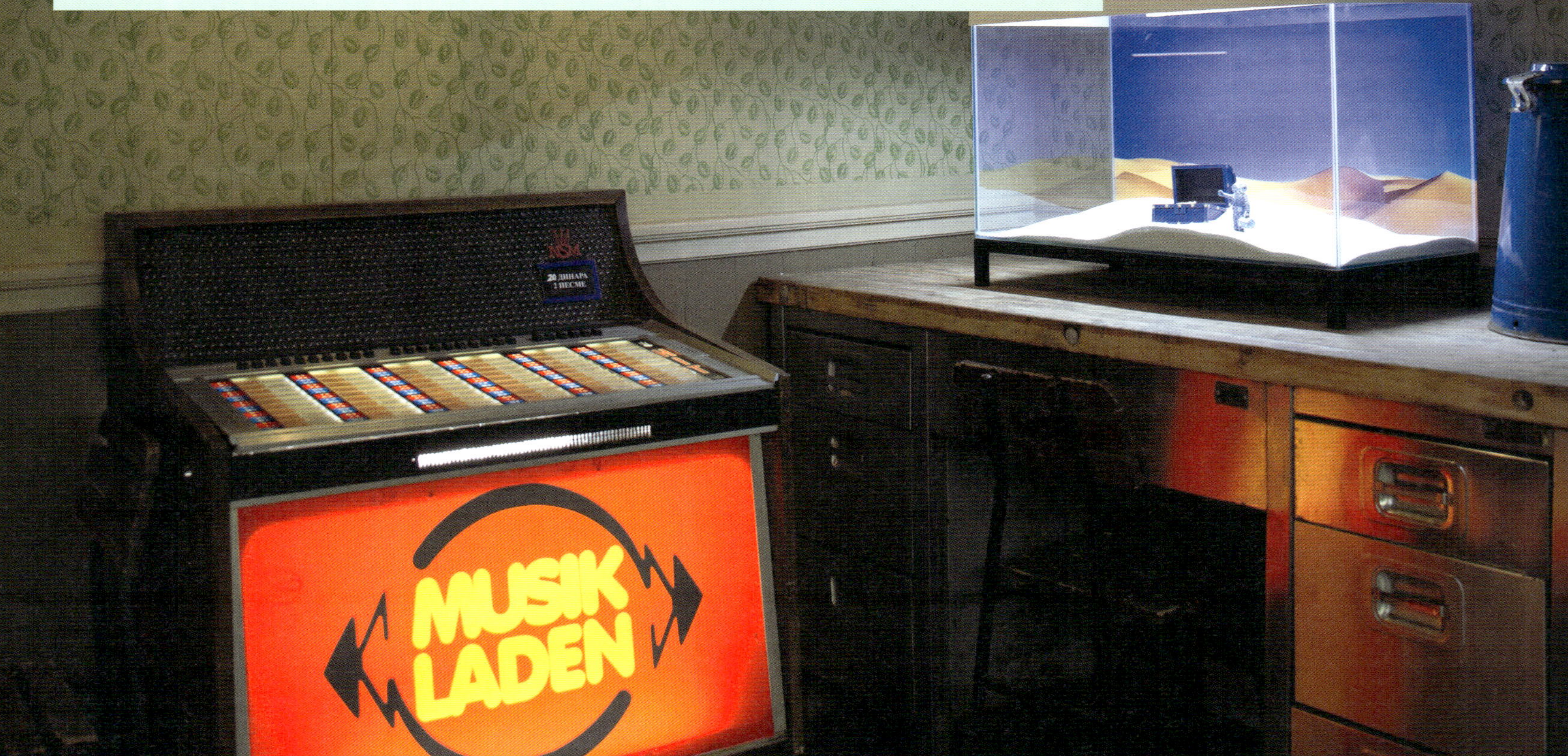

man zoo setting, brought to "be seen by others for their gratification and education" (Greenalgh 1988, 89) "At the Paris Expositions Universelles of 1889 and 1900 and the colonial exposition of 1931, 'natives' from the French colonies such as Indochina, Senegal, Dahomey and New Caledonia traveled to the French capital in order to bring to life the pavilions, gardens and reconstituted villages featured at these imperial exhibits" (Van Troi 2015, 163) They made such an attraction that Paul Morand, diplomat and writer with a racist viewpoints wrote that, during the time of those exhibitions: "Paris belonged to the negroes [and] the yellow raw fish eaters". (Morand 1931, 79).

The vast richness of the colonies, as shown in those exhibitions, had to impress all categories of French citizens who could possibly enhance their exploitation. So there had to be something special for each of them, in order to enable them to imagine themselves as potential future soldiers, merchants, plantation owners, missionaries, educators, scientific researchers, or simply hobby hunters and explorers of exotic places. So, the range of products allegedly from the colonies varied from "Banania" drink for children to expensive jewelry for upper-class colonialists. Banania was made of banana flour, cocoa, crushed grain, and sugar, featuring a Senegalese marksman wearing a bright red fez saying "Y'a bon" (imaginary pidgin French or 'petit nègre'), while "French jewelry designers like Van Cleef and Arpeis introduced a new line of necklaces, bracelets, and earrings of French colonial inspiration", so that, from the 1931 exhibition "slave collars, ivory and coral earrings, and enameled brooches became fashionable" (August 1982, 153)

The first official international colonial exhibition was held in Amsterdam from May 1 to October 1, 1883. at today's Museumsplain. Its title was "The International Colonial and Export Exhibition", and it showed a wealth of 28 different nations presenting their colonial trade. The curator behind the event which drew at least a million visitors and was Edouard Agostini, who had previously been involved in organizing the 1878 Exposition Universelles in Paris. The follow-up to that exhibition in other colonizing countries was the "Colonial and Indian Exhibition", held in London in 1886, the "Philippines Exposition", held in Madrid in 1887, "Exposição Insular e Colonial Portuguesa" in Oporto in 1894, the British Empire Exhibition in London, in 1924, and in France the "Exposition Internationale et colonial" in Lyon in 1894, then in the occupied Hanoi in 1902, Marseille 1906, Paris 1907, and so on, leading to the 1931 Paris exhibition, for which the first plans and projections were made back in 1912, on the initiative of Albert Lebrun, Minister of Colonies.

The catalog of the exhibition was quite clear in its message, sent to 33 million visitors: "Colonization is legitimate. It is beneficial. These are the truths that are inscribed on the walls of the pavilions at the Bois de Vincennes" (Olivier 1931, 11). According to Patricia Morton, "the exposition had two educational goals: first, to stimulate French business to invest in the colonies, and second, to overcome the apathy and even hostility that the French public felt toward its colonial empire", because "national pride was at stake, and the exposition was meant to counter the image of the *casanier* (stay-at-home), the lethargic French who cared nothing for their colonial holdings" (Morton 1998, 357). At the exhibition, which was to convince French youth to move into the Colonies, "the visitors could marvel in front of the displays that highlighted the power of their nation overseas, and absorb the national discourse according to which 'inferior' peoples would 'progress' accordingly through the gift of Western modernity". (Sauvage 2010, 106)

"To colonize does not mean merely to construct wharves, factories, and railroads," wrote Le Maréchal Hubert Lyautey, Commissioner General of the exposition, "it means also to instill a humane gentleness in the wild hearts of the savannah or the desert." (Lyautey 1931, n.p.) Maréchal Lyautey had a deep knowledge of the colonies, being the first Resident-General of the French protectorate in Morocco, which lasted from 1912. to 1956. He was in office there from 1912 to 1925, with the exception of the time in 1917, when he was France's Minister of War for three months. His influence helped to ensure that Morocco would acquire a significantly different legal position as a colony than Algeria. Instead of the assimilation policy, that was enacted in Algeria, he was insisting on the fullest application of association policy, which dictated the strict physical, political, social and cultural segregation of natives from the 'civilized' French settlers.

The end of Maréchal Lyautey's official duties in Morocco came with the French military intervention in the Rif war between the Spanish colonial forces and the Berber peoples inhabiting the region of northern Morocco, led by Muhammad Abd el-Krim. When Lyautey's heard that Maréchal Philippe Pétain, who was then Inspector-General of the Army, was to command that intervention, he felt offended, resigned from his post and went back to France. However, on returning, he had to face significant cultural opposition to his ideas on French identity. "No coherent political or social attitude (among the Surrealists) however, made its appearance until 1925; that is to say (and it is important to stress this) until the outbreak of the Moroccan war", André Breton had addressed the question 'What is Surrealism?' to a public audience in Brussels, on 1 June 1934. That specific war was, according to Breton, re-arousing surrealists' joint "hostility to the way armed conflicts affect man", faced them with "the necessity of making a public protest", and "created a precedent that was to determine the whole future direction of the movement" (Breton 1989, 116 - 117). It also ended their first, as he characterized it, "purely intuitive epoch" (1919–24) and made them enter into the second, "reasoning epoch" (1925–34). (Ibid.) The Colonial Exhibition in 1935 would make them soon enter into the third epoch of direct action. They invited the audience not to visit it, and, in collaboration with other anti-colonial groups they made a counter-exhibition, addressing the actual state of affairs at the colonies.

The Leaflet: "Ne visitez pas l'Exposition Coloniale!"/ "Do not visit the Colonial Exhibition", was conceived by André Breton, Paul Eluard, Louis Aragon, and Maxime Alexandre, and co-signed by Benjamin Péret, Georges Sadoul, René Char, Yves Tanguy, Pierre Unik, André Thirion, René Crevel and George Malkine. It was later followed by another text, entitled "First Assessment of the Colonial Exhibition". Sascha Bru, in his book "The European Avant-Gardes, 1905–1935 stressed, as the most important issue in the first text, the criticism of the manner in which the exhibition presented its content: "the way in which colonized regions were presented to people in France, as if these were tropical paradises where even uneducated (male) colonizers awaited an easy life with local women all too willing to serve them" (Bru 2018, 152) In order to show the exactly opposite, Surrealists joined the "League against Imperialism and Colonial Oppression" and made an exhibition entitled: "The truth about the Colonies", which was to show that the colonies were a place of utmost horror: exploitation, oppression, forced labor and death.

There were also other critiques of the exhibition from the organized left, even more harsh. According to the "Ligue de Defense de la Race Negre" (LDRN), architectural pastiches, such as the 'Fontaine des totems' and the Pavilion of French West Africa were reduced to "crude caricatures of the art of colonized people's ancestors", while according to the statements of the Vietnamese "Comite de Lutte", the staged spectacles going on in the framework of the exhibition were using indigenous participants just "like a herd of strange beasts for the pleasure of the eyes of the spectators". (Blake 2002, 37) The members of the "Parti Communiste Francais" (PCF) distributed a pamphlet titled "The Real Guide to the Colonial Exhibition: France's civilizing mission clarified in a few pages", in which they quoted the official data supplied at the exhibition with data collected on the ground by activist's groups, that made a completely opposite story.

In the New York MOMA collection, a copy of the leaflet: " Do not visit the Colonial Exhibition!" is listed as an artwork. If that were in accordance with his own intentions, Breton would be an artist who was totally blinded by his wish to erase the difference between activism and art. But I doubt that, since, in contrast to the other activists, the surrealists did not only want to correct the view on the colonies the official exhibition was providing, but to go beyond the realm of colonial phantasies and show all the traumatic features of everyday life in the colonies, as their actual 'truth'. What they loathed and actually tried to point towards was the further exploitation of colonial subjects that goes on beyond the extraction of their physical labor, and the natural resources they have been proclaimed too ignorant and uncivilized to extract for themselves. The 'Colonial' exhibitions were also the extraction zones - venues of commercial exploitation of the aesthetic codes in the clothing styles, music, dances and artefact-making of the colonized, which got appropriated and copyrighted by companies from colonizing states. Instead, at the exhibition they made, the surrealists have equally treated all the African ceremonial 'fetish' objects and the European ritual objects labeled as 'catholic fetish', in displays made to" redistribute the sensible".

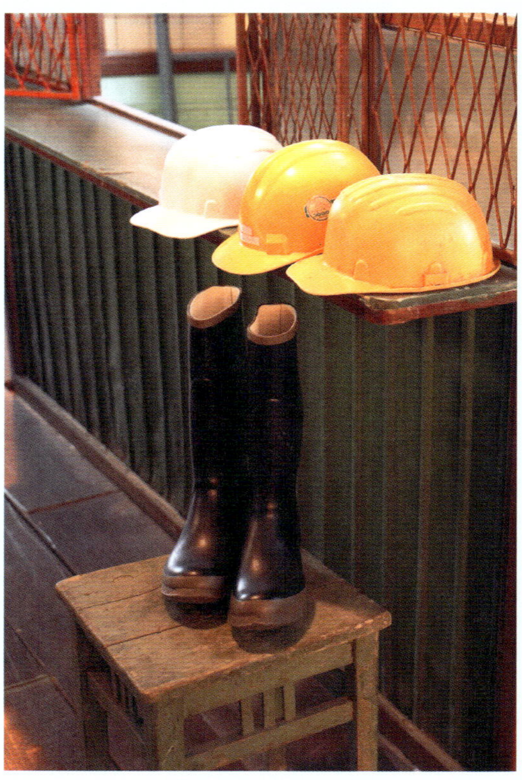

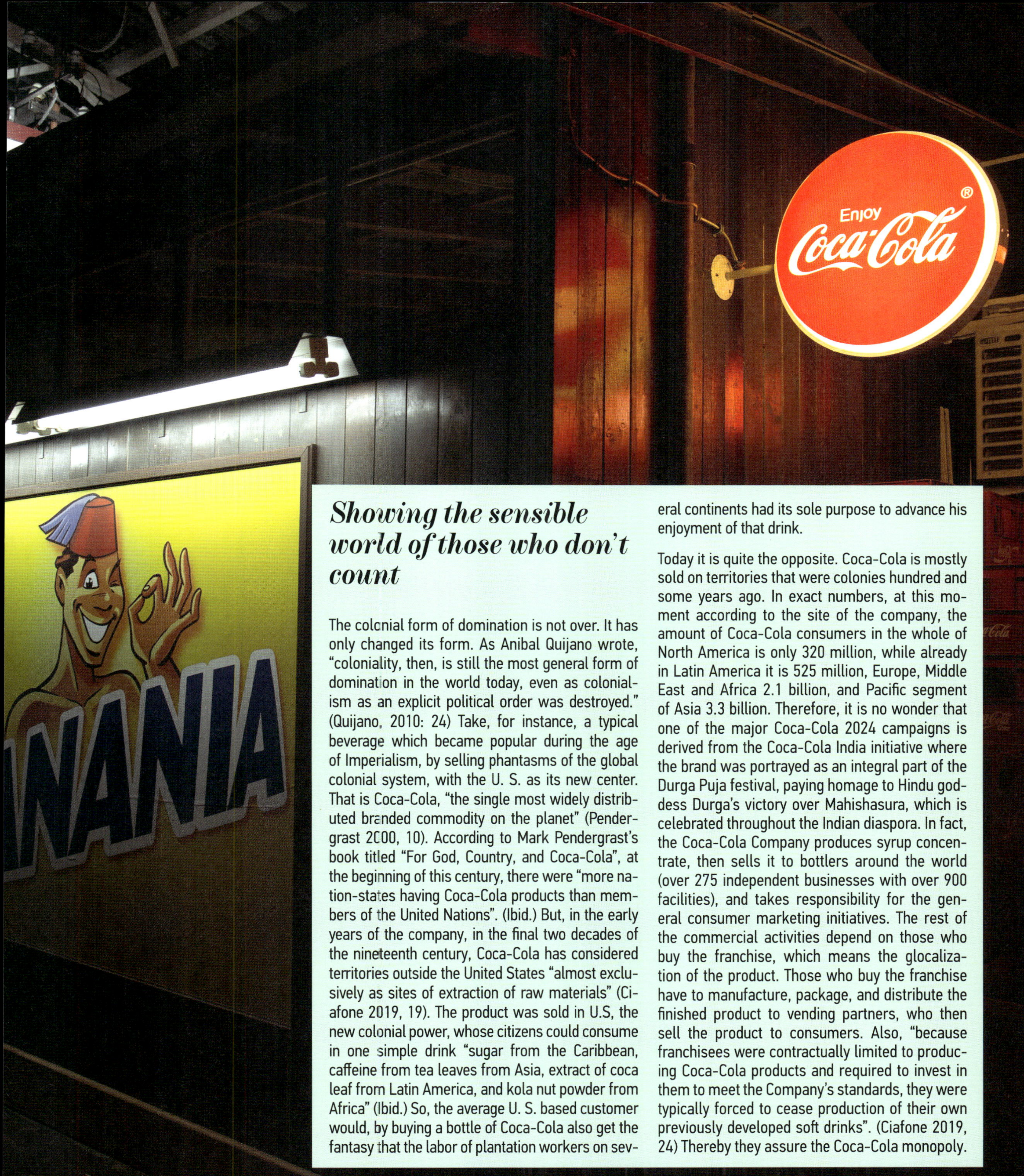

Showing the sensible world of those who don't count

The colonial form of domination is not over. It has only changed its form. As Anibal Quijano wrote, "coloniality, then, is still the most general form of domination in the world today, even as colonialism as an explicit political order was destroyed." (Quijano, 2010: 24) Take, for instance, a typical beverage which became popular during the age of Imperialism, by selling phantasms of the global colonial system, with the U. S. as its new center. That is Coca-Cola, "the single most widely distributed branded commodity on the planet" (Pendergrast 2000, 10). According to Mark Pendergrast's book titled "For God, Country, and Coca-Cola", at the beginning of this century, there were "more nation-states having Coca-Cola products than members of the United Nations". (Ibid.) But, in the early years of the company, in the final two decades of the nineteenth century, Coca-Cola has considered territories outside the United States "almost exclusively as sites of extraction of raw materials" (Ciafone 2019, 19). The product was sold in U.S, the new colonial power, whose citizens could consume in one simple drink "sugar from the Caribbean, caffeine from tea leaves from Asia, extract of coca leaf from Latin America, and kola nut powder from Africa" (Ibid.) So, the average U. S. based customer would, by buying a bottle of Coca-Cola also get the fantasy that the labor of plantation workers on sev-eral continents had its sole purpose to advance his enjoyment of that drink.

Today it is quite the opposite. Coca-Cola is mostly sold on territories that were colonies hundred and some years ago. In exact numbers, at this moment according to the site of the company, the amount of Coca-Cola consumers in the whole of North America is only 320 million, while already in Latin America it is 525 million, Europe, Middle East and Africa 2.1 billion, and Pacific segment of Asia 3.3 billion. Therefore, it is no wonder that one of the major Coca-Cola 2024 campaigns is derived from the Coca-Cola India initiative where the brand was portrayed as an integral part of the Durga Puja festival, paying homage to Hindu goddess Durga's victory over Mahishasura, which is celebrated throughout the Indian diaspora. In fact, the Coca-Cola Company produces syrup concentrate, then sells it to bottlers around the world (over 275 independent businesses with over 900 facilities), and takes responsibility for the general consumer marketing initiatives. The rest of the commercial activities depend on those who buy the franchise, which means the glocalization of the product. Those who buy the franchise have to manufacture, package, and distribute the finished product to vending partners, who then sell the product to consumers. Also, "because franchisees were contractually limited to producing Coca-Cola products and required to invest in them to meet the Company's standards, they were typically forced to cease production of their own previously developed soft drinks". (Ciafone 2019, 24) Thereby they assure the Coca-Cola monopoly.

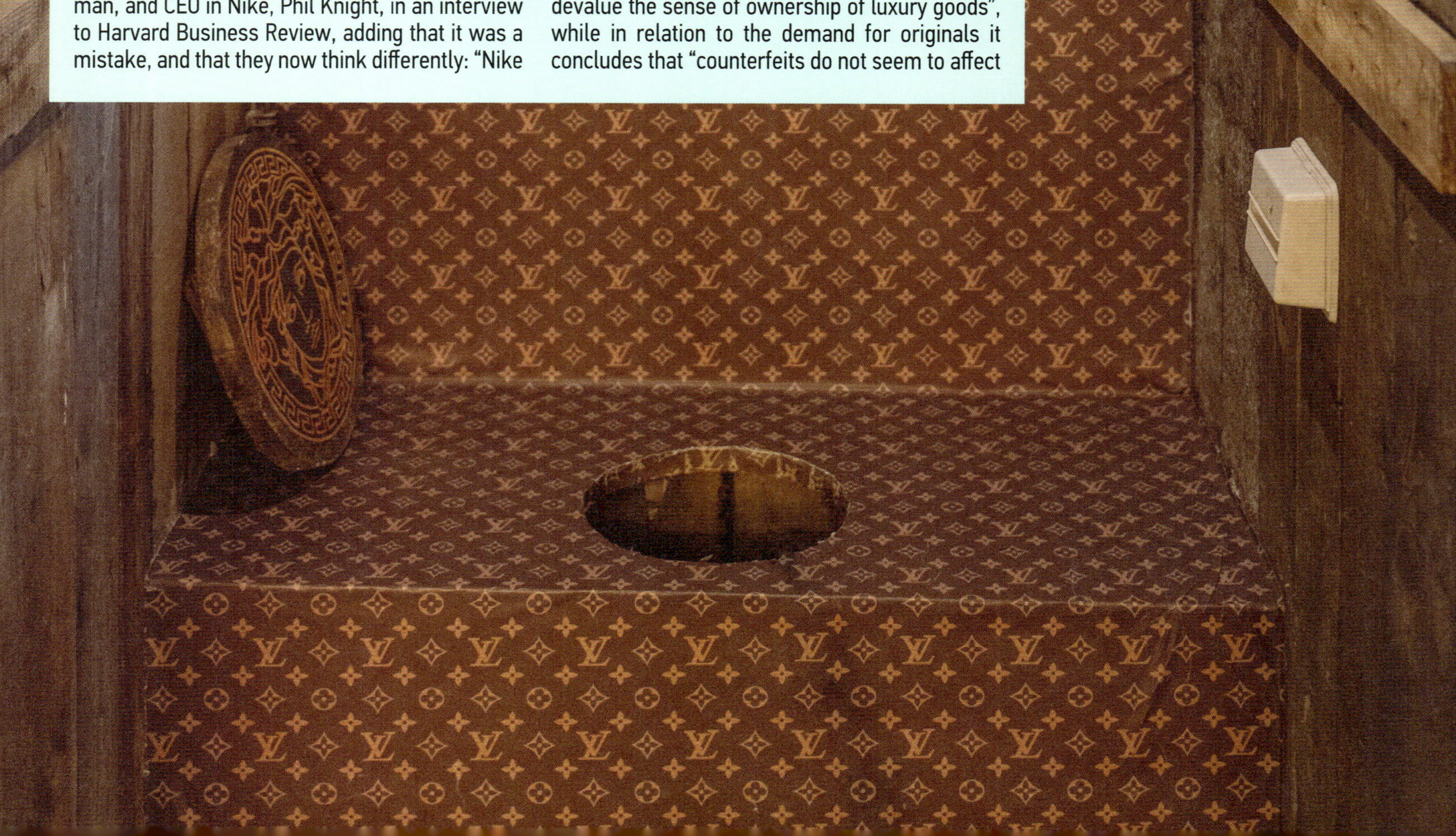

As Adam Arvidsson, author of the book "Brands: Meaning and Value in Media Culture" wrote, "brands now provide a source of meaning and a 'community', capable of replacing those supposedly lost in the modernization process". (Arvidsson 2006, 5) Globally distributed brands can provide a homely feeling to those customers who are used to consuming them on daily basis wherever they would be, including the military trenches, for instance, since Coca-Cola and Lucky Strike developed special arrangements with the U.S. Army already during WWII. That goes for those who have conventional identities, obtained by simply adjusting to the immediate surroundings and acquiring a sense of belonging from it. On the other hand, for those who use brands to become visually distinct, and develop a different identity, some brands can really help in a total remake. Hal Foster has, in a supplement to his "Design and Crime" book, wrote that "today you don't have to be filthy rich to be projected not only as designer but as designed". To become designed according to your wildest fantasies, you can even alter "your sagging face (designer surgery) or your lagging personality (designer drugs), your historical memory (designer museums) or your DNA future (designer children)". (Foster 2002, 192) The use of designer brands is just the first step in that.

"For years we thought of ourselves as a production-oriented company", said the founder, chairman, and CEO in Nike, Phil Knight, in an interview to Harvard Business Review, adding that it was a mistake, and that they now think differently: "Nike is a marketing-oriented company, and the product is our most important marketing tool". (Klein 2000: 44) Hartmut Böhme has extended the Nike brand issue in his book titled "Fetishism and Culture", explaining that "the manufacturing company is not so much selling the shoes, but instead the brand they carry, the design, lifestyle, sense of identity, fashion and sense of belonging to cultural groups that are attached to the brand and not the shoe" (Böhme 2014, 106). That makes it "a cultural artefact, a switch in the circuit of symbolic values", and not just a "functional device".

Therefore, an outhouse with a Versace logo on the toilet lid, and Louis Vuitton-themed wallpaper pasted on its walls, such as the one at the "Exposition Coloniale", necessarily adds quite some class to the experience of using it, and some status to the user, regardless of the question if it is a counterfeit. Namely, as several empirical researches of Luuk van Kempen, a development economist specialized in behavioral aspects of poverty, have shown, a counterfeit luxury brand's product is quite sometimes the optimal choice for status-minded consumers with budget constraints. On the other hand, as the very frequently quoted and much-discussed text "Do counterfeits devalue the ownership of luxury brands?" by Arghavan Nia and Judith Lynne Zaichkowsky concludes related to the customer experience, it turns out that, "in general, counterfeits may not devalue the sense of ownership of luxury goods", while in relation to the demand for originals it concludes that "counterfeits do not seem to affect demand for originals, due to the exclusivity, durability and better quality of original luxury brands". (Nia and Zaichkowsky 2000, 495)

Anyway, while sitting on that Versace/Vuitton branded toilet, one can enjoy the view on the backside of the huge lit letter sign "Europe[tm]", which would then demarcate this uncanny zone as, in fact, a kind of a Eurozone. To make this sense of belonging to Europe even stronger among visitors, each of the songs one can play on a jukebox in the cantina has "Europe" in the title: So, one can insert a coin and listen to the "European Son", a 1966. song by the Velvet Underground, produced by Andy Warhol; to "Insieme: 1992" by Toto Cutugno, the winning song of the Eurovision Song Contest 1990, in Zagreb, Yugoslavia; "Evropa Čoček" by the Džambo Aguševi Orchestra, a Balkan brass song composed by the "Funky Tiger of Macedonia"; "Trans Europe Express", by Koto (Kraftwerk cover from 1990); "Fortress Europe", by Asian Dub Foundation, from the soundtrack of the 2002 Jonathan Demme film "The Truth About Charlie"; to "Europa" by Carlos Santana, "Radio Free Europe" by R. E. M, etc. If "Europe" is mainly a trademark, and in public diplomacy today there is a tendency towards branding nations and regions, then this looks like a kind of mock campaign to franchise the brand to the candidate countries to join the EU, which have more and more problems of demand, when distributing it. Namely, as Kortenska, Steunenberg & Sircar wrote in a 2019 article on elite and citizen discourses on European integration in Serbia, the proclaimed key components of the EU's enlargement strategy are "justice, stability, and 'returning to Europe'", but, in Serbia, that does not "filter down to citizens, whose attitudes are based on opportunity and pragmatism". (Kortenska et al. 2019, n.p.) So, there is a significant gap between the discourses of ordinary people and of the elites who try to sell them the franchised idea of Europe as the cradle of democratic traditions and personal liberties. According to Kiossev, these elites are characteristic of the "self-colonizing cultures" (Kiossev 1999, 114–118), as a "special brand of self-reinforcing peripherally, neatly connected with narratives of fidelity to the European project", which they believe to be based "on the Enlightenment foundations of liberalism, human rights, and civic ethos"." (Huigen and Kołodziejczyk 2023: 2)

So, the political elites argue that insisting on a European identity is necessary for the symbolic constitution of the social world in the applicant countries, and that it has to be debated in economic and legal terms. But where is it in the sensorial and everyday phenomenological experience? What kind of sensorial world exists behind the big lighted letter sign "Europe[tm]"? that cannot be simply explained, analyzed and interpreted, it has to be shown; demonstrated. And that demonstration has to answer the common question to the Gastarbeiter (foreign or migrant workers), asked by friends from home: "how is life there?" Aleksandar Denić, being a Gastarbeiter himself, has offered this quite dystopian demonstration.

Wandering through the setting of the installation, one also encounters a billboard for West cigarettes and Wild Turkey bourbon whiskey, a banner advertising the Banania drink, and glowing advertisements for Schwarzkopf hair care products and Coca-Cola. Texaco and Rosneft branded used oil drums are placed next to the vacant phone booth, painted in the colors of the Ukrainian flag, which in regular intervals rings in a very loud manner, but, since the receiver is disconnected, it is not possible to answer the call, nor to stop the ringing in any other way. The military or hospital-style up and down metal bed squeezed into the kiosk has, instead of mattresses, packages of offers leaflets from Lidl, with quite recognizable designs. On the bed, as well as in the bathroom/sauna there are clothes left, as well as some shoes, rubber boots and construction helmets. There are visible signs of use but no signs of any personalization of those spaces, which seems a bit puzzling. Since the air conditioner in the room is on, and the water in the bathroom is running, the whole setting seems as if its regular users have just suddenly left, taking all personal belongings with them. And it seems that someone is constantly calling them on the phone whose receiver is out of function. But there is no script to the story, so questions of this kind cannot be answered.

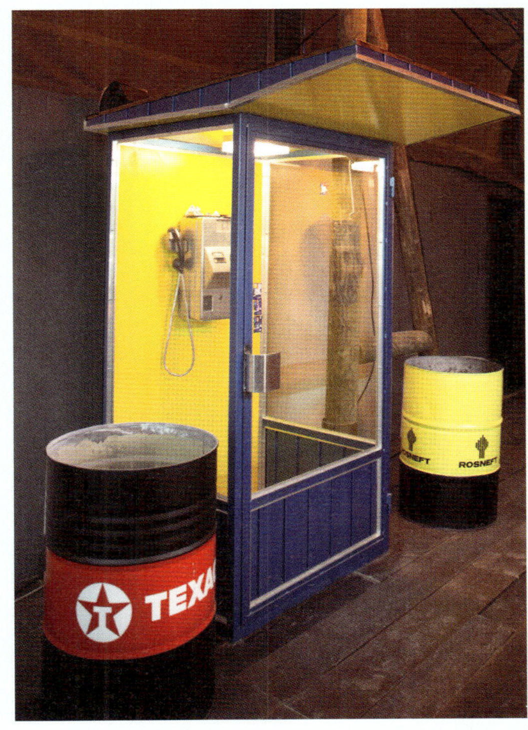

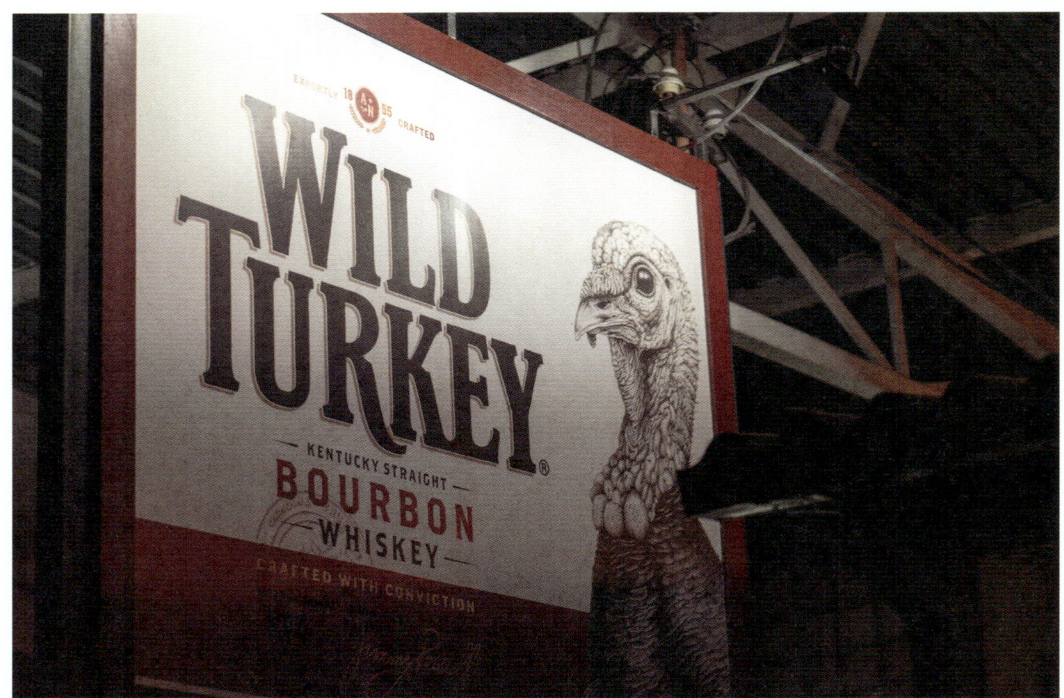

The feeling with which one leaves the installation, or uses one of many surfaces in its structure to sit and rest before continuing the stroll among other pavilions, is quite physical. Regardless of the abundance of signifiers scattered around, and the provocative title of the show, what really strikes the visitor are the sounds, the smells, the temperature in the cooled-down room versus the temperature in the back passage which is heated by the engine of the used up air conditioner, the moistness in the bathroom, the way in which each local light looks and how much light it provides, the ways in which the fence on the entrance was welded and painted, or the electric cables tied into knots, and those carefully and precisely planned vistas one encounters moving through the space. All that in synergy makes what Rancière calls "a specific regime of the sensible, which is extricated from its ordinary connections and is inhabited by a heterogeneous power, the power of a form of thought that has become foreign to itself". (Rancière 2004, 22–23) If, for Rancière, politics aims towards giving a voice to those that do not count, aesthetics provides them with a way to show their sensible world. The aesthetic segment of this installation does precisely that.

According to Rancière, "there is politics when there is a part of those who have no part", for instance, "a part or party of the poor".(Rancière 1999: 11) Politics happens because that part does not count as an equal part of society (instead of poor, that could be migrants, or, historically women, slaves, foreigners), and that exclusion is essential for the existence of a political community. Social consensus is always based on exclusion. In other words, "politics arises from a count of community 'parts', which is always a false count, a double count, or a miscount" (Rancière 1999: 2), but only in rare and occasional moments that fact becomes clear. Also, besides showing that inequality exists in a society it is necessary to show that equality is to be a presupposition. In order to deal with inequality, by including the part that has no part, one has to be able to see them, those invisible parts of the society, and also to see from their standpoint, in order to question the hierarchical structure of the society exactly from that standpoint. That is the way in which aesthetics and politics intervene into the symbolic constitution of the social world.

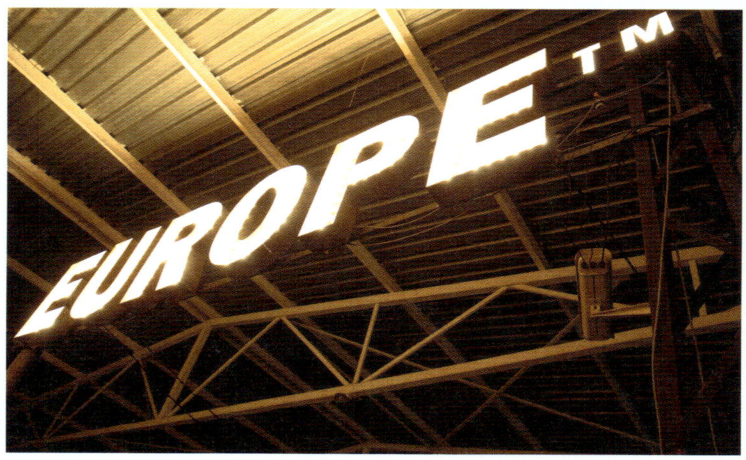

Used literature:

1. Aldrich, R. 2009. Colonial Museums in a Postcolonial Europe, African and Black Diaspora: An International Journal, 2:2, 137-156.
2. Arvidsson, A. 2006.Brands: Meaning and Value in Media Culture. London: Routledge.
3. Asher, M. 1983. Writings 1973–1983 on Works 1969–1979, ed. Benjamin H.D. Buchloh. Halifax: Nova Scotia College of Art and Design/ Museum of Contemporary Art, Los Angeles.
4. August, T. 1982."The Colonial Exposition in France: Education or Reinforcement?" Proceedings of the Meeting of the French Colonial Historical Society Vol. 6/7 (1982), 147-154.
5. Benjamin, W. "Unpacking my Library: A Talk about Bal, Book Collecting," in Illuminations. New York: Schocken Books, 1969, 59-67.
6. Bhaba, H. 1994.The Location of Culture. London, New York: Routledge.
7. Bishop, C. 2006. "The Social Turn: Collaboration and Its Discontents," Artforum, vol. 44, no. 6 (February 2006)
8. Bourriaud, N. 2002. Relational Aesthetics. Dijon: Les Presses du réel.
9. Böhme, H. 2014. Fetishism and Culture: A Different Theory of Modernity. Berlin and Boston: De Gruyter.
10. Breton, A. 1989. "What is Surrealism?", in Rosemont, F. (ed.), What is Surrealism?. London: Pluto, 1989.
11. Bru, S. 2018. The European Avant-Gardes, 1905–1935. Edinburgh: Edinburgh University Press.
12. Cavell, S. 1989. This New Yet Unapproachable America: Lectures after Emerson and Wittgenstein. Albuquerque: Living Bath Press.
13. Carnevale F, and Kelsey, J. 2007. "Art of the Possible: Fulvia Carnevale and John Kelsey in Conversation with Jacques Rancière," Artforum, vol. 45. no. 7 (March 2007).
14. Ciafone. A. 2019. Counter-Cola: A Multinational History of the Global Corporation. Oakland, California: University of California Press.
15. Crary, J. 1990. Techniques of the Observor: On Vision and Modernite in the Nineteenth Century. Cambridge, Mass.: MIT Press.
16. Doherty, C. 2004. "The Institution is Dead! Long Live the Institution! Contemporary Art and New Institutionalism," Engage 15 (Summer 2004).
17. Knox, P. 1993."Capital, Material Culture and Socio-Spatial Differentiation'. In Knox, P. 1993. (ed.). The Restless Urban Landscape, Englewood Cliffs NJ: Prentice Hall, 1–34.
18. Ferraz de Matos, P, Birkalan-Gedik, H, Barrera-González, A. and Vail, P. 2022. "World Fairs, Exhibitions and Anthropology - Revisiting Contexts of Post-colonialism". Anthropological Journal of European Cultures Volume 31, No. 2 (2022): 1-14.
19. Freud, S. (1933). New Introductory Lectures On Psycho-Analysis. The Standard Edition of the Complete Psychological Works of Sigmund Freud, Volume XXII (1932-1936): New Introductory Lectures on Psycho-Analysis and Other Works, 1-182.
20. Gómez-Barris, M. 2017. The Extractive Zone - Social Ecologies and Decolonial Perspectives. Durham and London: Duke University Press.
21. Hoffenberg, P.H. 2001. An Empire on Display: English, Indian, and Australian Exhibitions from the Crystal Palace to the Great War. Berkeley and Los Angeles: University of California Press.
22. Huigen S. and Kołodziejczyk D. (eds.) 2023. East Central Europe Between the Colonial and the Postcolonial in the Twentieth Century. Cham: Palgrave Macmillan.
23. Gordillo, G. 2013 "The Void: Invisible Ruins on the Edges of Empire", Imperial Debris: On Ruins and Ruination, edited by A. L. Stoler . Durham: Duke University Press, 227–251.
24. Kabakov, I. 1995 On the Total Installation. Ostfildern, Germany: Cantz Verlag.
25. Kiossev, A. 1999. Notes of Self-Colonising Cultures. In Pejić, B.and Elliott, D. (Eds.) After the Wall - Art and Culture in Post-communist Europe. Stockholm: Moderna Museet. 114–118.
26. Klein, N. 2000. No Logo. Taking Aim at the Brand Bullies. London: Flamingo.
27. Knox, P. 1993. "Capital, material culture and socio-spatial differentiation". In P. Knox (ed.), The Restless Urban Landscape, Englewood Cliffs NJ: Prentice Hall, 1–34.
28. Kristeva, J. 1991. Strangers to Ourselves. New York: Columbia University Press.
29. Küppers-Lissitzky, S. 1967. El Lissitzky: Life, Letters, Text. Greenwich, Conn.: New York Graphic Society.
30. Marx, K. 1975. Economic and Philosophic Manuscripts of 1844, in Karl Marx and Friedrich Engels, Collected Works, vol. 3, Marx and Engels, 1843—1844. New York: International Publishers.
31. Marx, K. 1992. Capital, Vol III: A Critique of Political Economy. New York: Penguin Classics.
32. Masschelein, A.2011. The Unconcept. The Freudian Uncanny in the Late-Twentieth Century Theory. Albany: State University of New York.
33. Morand, P. 1931. 1900. Paris: Flammarion.
34. Morton, P. A. 1998. "National and Colonial: The Musée des Colonies at the Colonial Exposition, Paris, 1931". The Art Bulletin, Vol. 80, No. 2 (Jun., 1998), 357-377
35. Nia, A., & Zaichkowsky, J. 2000. "Do counterfeits devalue the ownership of luxury brands?", in Journal of Product and Brand Management, 9(7), 485-497
36. Olivier, M. 1931. "Avant-Propos," Le Livre d'Or de l'Exposition Coloniale Internationale de Paris. Paris: Librairie Ancienne Honoré Champion.
37. Pendergrast, M. 2000. For God, Country, and Coca-Cola: The Definitive History of the Great American Soft Drink and the Company That Makes It. New York: Basic Books.
38. Podoroga, V. 2003. Notes on Ilya Kabakov's 'On the Total Installation' Third Text, Vol. 17, Issue 4, 2003, 345–352
39. Pugliese, J. 2009."Crisis Heterotopias and Border Zones of the Dead", Continuum: Journal of Media & Cultural Studies, 23.5 (2009), 663–79.
40. Rancière, J. 1999. Disagreement: Politics and Philosophy, Minneapolis: University of Minnesota Press.
41. Rancière, J. 2004. The Politics of Aesthetics. London: Continuum Books.
42. Rancière, J. 2010. Dissensus: On Politics and Aesthetics. Continuum.
43. Sauvage, A. 2010."To be or not to be Colonial: Museums Facing Their Exhibitions". Culturales, vol. VI, núm. 12, julio-diciembre, 2010, pp. 97-116
44. Quijano, A. 2010. "Coloniality and Modernity / Rationality",in Walter D. Mignolo, W. D. and Escobar, A. (eds.) 2010. Globalization and the Decolonial Option.London and New York: Routledge, 22 - 32.
45. Van Troi, T. 2015. "How 'Natives' Ate at Colonial Exhibitions in 1889, 1900 and 1931". French Cultural Studies 2015, Vol. 26(2), 163 –175
46. van Wesemael, P. 2001. Architecture of Instruction and Delight: A Socio-historical Analysis of World Exhibition as a Didactic Phenomenon (1798-1851-1970). Rotterdam: OIO Publishers.

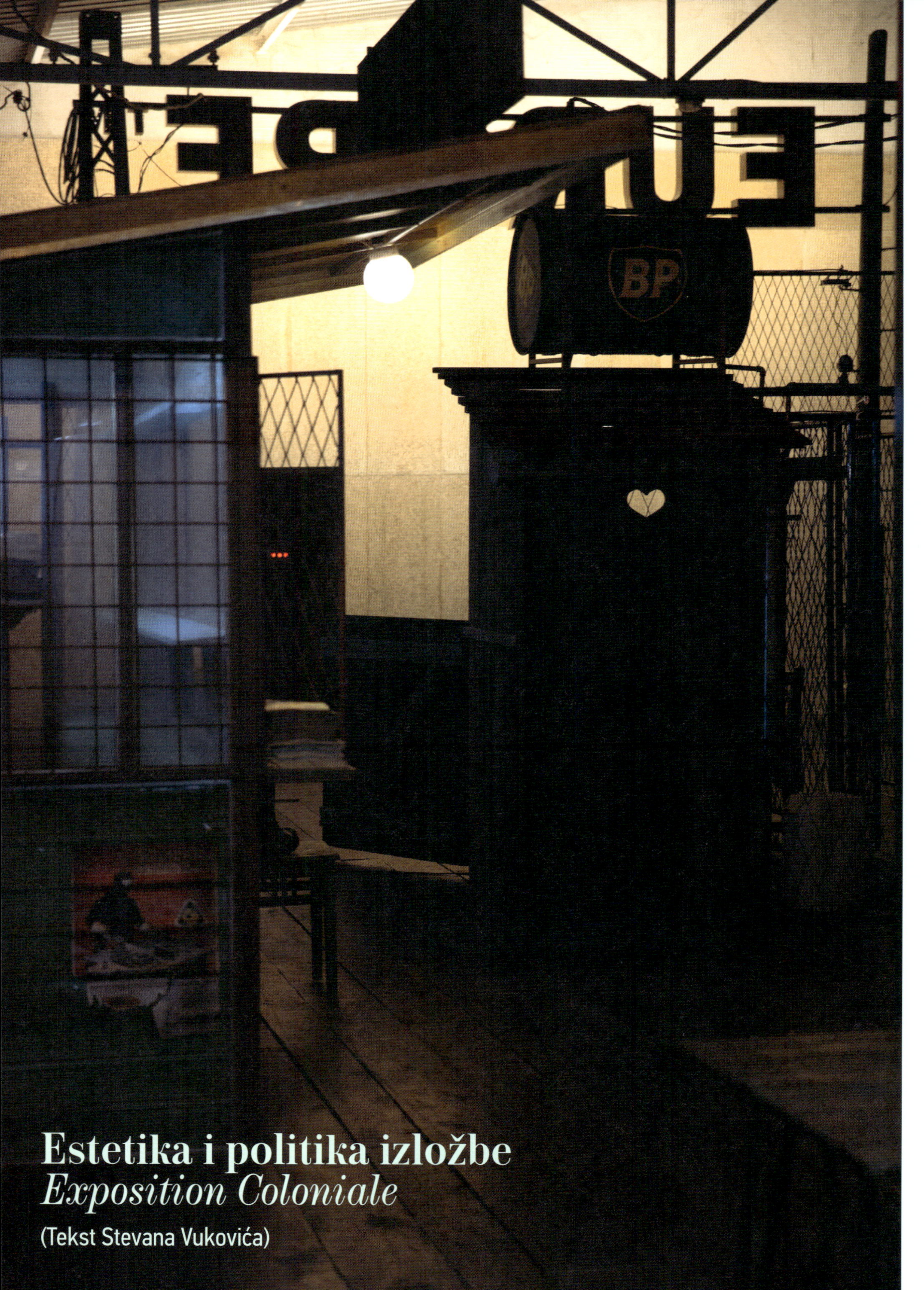

Estetika i politika izložbe
Exposition Coloniale

(Tekst Stevana Vukovića)

„Kritička umetnost je umetnost koja ima za cilj da proizvede novu percepciju sveta i da, stoga, stvori rešenost za njegovu promenu. Ova šema, naizgled veoma jednostavna, u stvari je rezultat tri procesa: prvog, da se načini čulna forma 'stranosti'; drugog, da se razvije svest o razlogu za tu stranost; i trećeg, da se pojedinci mobilišu usled te svesti.“

(Rancière 2010, 142)

„*U stranoj zemlji u sopstvenoj domovini*“

Kako sam zakoračio u totalnu instalaciju Aleksandra Denića, pod naslovom *Exposition Coloniale*, koja je po prvi put bila postavljena u nekadašnjem skladištu na periferiji Beograda da bi je na brzinu testirali, razmontirali i prevezli do Paviljona Srbije na 60. Bijenalu u Veneciji, pale su mi na pamet reči iz knjižice Luja Aragona, one koje su postale moto knjige Julije Kristeve *Stranci sebi samima*. Naime, osećao sam da sam „u stranoj zemlji u sopstvenoj domovini.“ Znajući da ću ući u instalaciju, izvedenu na osnovu Denićevih iskustava scenskog dizajna za pozorišne događaje, pripremio sam se na nešto u potpuno drugom vizuelnom kodu, nešto mnogo udaljenije od toga na šta bih naleteo šetajući po nekom urbanom predgrađu.

Postavka je bila veoma blizu nekim samoregulisanim i samoizgrađenim delimično urbanim rubnim naseobinama, koje su vrlo česte u zemlji u kojoj trenutno obitavam i mnogim drugim koje sam posetio, ali je bila svedena na potpuni minimum funkcija i pogodnosti i delovala je kao turobna, zastrašujuća i napuštena. Sa druge strane, bila je potpuno kolonizovana predstavama brendova, u dijapazonu od Koka-Kole do Švarckopfa, Vesta i burbona Vajld Turki do Teksakoa, Britanskog petroleja i Rosnefta, Versaćea i Luj Vitona, od čega je ponešto bilo na recikliranim predmetima, kao što je bure u kome se obično sakuplja kišnica za improvizovani tuš. Čak je i svetleći znak koji je označavao Evropu bio potpuno okrenut ka zidu i imao natpis „Europe™“, ne kao naziv teritorije kojoj neko pripada, već kao robna marka u poslovanju franšizama.

Ova postavka paraarhitektonskih objekata i instalacija nije proizvedena samo za poglede posetilaca da bi ih fascinirala ili zavela, ni da predstavi ili ilustruje neku ideju. Rad je očigledno bio formatiran kao totalna instalacija — „sasvim reprocesiran prostor“ (Kabakov 1995, 127), čije osobine, po interpretacijama nekadašnjeg ruskog filozofa Valerija Podroge „ne mogu biti shvaćene, nego samo prepoznate“ i to je „skoro uvek trenutno“ (Podoroga 2003, 351). Načinjen je da bi „učinio posetioca aktivnim“, što je Lisicki očekivao od sopstvenih instalacija (Küppers-Lissitzky 1967, 362); ali i Alan

Kaprov od okruženja (environments) koje je sam pravio. U brošuri pod nazivom *Beleške o stvaranju totalne umetnosti* iz 1958, Kaprov je čak dao instrukcije posetiocima, pišući da „na ovu ovde prisutnu izložbu ne dolazimo da bismo gledali u neke stvari“, već „da bismo bili okruženi njima, i postali deo toga što nas okružuje.“ (Kaprow 2003, 10–11)

Blisko logici okruženja, ovaj rad se ne oslanja na niz unapred određenih aktivnosti koje bi posetioci trebalo da izvode, kao što je to slučaj u većini dela relacione umetnosti, koje koriste postojeće „forme društvenosti“, kako ih je Burijo nazvao (Bourriaud 1998, 13), pozivajući posetioce na setove akcija kao što su, recimo, spuštanje niz tobogan, lebdenje ili kuvanje. Štaviše, ovaj rad je načinjen sa namerom da se izbegnu ta dva tipa grešaka, koje je Kler Doerti pripisala relacionoj umetnosti. Jedan od njih se tiče već opisanog „procepa između retorike angažovanja i aktuelnog doživljaja rada“, koji će „pre voditi ka impotentnoj participaciji, nego dinamičnom iskustvu.“ (Doherty 2004, 6) Drugi je u tome da izložbe tog tipa „mogu da deluju kao nova participativna iskustva, pre nego nešto po sebi.“ (Ibid.) Kler Bišop je još razjasnila tu drugu grešku pišući da bi, u relacionoj umetnosti „umetnik trebalo da se liši svog autorskog prisustva, omogućavajući učesnicima projekta da progovore preuzimajući tu funkciju)“, sledeći ideju da bi umetnost trebalo da se izvuče iz domena 'nekorisnog' i da se sjedini sa nekim društvenim praksama.“ (Bishop 2006, 183)

Autorsko prisustvo je prilično jasno na ovoj postavci nazvanoj *Exposition Coloniale*, čak iako poziva publiku da stupi u fizički odnos sa svakim elementom postavke, bez toga da je nekim scenarijem unapred zadano šta bi neko mogao da radi. Kao u Denićevom scenografskom radu, koji je u potpunosti svet za sebe, samodovoljan, tako da ko god da nešto izvodi samo treba taj svet da naseli i narativ koji u njemu treba da se izvede će naći svoje mesto. U ovom specifičnom slučaju taj rad se sastoji od male sobe (bez toaleta i kupatila), kioska, kafane, poljskog kupatila, javnog kupatila sa saunom, telefonske govornice i javnog aparata za slikanje. Dovoljno za prostog radnog čoveka da se između smena teškog rada odmori negde gde baš i ne pripada (bez obzira što, možda, potiče sa tog mesta). Razlika spram njegovog scenografskog rada za pozorište je upravo u činjenici da u ovoj postavci nema scene koja bi se mogla videti sa distance, niti scenarija, glumaca ili režisera.

Tokom njegovih saradnji sa pozorišnim režiserom Frankom Kastorfom, uvek je bilo jasno da su procedure za njihov zajednički rad izvedene iz principa Bertolda Brehta, koje je objasnio u knjižici zabeleški za operu *Mahagoni*, kojima je, po Daglasu Kelneru „razlikovao svoje razdvajanje reči, muzike i scene od vagnerovskog Gezamtkunstverka, koji je spajao

41

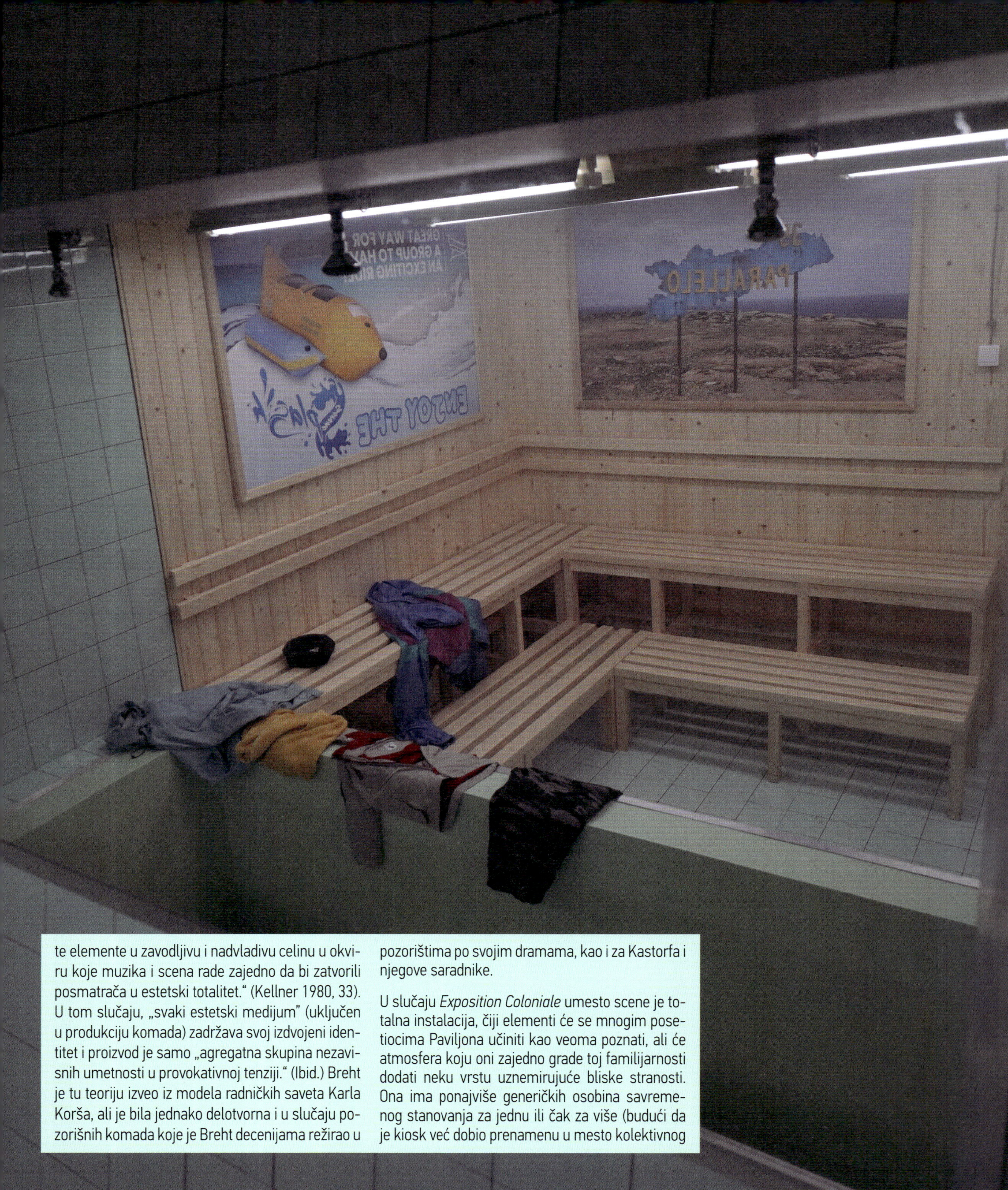

te elemente u zavodljivu i nadvladivu celinu u okviru koje muzika i scena rade zajedno da bi zatvorili posmatrača u estetski totalitet." (Kellner 1980, 33). U tom slučaju, „svaki estetski medijum" (uključen u produkciju komada) zadržava svoj izdvojeni identitet i proizvod je samo „agregatna skupina nezavisnih umetnosti u provokativnoj tenziji." (Ibid.) Breht je tu teoriju izveo iz modela radničkih saveta Karla Korša, ali je bila jednako delotvorna i u slučaju pozorišnih komada koje je Breht decenijama režirao u pozorištima po svojim dramama, kao i za Kastorfa i njegove saradnike.

U slučaju *Exposition Coloniale* umesto scene je totalna instalacija, čiji elementi će se mnogim posetiocima Paviljona učiniti kao veoma poznati, ali će atmosfera koju oni zajedno grade toj familjarnosti dodati neku vrstu uznemirujuće bliske stranosti. Ona ima ponajviše generičkih osobina savremenog stanovanja za jednu ili čak za više (budući da je kiosk već dobio prenamenu u mesto kolektivnog stanovanja) osoba u nevolji, ali to ne izaziva baš taj osećaj boravka kod kuće, pa čak ni boravka u nečijoj kući. Takođe nema jasnih indikatora prisustva bilo koga ko bi ovo smatrao domom, makar samo privremeno, iako sve što se nalazi uokolo deluje kao da se već neko duže vreme koristi (od kuhinje, preko kupatila, klupa, pa do telefonske govornice). Nema znakova prisvanja stvari i prostora, bilo od strane neke konkretne osobe, niti indikatora koji bi upućivali na neku specifičnu grupu ljudi, i nema takvih stvari uokolo koje bi nekome mogle da budu od ličnog značaja.

Dakle, ima samo jedno logično rešenje pitanja „Ko bi bili korisnici tog prostora?" – sami posetioci Paviljona. Ko god da uđe u instalaciju je prava osoba na pravom mestu ili upravo ona za koju je to mesto načinjeno. Taj stranac ili „tuđinac, imigrant, ekspatriot, osoba iz dijaspore, emigrant, azilant ili izbeglica", o kojima je Adriano Pedrosa pisao, određujući naslov i glavnu temu 60. Bijenala u Veneciji, nastanjen je u svakom pojedinačnom posetiocu. Po rečima Julije Kristeve, negde duboko unutar nas „znamo da smo stranci mi sami i da samo uz takvu podršku možemo da pokušamo da živimo sa drugima." (Kristeva 1991, 170) Samo kada stranca nađemo u sebi samima možemo stvarno da mislimo o uslovima koji su doveli mnoge ljude oko nas u tu situaciju da budu viđeni kao stranci, kao i da iskuse potpuni gubitak javnog interesa za uslove u kojima takvi stranci žive. „Dok geta i slamovi nikako baš nisu nove komponente urbane strukture", pisao je Pol Noks pre više decenije, iako su te reči aktuelne i danas „pejzaži isključenih su bez presedana u intenzitetu kombinovanja siromaštva, nasilja, očaja i izolacije." (Knox 1993b, 231)

Stoga, kao što je Analin Mašelajn već pisala, pozivajući se na Frojdovo tumačenje fenomena strane bliskosti (Das Unheimliche), na osnovu koga je Julija Kristeva izgradila svoje sopstveno, „osnovno Frojdovo tumačenje 'poznatog koje je postalo strano' ne može se odvojiti od jednog od najvažnijih pojmova u mnogim diskursima 20. veka: otuđenja kao ekonomskog, političkog, psihološkog i egzistencijalnog stanja." (Masschelein 2011, 136) Kako može neko ko je je žrtva prisilne migracije i/ili prisilnog rada – trgovine u svrhu eksploatacije radne snage, da ne bude otuđen i da se oseća kao kod kuće kad god bi neka kompanija, državna institucija ili međunarodna humanitarna organizacija našla ili obezbedila mesto na kome bi mogao privremeno da se smesti? U kupatilu instalacije *Exposition Coloniale* je poster sa 35. paralele, na ostrvu Lampeduza koje je postalo simbol besmislenih smrti afričkih migranata, koji su pokušavali da se dočepaju Evrope bilo kakvim sredstvima. Naime, tokom noći 3. oktobra 2013, drveni čamac sa utvrđenim kapacitetom od 35 osoba napunjen je toliko da je u njega stalo oko 500 osoba koje su iz Eritreje, So-

malije i Gane morale da krenu u traganju za azilom put Zapada. Brod je potonuo blizu obale tog italijanskog ostrva i njih 368 se udavilo. Čak i pre tog tragičnog događaja Jozef Puljeze je, uzimajući u obzir istoriju Lampeduze kao sabirnog logora, odredio taj prostor kao strano mesto ostrva za odmore/kažnjeničku koloniju, u kojoj, neposredno pored turista koji uživaju u svom odmoru, migranti žive svoje živote „ostajući nevidljivi za osobe iz Prvog sveta, iako su neposredno postavljeni u njihovo polje viđenja." (Pugliese 2009, 664) Nakon tragičnog događaja Federika Macara je napisala nastavak tog teksta, pišući da „u pokušaju da se te dve prostorne dimenzije drže odvojene, ali ipak i koegzistirajuće, Lampeduza se polako transformisala u 'treći prostor', kombinaciju realnog i imaginarnog prostora, gde migranti alternativno okupiraju prostore 'vidljivosti' i 'nevidljivosti', zavisno od toga ko posmatra i iz koje perspektive." (Mazzara 2015, 452)

Ova mešavina „realnog i imaginarnog prostora" vraća nas na izjavu Julije Kristeve, shodno kojoj se „uznemirujuća bliska stranost dešava kada se granice između imaginacije i realnosti izbrišu." (Kristeva 1991, 188) Zato je bitno naglasiti da u instalaciji *Exposition Coloniale* nema redimejd objekata. Sve je dizajnirao umetnik i proizveo u skladu sa svojim estetskim kodom, ali su materijali i principi izrade bili isti kao za predmete praktične upotrebe. Zato ovaj prostor nije samo scenski rekvizit. On je nastanjiv, prepoznatljiv kao najbazičnije improvizovano mesto za boravak, sasvim obično, ali, s druge strane, sasvim uznemirujuće bliske stranosti. To odgovara tezi Stenlija Kavela o „uznemirujućoj bliskoj stranosti običnog", kao nekoj vrsti „dekreacije" obične stvarnosti, receptivnosti za „nešto blisko, okupirano nečim drugim bliskim." (Cavell 1989, 47) Za Marksa, stanovanje radnika je paradigma za to: „stanovanje koje ostaje strana sila i koje se njemu podaje samo ukoliko se on podaje sopstvenoj krvi i znoju – stanovanje koje on ne može da smatra za sopstveno ognjište – na kome bi konačno mogao da uzvikne 'Ovde sam kod kuće' – već gde nalazi sebe u nečijoj tuđoj kući, u kući tog stranca koji ga stalno nadgleda i izbacuje ga ako ne plati kiriju." (Marx 1975, 314).

Izlaganje zone ekstrakcije

Kao što je Karl Marks svojevremeno opazio, kapitalistički sistem „nemilice troši ljudska bića… spremnije nego druga sredstva za proizvodnju, trošeći ne samo njihovo meso i krv, nego i nerve i mozak takođe." (Marx 1992, 182). Kapital oduzima ljudima vlasništvo, podređuje ih različitim vrstama nasilja, patnje i nebrige, koji proizvode „ljudske ruine koje [kapitalističko] osvajanje ostavlja po prostoru" (Gordillo 2013, 246). Preciznijim terminima, „kolonijalni kapitalizam je glavni katastrofični događaj koji je progutao resurse planete, diskurzivno stvarajući rasno određena tela u geografijama razlike, sistematski uništava kroz otimanje imovine, porobljavanje, a potom oblikuje planetu kao korporativnu bio-teritoriju." (Gómez-Barris 2017, 4) On mapira celu planetu da bi identifikovao i označio potencijalne zone ekstrakcije, da bi ih eksploatisao do njihovih krajnjih granica, bez obzira na istorije kojima su te zone bile svedoci, i bez poštovanja pravnih i običajnih principa koji regulišu načine njihove upotrebe.

Najranije mape takve korporativne bio-teritorije bile su predstavljene na Kolonijalnim izložbama, čiji je vrhunac popularnosti bio pre sto godina. Njihov glavni prethodnik bila je izložba održana 1851. u Kristalnoj palati u Londonu (*Velika izložba dela industrije svih naroda*), koju je sledio Sajam u Kristalnoj palati u Njujorku 1853, pa Univerzalne izložbe 1889. i 1900. u Parizu i mnoge druge. Njihova ekonomska, društvena i politička uloga je bila da pospeše „proizvodnju, trgovinu i potrošnju, uz dodatne socio-kulturne aspekte." (van Wesemael 2001, 21). Kao što je Hofenberg pisao, „izložbe su bile u srcu imperijalnih i nacionalnih, socijalnih i komercijalnih poduhvata tokom viktorijanske i edvardijanske ere" (Hoffenberg 2001, 20) i to tako da su „imperijalni, kolonijalni i nacionalni inventari bili vezani za izložbe, zvaničnim testovima i izveštajima komisija, potrošnjom, turizmom i javnim proslavama." (Ibid, XV)

Tokom ekonomske krize 1930-ih takav izloženi format koristile su glavne imperijalističke države da „promovišu ideje carstva i imperijalizma, za koje su mislili da su suštinske za modernitet i progres' i da „pokažu benefite kolonijalizma za kolonizatore." (Ferraz de Matos at all 2022, 3) Nadalje, „muzeji, koji su izuzetno brzo oformljeni radi promovisanja kolonijalizma, bili su veoma ponosni u pokazivanju blaga kolonija", tako da su „njihovi graditelji, sponzori i kustosi imali nameru da pokažu ponos imperije, da pridobiju publiku ne baš entuzijastičnu za misije civilizovanja 'divljaka', da razviju resurse oko kojih se razvijaju državne zastave, da poduče publiku o opskurnim ćoškovima

velike Britanije ili najveće Francuske, da stimulišu razne imperijalne vokacije." (Aldrich 2009, 138)

Između 1889. i 1914, čak i one izložbe koje nisu bile nazivane Kolonijalnim počele su da uključuju grupe ljudi iz kolonija, na način svojevrsnog zoološkog vrta, čija je svrha bila „biti izložen drugima radi njihovog zadovoljstva i obrazovanja." (Greenalgh 1988, 89) „Na pariskim Univerzalnim izložbama 1889. i 1900. i na *Kolonijalnoj izložbi* iz 1931, 'urođenici' iz francuskih kolonija, kao što su Indokina, Senegal, Dahomi i Nova Kaledonija, putovali su do glavnog grada Francuske da bi doneli život u sve te paviljone, bašte i rekonstruisana sela, koji su bili prikazani na tim imperijalnim izložbama." (Van Troi 2015, 163) Oni su bili takva atrakcija da je Pol Morand, diplomata i pisac sa rasističkim stanovištima, napisao da je za vreme tih izložbi: „Pariz pripadao crncima [i] žutim jedačima žive ribe." (Morand 1931, 79)

Veliko bogatstvo kolonija, kakvo je pokazano na tim izložbama, trebalo je da impresionira sve kategorije francuskih građana koji bi možda mogli da povećaju stepen njihove eksploatacije. Tako da je tamo moralo da bude nešto posebno za svaku od njih, da bi mogli da se zamisle kao potencijalni vojnici, trgovci, vlasnici plantaža, misionari, edukatori, naučni istraživači ili samo lovci hobisti i istraživači egzotičnih mesta. Tako se dijapazon proizvoda prostirao od Bananija, pića za decu, do skupog nakita za više klase kolonijalista. Bananija je pravljena od brašna od banane, mlevenih orašastih plodova i šećera, a na etiketi je bio vojnik, strelac iz Senegala koji je nosio svetlo-crveni fes i izgovarao „Y'a bon" (na imaginarnom pokvarenom francuskom jeziku – osoba sagledavana kao 'petit nègre'), dok su „francuski dizajneri nakita, poput Van Klefa i Arpersa, uveli nove linije ogrlica, narukvica i minđuša inspirisanih francuskim kolonijama", tako da su od izložbe 1931. godine „robovske ogrlice, minđuše od slonovače i korala i emajlirani broševi postali popularni." (August 1982, 153)

Prva zvanična međunarodna kolonijalna izložba bila je održana u Amsterdamu od 1. maja do 1. oktobra 1883, na mestu gde je danas Trg muzeja. Njen naziv bio je *Međunarodna kolonijalna i izvozna izložba* i na njoj je pokazano bogatstvo 28 različitih naroda, koji su pokazivali svoju trgovinu sa kolonijama. Kustos koji je stajao iza ovog događaja, koji je doveo bar million posetilaca, bio je Eduard Agostini, ranije uključen u organizovanje *Univerzalne izložbe* u Parizu 1878. Tu izložbu su potom sledile druge kolonizatorske zemlje, tako da je *Kolonijalna i indijska izložba* bila održana u Londonu 1886, *Filipinska izložba* u Madridu 1887, *Exposição Insular e Colonial Portuguesa* u Oportu 1894, *Izložba britanske imperije u Londonu* 1924, a u Francuskoj su održane *Exposition internationale*

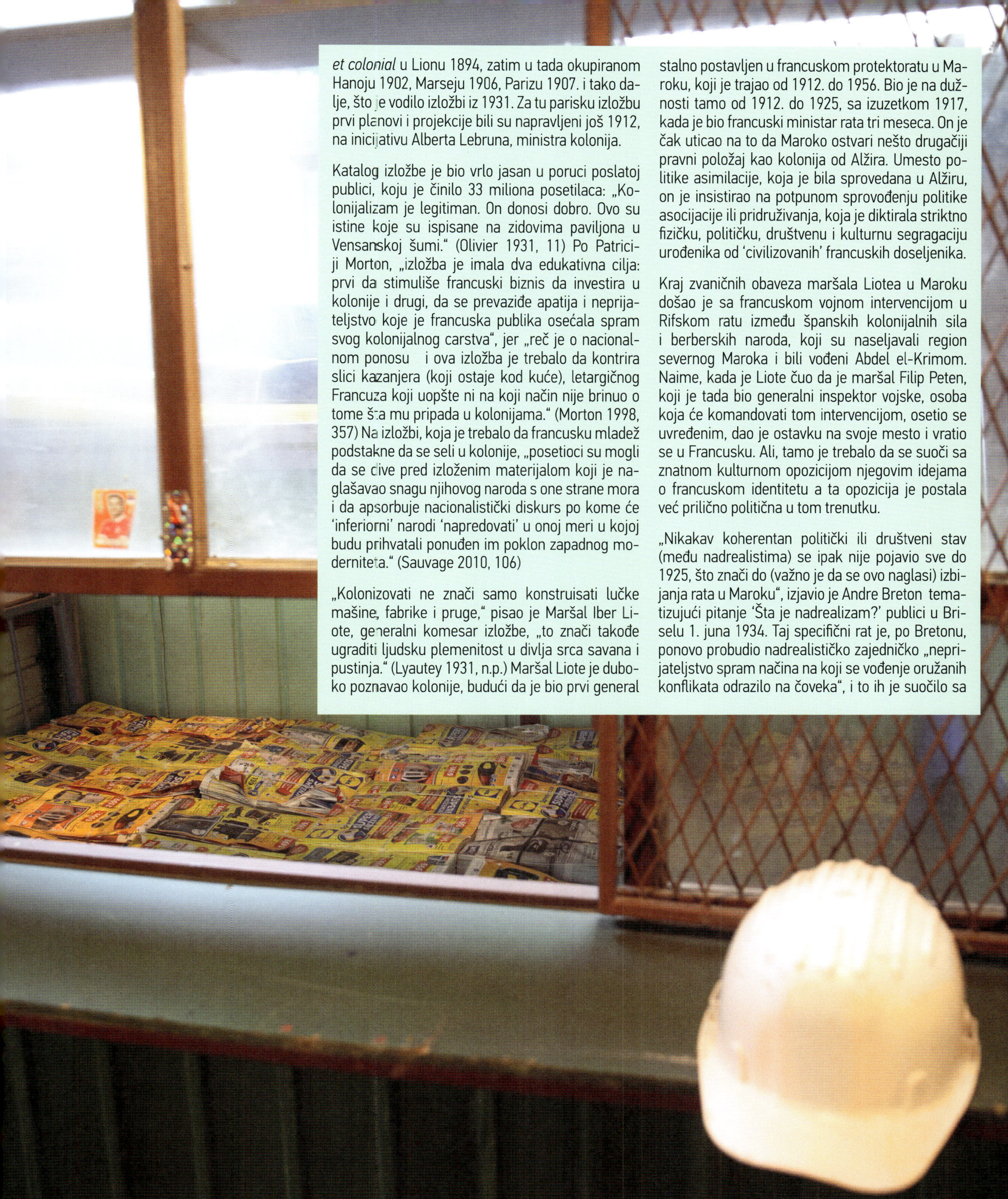

et colonial u Lionu 1894, zatim u tada okupiranom Hanoju 1902, Marseju 1906, Parizu 1907. i tako dalje, što je vodilo izložbi iz 1931. Za tu parisku izložbu prvi planovi i projekcije bili su napravljeni još 1912, na inicijativu Alberta Lebruna, ministra kolonija.

Katalog izložbe je bio vrlo jasan u poruci poslatoj publici, koju je činilo 33 miliona posetilaca: „Kolonijalizam je legitiman. On donosi dobro. Ovo su istine koje su ispisane na zidovima paviljona u Vensanskoj šumi." (Olivier 1931, 11) Po Patriciji Morton, „izložba je imala dva edukativna cilja: prvi da stimuliše francuski biznis da investira u kolonije i drugi, da se prevaziđe apatija i neprijateljstvo koje je francuska publika osećala spram svog kolonijalnog carstva", jer „reč je o nacionalnom ponosu i ova izložba je trebalo da kontrira slici kazanjera (koji ostaje kod kuće), letargičnog Francuza koji uopšte ni na koji način nije brinuo o tome šta mu pripada u kolonijama." (Morton 1998, 357) Na izložbi, koja je trebalo da francusku mladež podstakne da se seli u kolonije, „posetioci su mogli da se dive pred izloženim materijalom koji je naglašavao snagu njihovog naroda s one strane mora i da apsorbuje nacionalistički diskurs po kome će 'inferiorni' narodi 'napredovati' u onoj meri u kojoj budu prihvatali ponuđen im poklon zapadnog moderniteta." (Sauvage 2010, 106)

„Kolonizovati ne znači samo konstruisati lučke mašine, fabrike i pruge," pisao je Maršal Iber Liote, generalni komesar izložbe, „to znači takođe ugraditi ljudsku plemenitost u divlja srca savana i pustinja." (Lyautey 1931, n.p.) Maršal Liote je duboko poznavao kolonije, budući da je bio prvi general

stalno postavljen u francuskom protektoratu u Maroku, koji je trajao od 1912. do 1956. Bio je na dužnosti tamo od 1912. do 1925, sa izuzetkom 1917, kada je bio francuski ministar rata tri meseca. On je čak uticao na to da Maroko ostvari nešto drugačiji pravni položaj kao kolonija od Alžira. Umesto politike asimilacije, koja je bila sprovedana u Alžiru, on je insistirao na potpunom sprovođenju politike asocijacije ili pridruživanja, koja je diktirala striktno fizičku, političku, društvenu i kulturnu segragaciju uroćenika od 'civilizovanih' francuskih doseljenika.

Kraj zvaničnih obaveza maršala Liotea u Maroku došao je sa francuskom vojnom intervencijom u Rifskom ratu između španskih kolonijalnih sila i berberskih naroda, koji su naseljavali region severnog Maroka i bili vođeni Abdel el-Krimom. Naime, kada je Liote čuo da je maršal Filip Peten, koji je tada bio generalni inspektor vojske, osoba koja će komandovati tom intervencijom, osetio se uvređenim, dao je ostavku na svoje mesto i vratio se u Francusku. Ali, tamo je trebalo da se suoči sa znatnom kulturnom opozicijom njegovim idejama o francuskom identitetu a ta opozicija je postala već prilično politična u tom trenutku.

„Nikakav koherentan politički ili društveni stav (među nadrealistima) se ipak nije pojavio sve do 1925, što znači do (važno je da se ovo naglasi) izbijanja rata u Maroku", izjavio je Andre Breton tematizujući pitanje 'Šta je nadrealizam?' publici u Briselu 1. juna 1934. Taj specifični rat je, po Bretonu, ponovo probudio nadrealističko zajedničko „neprijateljstvo spram načina na koji se vođenje oružanih konflikata odrazilo na čoveka", i to ih je suočilo sa

„nužnošću da se napravi javni protest" i „stvorilo presedan koji je trebalo da odredi celokupno buduće usmerenje pokreta." (Breton 1989, 116–117) Ono je takođe završilo njihovu prvu, kako je on to karakterizovao, „čisto intuitivnu epohu" (1919–24) i naveo ih je da uđu u drugu, „epohu rezonovanja" (1925–34). (Ibid.) Kolonijalna izložba iz 1931. će ih uskoro naterati da uđu u treću – epohu neposrednih akcija. Pozvali su publiku da ne posećuje tu izložbu, da bi u saradnji sa drugim antikolonijalnim grupama stvorili kontraizložbu, koja je tematizovala aktuelno stanje stvari u kolonijama.

Letak *Ne visitez pas l'Exposition Coloniale! / Nemojte da posetite kolonijalnu izložbu* osmislili su Andre Breton, Pol Elijar, Luj Aragon i Maksim Aleksander, a onda su ga potpisali i Benžamin Pere, Žorž Sadul, Rene Šar, Iv Tangi, Pjer Unik, Andre Tirion, Rene Klevel i Žorž Malkin. Kasnije je letak bio praćen tekstom pod naslovom *Prva procena kolonijalne izložbe*. Saša Bru, u svojoj knjizi *Evropske avangarde, 1905–1935,* stavio je naglasak na rodni aspekt kritike načina na koji je predstavljen sadržaj te izložbe, kako je to bilo formulisano u prvom njihovom tekstu, a to je: „način na koji su kolonizovani bili predstavljeni ljudima u Francuskoj, kao da su to tropski rajevi u kojima čak i neobrazovane (muške) kolonizatore čeka lak život sa lokalnim ženama koje su voljne da im služe." (Bru 2018, 152) Da bi prikazali da je to sve potpuno suprotno, nadrealisti su se pridružili Ligi protiv imperijalizma i kolonijalne opresije i napravili izložbu *Istina o kolonijama*, koja je pokazivala da su kolonije bile mesto krajnjeg užasa: eksploatacije, opresije, prisilnog rada i smrti.

Bile su i druge kritike Kolonijalne izložbe od strane organizovane levice, i to čak mnogo žešće. Prema Ligi za odbranu crnačke rase (LDRN), arhitektonski pastiši, kao što je to bila 'Fontana totema' i Paviljon francuske Zapadne Afrike, bili su svedeni na „grube karikature umetnosti predaka kolonizovanih naroda, dok su se, prema stavovima vijetnamskog Borbenog komiteta, inscenirani spektali u okviru izložbe odvijali tako što su urođenici koji su u njima učestvovali bili korišćeni „kao stado čudnih zveri, za zadovoljstvo u očima posmatrača." (Blake 2002, 37) Članovi Komunističke partije Francuske (PCF) distribuirali su pamflet pod nazivom *Pravi vodič za Kolonijalnu izložbu: civilizujuća uloga Francuske razjašnjena na nekoliko strana*, u kome su citirali oficijalne podatke dobijene na izložbi i dopunjene podacima koje su na terenu sakupile grupe aktivista, a koji su pružali potpuno suprotnu priču.

U zbirci Njujorškog muzeja MOMA primerak letka *Nemojte da posetite Kolonijalnu izložbu* zaveden je kao umetničko delo. Da je to u skladu sa njegovim intencijama, Breton bi bio umetnik potpuno zaslepljen svojom željom da izbriše razliku izme-

đu aktivizma i umetnosti. Ali, sumnjam, budući da, za razliku od drugih aktivista, nadrealisti nisu želeli samo da koriguju stav o kolonijama kakav je pružen na oficijelnoj izložbi i da prodru iza područja kolonijalnih fantazija, već da prikažu sve traumatične karakteristike svakodnevnog života u kolonijama kao njihovu 'istinu'. To što su oni mrzeli i u stvari pokušavali da istaknu je da dalja eksploatacija kolonijalnih podanika ide dalje od ekstrakcije njihovog fizičkog rada i prirodnih resursa, za koje su bili prikazani kao nedovoljno obrazovani i civilizovani da ih sami eksploatišu. Kolonijalne izložbe su takođe bile zone ekstrakcije – mesta komercijalne eksploatacije estetskih kodova u načinu oblačenja, muzici, plesu, kao i stvaranju artefakata, koji su preuzeti od urođenika i zaštićeni autorskim pravom od strane kompanija iz kolonizatorskih država. Na izložbi koju su organizovali nadrealisti jednako su tretirani afrički ceremonijalni 'fetiš' objekti i evropski ritualni predmeti označeni kao „katolički fetiš", i to u postavkama koje su bile načinjene da „redistribuiraju čulno".

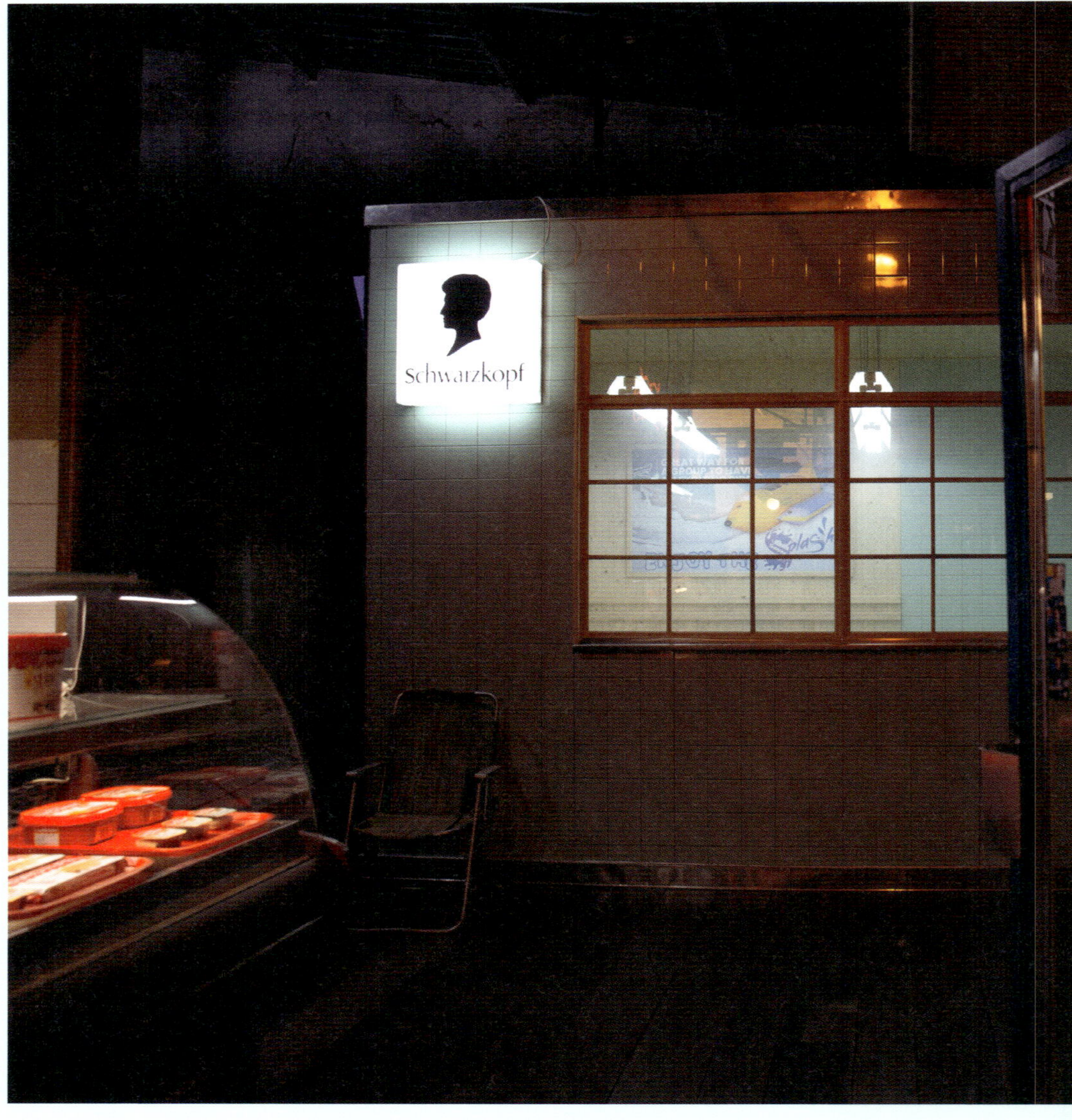

Pokazivanje čulnog sveta onih koji se ne računaju

Kolonijalna forma dominacije još nije došla do svog kraja, već je samo promenila formu. Kao što je Anibal K jano pisao, „kolonijalnost je, onda, još uvek najopštija forma dominacije u svetu današnjice, sada kada je kolonijalizam kao eksplicitan politički režim već razoren." (Quijano 2010, 24) Uzmimo na primer tipično piće koje je postalo uspešno u dobu imperijalizma, prodajući fantazme o globalnom kolonijalnom sistemu sa SAD kao njegovim novim centrom. To je Koka-Kola, „najrasprostranjenija brendirana roba na planeti." (Pendergrast 2000, 10) Prema knjizi Marka Pendergrasta pod nazivom *Za Boga, zemlju i Koka-Kolu*, početkom ovog veka bilo je „više nacionalnih država koje su imale Koka-Kolu, nego što je bilo članica Ujedinjenih nacija." (Ibid.) Ali, u ranim godinama te kompanije, u poslednjim dekadama 19. veka, Koka-Kola je teritorije izvan SAD posmatrala „skoro isključivo kao mesta ekstrakcije sirovih materijala." (Ciafone 2019, 19) Proizvod je bio prodavan u SAD, novoj kolonijalnoj sili, čiji građani bi u jednom jednostavnom piću konzumirali „šećer sa Kariba, kofein iz lišća čaja iz Azije, ekstrakt lišća koke iz Latinske Amerike i prah oraha kola iz Afrike." (Ibid.) Tako je prosečna mušterija nastanjena u SAD mogla da, kupujući flašu Koka-Kole, dobije i fantaziju da je rad radnika na plantažama na nekoliko kontinenata imao za jedini cilj da obogati njegovo uživanje u tom piću.

Danas je prilično suprotno. Koka-Kola se uglavnom prodaje na teritorijama koje su pre sto i nešto godina bile kolonije. Prema podacima sa sajta kompanije, u ovom trenutku je broj konzumenata Koka-Kole u celoj Severnoj Americi samo 320 miliona, dok je u Latinskoj Americi 525 miliona, u Evropi sa Bliskim istokom i Afrikom je 2.1 milijarda, a u pacifičkom delu Azije 3.3 milijarde. Stoga nije čudo da je jedna od glavnih kampanja Koka-Kole za 2024. izvedena iz inicijative Koka-Kole Indija, gde se taj brend pojavljuje u okviru festivala Durga Puđa kao njegov integralni deo, slaveći pobedu Hindu boginje Durga nad Mahišasurom, što je prilično slavljeno svuda u indijskoj dijaspori. U stvari Koka-Kola proizvodi koncentrat sirupa, koji se zatim prodaje točionicama po celom svetu (to je preko 275 nezavisnih biznisa sa preko 900 pogona) i preuzima odgovornost za opšte inicijative marketinga kupcima. Sve ostalo je na onima koji kupe franšizu, što znači i glokalizaciju proizvoda, da bi se ostvarile i njegove lokalne osobine. Oni koji franšizu treba da proizvedu, upakuju i distribuišu gotovi proizvod partnerima koji onda to prodaju konzumentima. Takođe, „budući da su franšize

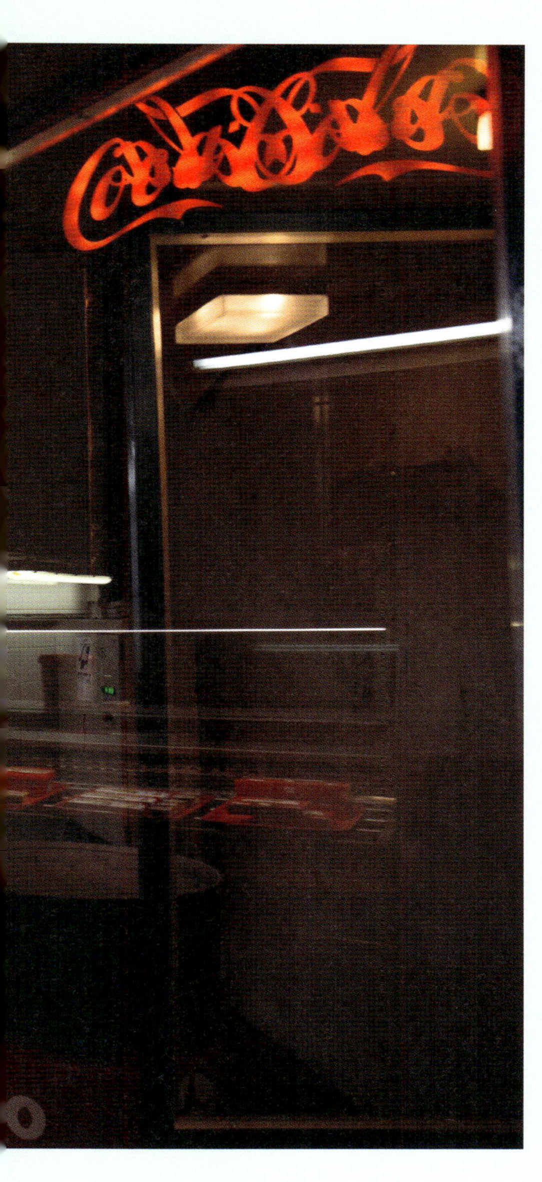

stalno bile limitirane u proizvodnji Koka-Kolinih proizvoda, traženo je od njih da investiraju da bi postigli standard kompanije, i oni su tako bili prisiljeni da se odreknu proizvodnje drugih sličnih bezalkoholnih pića koja su ranije proizvodili." (Ciafone 2019, 24) Na taj način je osiguran monopol Koka-Kole.

Kao što je Adam Arvidson, autor knjige *Brendovi: značenje i vrednost u medijskoj kulturi*, pisao, „brendovi danas obezbeđuju značenje i 'zajednicu', koja je u stanju da zameni onu koja se navodno izgubila u procesu modernizacije." (Arvidsson 2006, 5) Globalno distribuirani brendovi mogu da obezbede osećaj bivanja kod kuće kod onih mušterija koje su navikle da ih konzumiraju na dnevnoj bazi, gde god da se zateknu, pa bili to ivojni rovovi, pošto su, na primer, Koka-Kola i Laki Strajk razvili posebne vrste poslovnih ugovora sa američkom vojskom još tokom Drugog svetskog rata. To se tiče onih koji imaju konvencionalne identitete, koje su postigli prilagođavanjem neposrednom okruženju i ostvarili osećanje pripadnosti tom okruženju. S druge strane, kada je reč o onima koji koriste brendove da bi postali vizuelno različiti i da bi razvili drugačiji identitet, neki brendovi mogu da im pomognu da naprave totalni rimejk. Kako je Hal Foster, u dodatku svojoj knjizi *Dizajn i zločin*, napisao: „danas vam nije neophodno da budete jezivo bogati da biste se ne samo kao dizajner, nego i kao dizajniran." Da biste dizajnirali sebe shodno svojim najluđim fantazijama, možete čak da promenite „svoje mlitavo lice (plastična hirurgija) ili retardiranu ličnost (medikamenti), svoje istorijsko sećanje (muzeji), svoju DNK budućnost (usvajanje dece)." (Foster 2002, 192) Korišćenje brendova je samo prvi korak u tome.

„Godinama smo sebe smatrali za kompaniju koja je usmerena na proizvod", izjavio je osnivač, predsednik i izvršni direktor firme Najk, Fil Najt, u intervjuu za *Harvard biznis rivju*, dodajući kako je to bila greška i da sada misli drugačije: „Najk je marketinški usmerena filma i proizvod je naše najbitnije marketinško oruđe." (Klein 2000, 44) Hartmut Beme je o firmi Najk izneo svoj stav u knjizi *Fetišizam i kultura*, objašnjavajući da „ta proizvodna kompanija ne prodaje toliko patike, već umesto toga brend koji je razvila, dizajn, stil života, osećaj identiteta, modu i osećaj pripadnosti određenim kulturnim zajednicama vezanim za brend, a ne za patiku." (Böhme 2014, 106) To ga čini „artefaktom kulture, prekidačem u protoku simboličkih vrednosti, a ne samo 'funkcionalnom spravom'."

Stoga poljski WC sa Versaće logom na zaklopnoj dasci toaleta i Luj Viton tapetama na zidovima, kao što je ovaj postavljen u okviru *Exposition Coloniale*, nužno dodaje nešto prefinjenosti iskustvu njegovog korišćenja i neki status samom korisniku, bez obzira na dilemu da li je to original ili kopija. Naime,

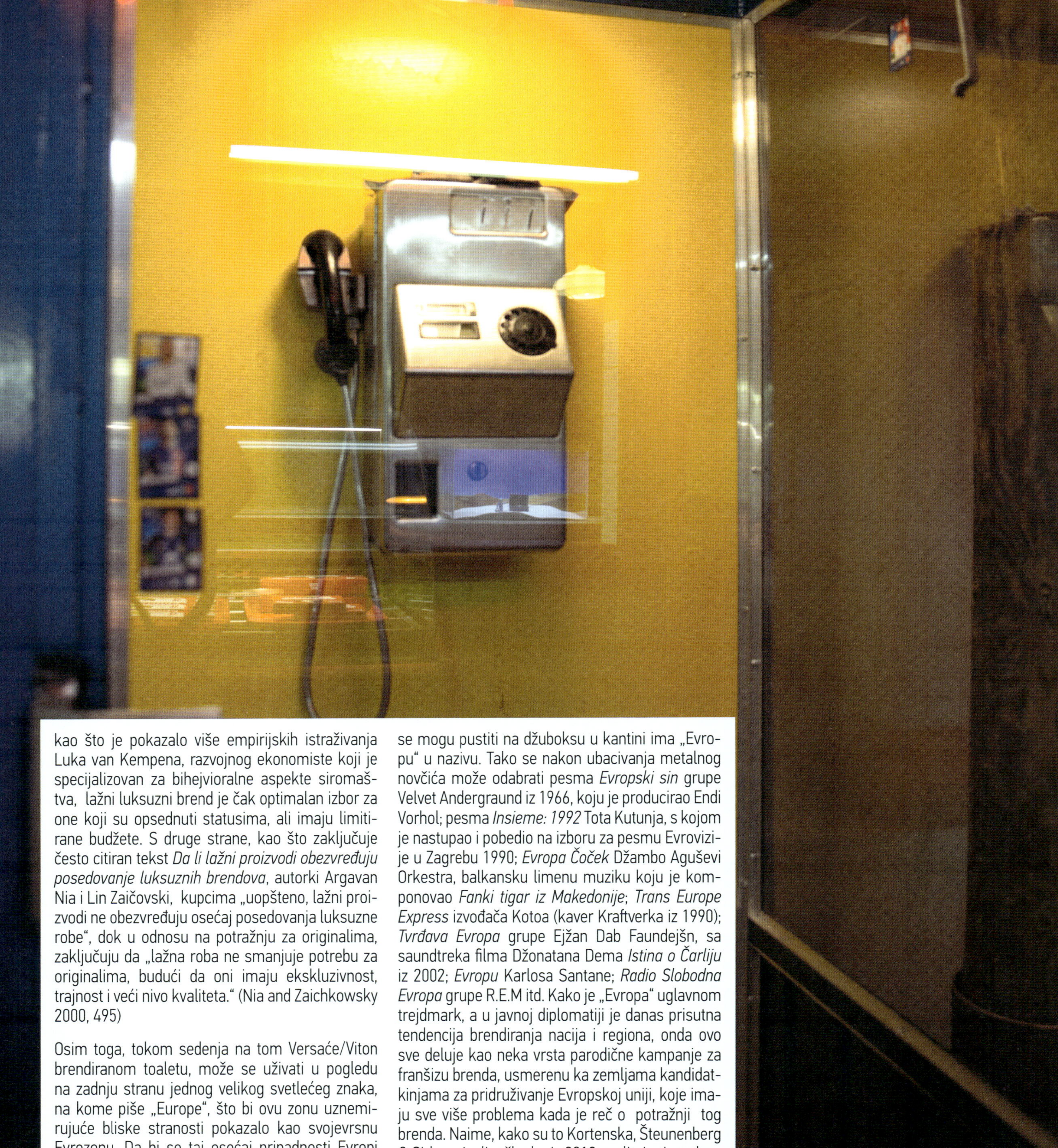

kao što je pokazalo više empirijskih istraživanja Luka van Kempena, razvojnog ekonomiste koji je specijalizovan za bihejvioralne aspekte siromaštva, lažni luksuzni brend je čak optimalan izbor za one koji su opsednuti statusima, ali imaju limitirane budžete. S druge strane, kao što zaključuje često citiran tekst *Da li lažni proizvodi obezvređuju posedovanje luksuznih brendova*, autorki Argavan Nia i Lin Zaičovski, kupcima „uopšteno, lažni proizvodi ne obezvređuju osećaj posedovanja luksuzne robe", dok u odnosu na potražnju za originalima, zaključuju da „lažna roba ne smanjuje potrebu za originalima, budući da oni imaju ekskluzivnost, trajnost i veći nivo kvaliteta." (Nia and Zaichkowsky 2000, 495)

Osim toga, tokom sedenja na tom Versaće/Viton brendiranom toaletu, može se uživati u pogledu na zadnju stranu jednog velikog svetlećeg znaka, na kome piše „Europe", što bi ovu zonu uznemirujuće bliske stranosti pokazalo kao svojevrsnu Evrozonu. Da bi se taj osećaj pripadnosti Evropi pojačao među posetiocima, svaka od pesama koje se mogu pustiti na džuboksu u kantini ima „Evropu" u nazivu. Tako se nakon ubacivanja metalnog novčića može odabrati pesma *Evropski sin* grupe Velvet Andergraund iz 1966, koju je producirao Endi Vorhol; pesma *Insieme: 1992* Tota Kutunja, s kojom je nastupao i pobedio na izboru za pesmu Evrovizije u Zagrebu 1990; *Evropa Čoček* Džambo Aguševi Orkestra, balkansku limenu muziku koju je komponovao *Fanki tigar iz Makedonije*; *Trans Europe Express* izvođača Kotoa (kaver Kraftverka iz 1990); *Tvrđava Evropa* grupe Ejžan Dab Faundejšn, sa saundtreka filma Džonatana Dema *Istina o Čarliju* iz 2002; *Evropu* Karlosa Santane; *Radio Slobodna Evropa* grupe R.E.M itd. Kako je „Evropa" uglavnom trejdmark, a u javnoj diplomatiji je danas prisutna tendencija brendiranja nacija i regiona, onda ovo sve deluje kao neka vrsta parodične kampanje za franšizu brenda, usmerenu ka zemljama kandidatkinjama za pridruživanje Evropskoj uniji, koje imaju sve više problema kada je reč o potražnji tog brenda. Naime, kako su to Kortenska, Šteunenberg & Sirkar pisali u članku iz 2019. o elitnim i građanskim diskursima o evropskoj integraciji u Srbi-

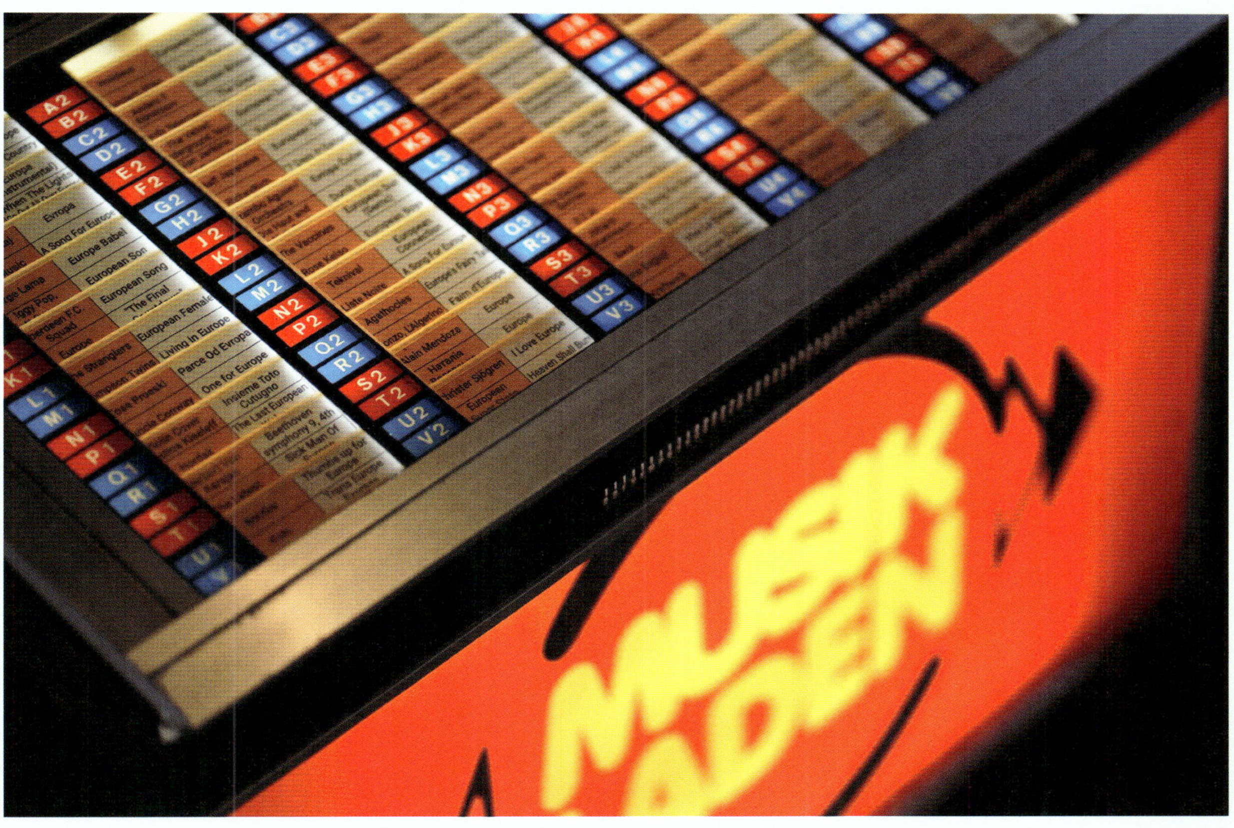

ji, proklamovane ključne komponente strategije proširenja Evropske unije su: „pravda, stabilnost i 'povratak u Evropu'", ali u Srbiji to „ne dopire do građana, čiji stavovi su zasnovani na oportunizmu i pragmatizmu." (Kortenska et al. 2019, n.p.) Tako, ovde vlada ozbiljan procep između diskursa običnih ljudi i elite koja pokušava da im proda neku franšizu Evrope kao kolevke demokratskih tradicija i ličnih sloboda. Po Kjosevu, ove elite karakterišu samokolonizujuće kulture (Kiossev 1999, 114–118) kao „poseban brend samostvorene perifernosti, brižno povezane sa narativima vernosti evropskom projektu", za koji oni veruju da treba da bude zasnovan na „prosvećenim stanovištima osnova liberalizma, ljudskih prava i građanskog etosa." (Huigen and Kołodziejczyk 2023, 2)

Tako političke elite tvrde da je insistiranje na evropskom identitetu nužno za simboličku konstrukciju društvenog sveta zemalja kandidata i da to treba da bude debatovano ekonomskim i pravnim terminima, ali gde je tu čulno i svakodnevno ljudsko iskustvo? Kakva vrsta čulnog sveta leži iza velikog osvetljenog znaka „Europe"? To se ne može lako i jednostavno objasniti, analizirati i interpretirati, već mora da bude pokazano, demonstrirano. A ta demonstracija mora da odgovori na uobičajeno pitanje postavljeno gastarbajteru (stranom radniku ili migrantu), koje mu postavljaju prijatelji kod kuće: „Kakav je život tamo?" Aleksandar Denić, budući sam gastarbajter, ponudio nam je prilično distopijsku demonstraciju toga.

Lutajući kroz postavku instalacije, nailazimo takođe na bilborde cigareta Vest i burbon viskija Vajld Turki, baner na kome se oglašava piće Bananija i svetleći oglas za preparate za negu kose Švarckopf, kao i za Koka-Kolu. Teksako i Rosneft su brendirali korišćenu burad za naftu, smeštenu pored prazne telefonske kabine obojene bojama ukrajinske zastave, koja zvoni u regularnim intervalima na veoma bučan način, ali, pošto slučalica nije vezana za aparat, nije moguće odgovoriti na poziv, niti zaustaviti zvonjavu na bilo koji drugi način. Metalni kreveti na sprat, poput bolničkih ili vojnih kreveta, ugurani su u kiosk i umesto dušeka imaju pakete Lidlovih lifleta sa popustima, veoma prepoznatljivog dizajna. Na krevetu, kao i u kupatilu/sauni, ima ostavljene odeće, kao i cipela, gumenih čizama i građevinskih šlemova. Ima vidljivih tragova upotrebe, ali ne i znakova personalizacije tih prostora, što deluje malo zagonetno. Klima uređaj je u sobi uključen, čuje se kako prska voda iz kupatila i ceo seting deluje kao da su njegovi regularni korisnici prosto iznenada nestali, noseći sve svoje lične stvari sa sobom. A deluje i da ih neko stalno zove na telefon čija slušalica nije u funkciji. Ali pošto nema ni scenarija ni priče, pitanja tog tipa ne mogu da budu odgovorena.

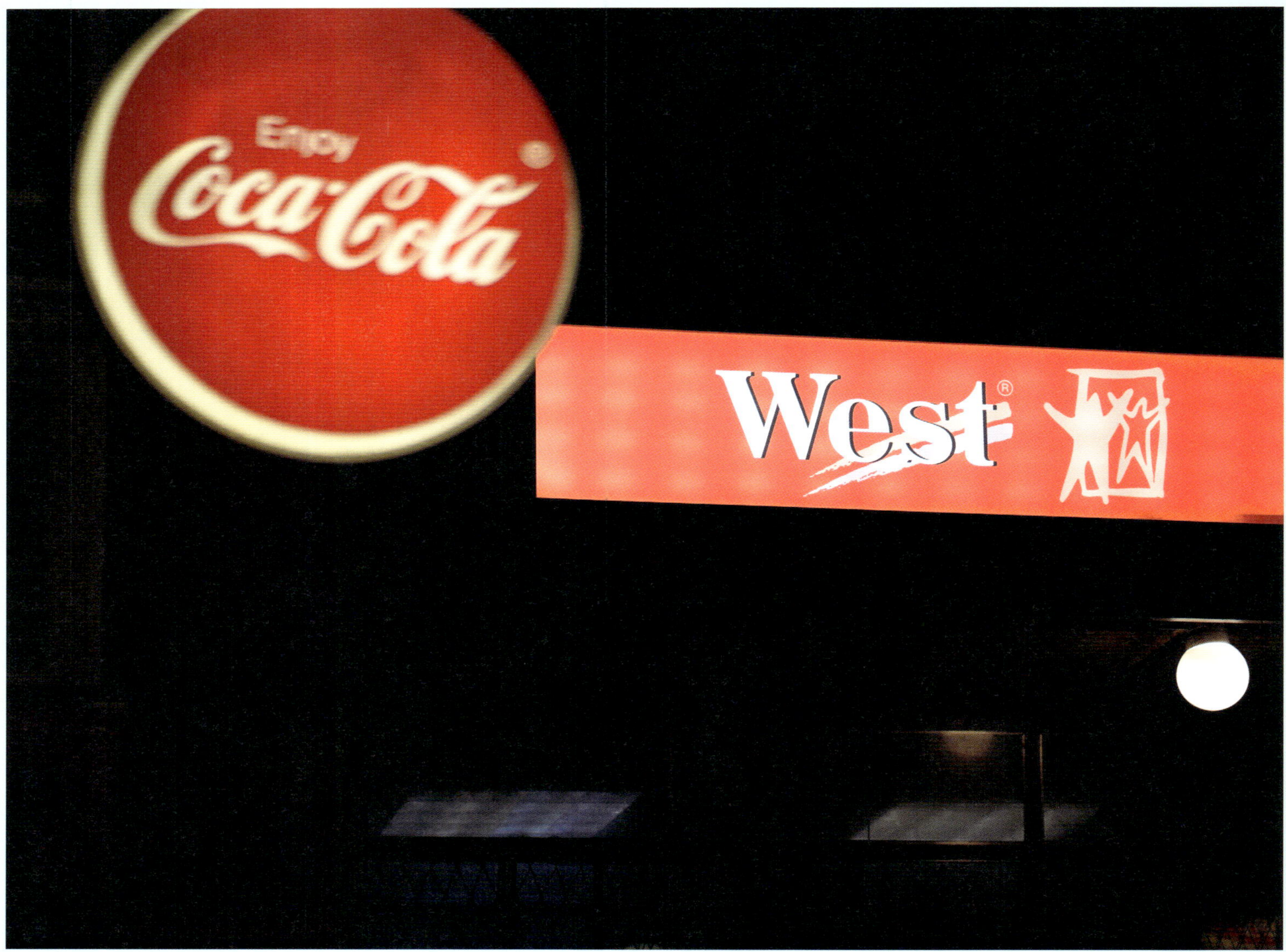

Osećaj sa kojim se napušta instalacija ili sedne na neku od više dostupnih površina u okviru njene strukture, pre nego li se nastavi šetanje među drugim paviljonima, veoma je fizički. Bez obzira na prekomerje označitelja koji se mestimično pojavljuju u okviru instalacije i na provokativni naziv izložbe, to što stvarno ostavlja utisak na posetioca su zvuci, mirisi, temperature ohlađene sobe nasuprot temperaturi u pasažu iza, koji greje motor dosta korišćenog klima uređaja, vlaga u kupatilu, način na koji svako pojedinačno lokalno svetlo izgleda i koliko svetlosti obezbeđuje, način na koji je ograda kod ulaza zavarena i obojena ili električni kablovi uvezivani u čvorove, i te veoma precizno isplanirane tačke pogleda na koje se nailazi prilikom kretanja kroz prostor. Sve je to u sinergiji toga što Ransijer zove „specifičnim režimom čulnog, koji se izbavlja od svojih običnih veza i postaje naseljen heterogenom moći, moći forme mišljenja koje je postalo strano sebi.“ (Rancière 2004, 22–23) Ukoliko za Ransijera politika teži ka tome da da glas onima koji se ne računaju, onda estetika treba da im omogući da se vidi njihov čulni svet. Estetski segment ove instalacije čini upravo to.

Prema Ransijeru, „ima politike tamo gde postoji deo za one koji nemaju udela“, na primer, „deo za one koji po podeli potpadaju među siromašne.“ (Rancière 1999, 11) Politika se dešava zato što neki neće biti uračunati kao jednak deo društva (umesto siromašnih, to mogu biti migranti ili, istorijski, žene, robovi, stranci) i zato što je to isključenje od suštinskog značaja za postojanje političke zajednice. Društveni konsenzus je uvek zasnovan na isključivanju. Drugim rečima, „politika izrasta iz računanja delova zajednice, što je uvek lažno računanje, duplo računanje, pogrešno računanje“ (Rancière 1999, 2), ali samo u retkim i povremenim trenucima to postaje jasno. Takođe, pored toga što je pokazivanje da nejednakost postoji u društvu nužno, takođe je nužno pokazati da je jednakost preduslov društva. Da bismo se bavili nejednakošću, uključujući one koji nemaju udela, treba biti u stanju videti ih, one nevidljive delove društva i takođe videti iz njihovog ugla posmatranja, da bi se hijerarhijska struktura društva problematizovala upravo sa tog stanovišta. To je način na koji estetika i politika intervenišu u simboličku konstrukciju društvenog sveta.

Korišćena literatura:

Aldrich, R. 2009. *Colonial Museums in a Postcolonial Europe, African and Black Diaspora: An International Journal*, 2:2, 137–156.

Arvidsson, A. 2006. *Brands: Meaning and Value in Media Culture*. London: Routledge.

Asher, M. 1983. *Writings 1973–1983 on Works 1969–1979*, ed. Benjamin H.D. Buchloh. Halifax: Nova Scotia College of Art and Design/ Museum of Contemporary Art, Los Angeles.

August, T. 1982. „The Colonial Exposition in France: Education or Reinforcement?" *Proceedings of the Meeting of the French Colonial Historical Society* Vol. 6/7 (1982): 147–154.

Benjamin, W. 1969. „Unpacking my Library: A Talk about Bal, Book Collecting,. In *Illuminations*. New York: Schocken Books: 59–67.

Bhaba, H. 1994.*The Location of Culture*. London, New York: Routledge.

Bishop, C. 2006. „The Social Turn: Collaboration and Its Discontents." *Artforum*, vol. 44, no. 6 (February 2006)

Bourriaud, N. 2002. *Relational Aesthetics*. Dijon: Les Presses du réel.

Böhme, H. 2014. *Fetishism and Culture: A Different Theory of Modernity*. Berlin and Boston: De Gruyter.

Breton, A. 1989. „What is Surrealism?" In Rosemont, F. (ed.), *What is Surrealism?*. London: Pluto.

Bru, S. 2018. *The European Avant-Gardes, 1905–1935*. Edinburgh: Edinburgh University Press.

Cavell, S. 1989. *This New Yet Unapproachable America: Lectures after Emerson and Wittgenstein*. Albuquerque: Living Bath Press.

Carnevale F, and Kelsey, J. 2007. „Art of the Possible: Fulvia Carnevale and John Kelsey in Conversation with Jacques Rancière." *Artforum*, vol. 45, no. 7 (March 2007).

Ciafone. A. 2019. *Counter-Cola: A Multinational History of the Global Corporation*. Oakland, California: University of California Press.

Crary, J. 1990. *Techniques of the Observor: On Vision and Modernite in the Nineteenth Century*. Cambridge, Mass.: MIT Press.

Doherty, C. 2004. „The Institution is Dead! Long Live the Institution! Contemporary Art and New Institutionalism." *Engage* 15 (Summer 2004).

Knox, P. 1993.„Capital, Material Culture and Socio-Spatial Differentiation." In Knox, P. 1993. (ed.). *The Restless Urban Landscape*, Englewood Cliffs NJ: Prentice Hall, 1–34.

Ferraz de Matos, P, Birkalan-Gedik, H, Barrera-González, A. and Vail, P. 2022. „World Fairs, Exhibitions and Anthropology - Revisiting Contexts of Post-colonialism." *Anthropological Journal of European Cultures* Volume 31, No. 2 (2022): 1–14.

Freud, S. 1933. *New Introductory Lectures On Psycho-Analysis. The Standard Edition of the Complete Psychological Works of Sigmund Freud*, Volume XXII (1932–1936): *New Introductory Lectures on Psycho-Analysis and Other Works*, 1–182.

Gómez-Barris, M. 2017. *The Extractive Zone - Social Ecologies and Decolonial Perspectives*. Durham and London: Duke University Press.

Hoffenberg, P.H. 2001. *An Empire on Display: English, Indian, and Australian Exhibitions from the Crystal Palace to the Great War*. Berkeley and Los Angeles: University of California Press.

Huigen S. and Kołodziejczyk D. (eds.) 2023. *East Central Europe Between the Colonial and the Postcolonial in the Twentieth Century*. Cham: Palgrave Macmillan.

Gordillo, G. 2013. „The Void: Invisible Ruins on the Edges of Empire." *Imperial Debris: On Ruins and Ruination*, edited by A. L. Stoler . Durham: Duke University Press, 227–251.

Kabakov, I. 1995 *On the Total Installation*. Ostfildern, Germany: Cantz Verlag.

Kiossev, A. 1999. „Notes of Self-Colonising Cultures." In Pejić, B. and Elliott, D. (eds.) *After the Wall – Art and Culture in Post-communist Europe*. Stockholm: Moderna Museet. 114–118.

Klein, N. 2000. *No Logo. Taking Aim at the Brand Bullies*. London: Flamingo.

Knox, P. 1993. „Capital, material culture and socio-spatial differentiation." In P. Knox (ed.), *The Restless Urban Landscape*, Englewood Cliffs NJ: Prentice Hall, 1–34.

Kristeva, J. 1991. *Strangers to Ourselves*. New York: Columbia University Press.

Küppers-Lissitzky, S. 1967. *El Lissitzky: Life, Letters, Text*. Greenwich, Conn.: New York Graphic Society.

Marx, K. 1975. „Economic and Philosophic Manuscripts of 1844." Иn Karl Marx and Friedrich Engels, *Collected Works*, vol. 3, Marx and Engels, 1843—1844. New York: International Publishers.

Marx, K. 1992. *Capital, Vol III: A Critique of Political Economy*. New York: Penguin Classics.

Masschelein, A. 2011. *The Unconcept. The Freudian Uncanny in the Late-Twentieth Century Theory*. Albany: State University of New York.

Morand, P. 1931. *1900*. Paris: Flammarion.

Morton, P. A. 1998. „National and Colonial: The Musée des Colonies at the Colonial Exposition, Paris, 1931." *The Art Bulletin*, Vol. 80, No. 2 (Jun, 1998), 357–377.

Nia, A., & Zaichkowsky, J. 2000. „Do counterfeits devalue the ownership of luxury brands?" In *Journal of Product and Brand Management*, 9(7), 485–497.

Olivier, M. 1931. „Avant-Propos." *Le Livre d'Or de l'Exposition Coloniale Internationale de Paris*. Paris: Librairie Ancienne Honoré Champion.

Pendergrast, M. 2000. *For God, Country, and Coca-Cola: The Definitive History of the Great American Soft Drink and the Company That Makes It*. New York: Basic Books.

Podoroga, V. 2003. „Notes on Ilya Kabakov's 'On the Total Installation'" *Third Text*, Vol. 17, Issue 4, 2003, 345–352

Pugliese, J. 2009. „Crisis Heterotopias and Border Zones of the Dead." *Continuum: Journal of Media & Cultural Studies*, 23.5 (2009), 663–79.

Rancière, J. 1999. *Disagreement: Politics and Philosophy*, Minneapolis: University of Minnesota Press.

Rancière, J. 2004. *The Politics of Aesthetics*. London: Continuum Books.

Rancière, J. 2010. *Dissensus: On Politics and Aesthetics*. Continuum.

Sauvage, A. 2010. „To be or not to be Colonial: Museums Facing Their Exhibitions." *Culturales*, vol. VI, núm. 12, julio-diciembre, 2010, pp. 97–116

Quijano, A. 2010. „Coloniality and Modernity / Rationality." In Walter D. Mignolo, W. D. and Escobar, A. (eds.) 2010. *Globalization and the Decolonial Option*. London and New York: Routledge, 22–32.

Van Troi, T. 2015. „How 'Natives' Ate at Colonial Exhibitions in 1889, 1900 and 1931." *French Cultural Studies* 2015, Vol. 26(2), 163–175.

van Wesemael, P. 2001. *Architecture of Instruction and Delight: A Socio-historical Analysis of World Exhibition as a Didactic Phenomenon (1798–1851–1970)*. Rotterdam: OIO Publishers.

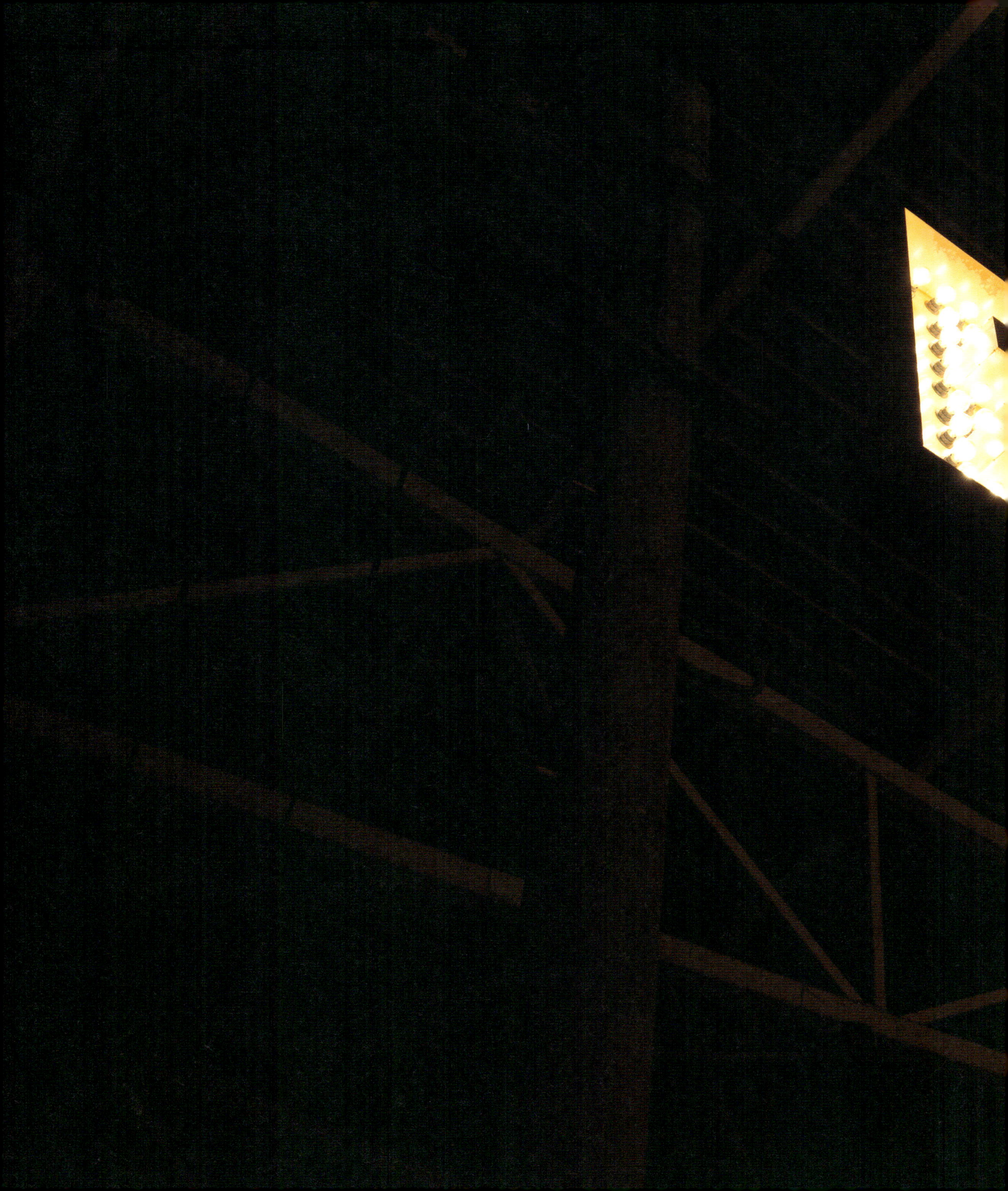

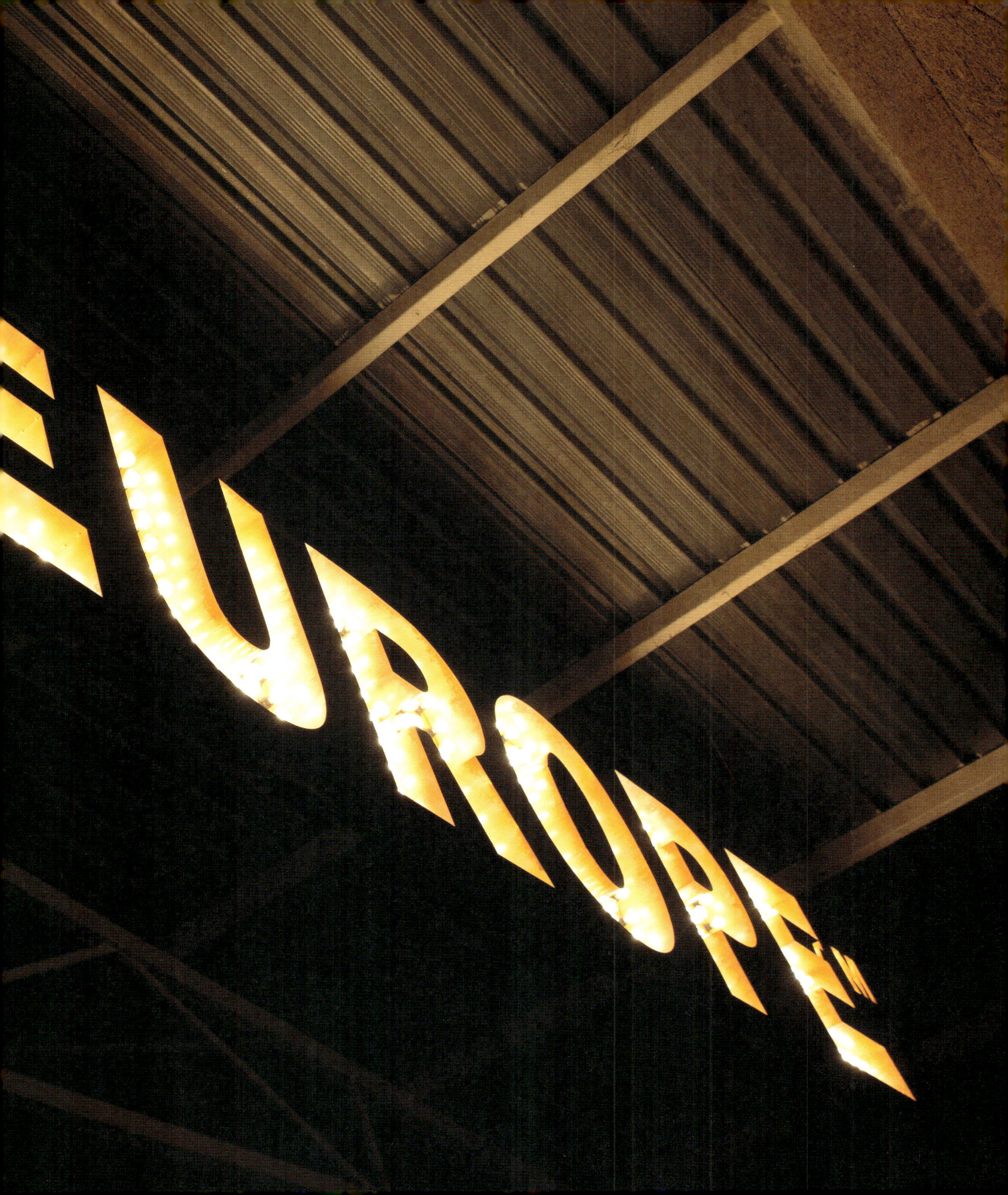
EUROPE

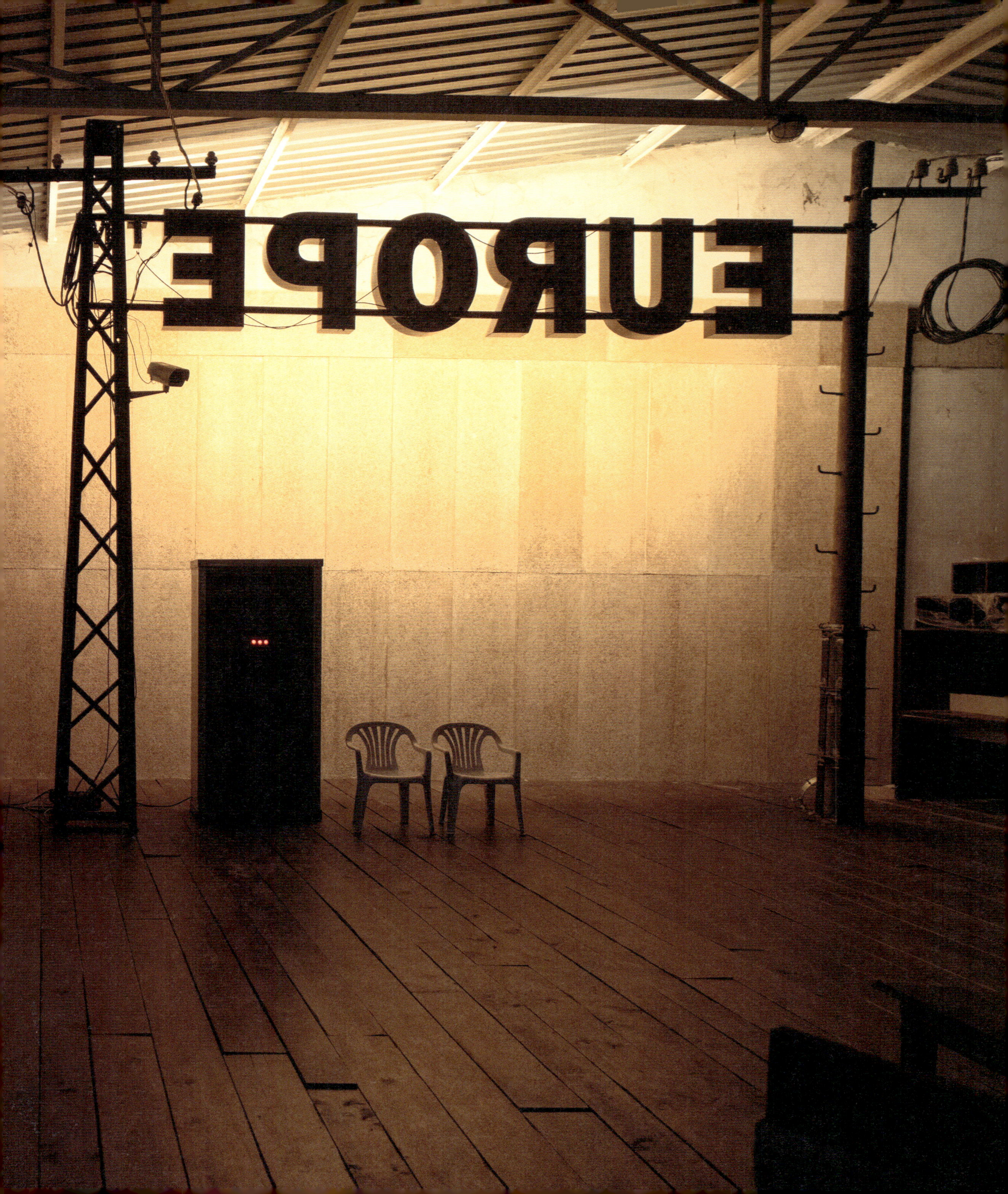

Christopher Yggdre

Europa, Europa !
Where the Simulacrum becomes a Palimpsest

"The man who finds his homeland sweet is still a tender beginner; he to whom every soil is as his native one is already strong; but he is perfect to whom the entire world is as a foreign land. The tender soul has fixed his love on one spot in the world; the strong man has extended his love to all places; the perfect man has extinguished his."
Hugues de Saint-Victor in *Didascalicon (1135)*

Audacicus! That's the word that immediately came to mind when I discovered Aleksandar Denić's project for the 60th edition of the Venice Biennale. Audacity is a quality in art, and Denić possesses it in abundance. I had the privilege of experiencing, in advance, in Belgrade, in December 2023, accompanied by the artist and curator Ksenija Samardžija, the total and immersive work "Exposition Coloniale", which will be presented for seven months from April to November 2024 in the former Pavilion of Yugoslavia (which became the Serbian Pavilion at the end of the 20th century) in the Giardini of Venice. The work was presented to me in the form of a model, with plans and sketches. The discovery of these simple elements evoked in me a sense of unease and discomfort. These are precisely the emotions I expect from a work of art. I expect it to challenge my certainties, my thought patterns, my comfort. I expect it to immerse me into a state of vertigo. I will long remember Denić's description of the work as he stood in front of his model. It seemed to come alive as he described the different architectures of the installation and the experiences each one entailed. It would be an understatement to say that the work "Exposition Coloniale" disturbed me. As I write these lines, the artwork has been fully realized in a warehouse in the suburbs of Belgrade. It now awaits transportation to Venice. In Paris, I study and look at photographs of the installation and watch a film in which the artist silently moves through the different modules of "Exposition Coloniale." The effect is striking. What existed as a plan now exists as a composite architecture offering a real, material, physical, sensory experience. The unease and vertigo are multiplied. I now eagerly await the arrival of spring to physically enter "Expostion Coloniale" and become one of the actors in a hybrid artwork where every detail is significant.

An examination of the title reveals some clues about the experience to be lived. It unveils the very nature of the work. It is a palimpsest that brings to the surface of collective memory facts that have long been repressed. For nearly a century, between the mid-19th and 20th centuries, Europeans traveled in droves to visit Colonial Exhibitions. These celebrated the conquests of the great colonial empires, including the United Kingdom, France, Belgium, the Netherlands, Portugal, and Spain. Denić's choice to name the work in French is not insignificant. The French colonial empire justified the subjugation of colonized peoples in the name of the universal principles inherited from the Enlightenment and the French Revolution. It was in the name of these "civilizing virtues" that France legitimized colonization, military expeditions, dispossession, acculturation, and massacres. Between 1889 and 1937, in less than fifty years, France organized no less than fourteen Colonial Exhibitions, attracting crowds from all over Europe. Before the advent of cinema, these exhibitions were one of the first mass entertainment industries. The most chilling thing is to discover that at these Colonial Exhibitions, entire villages from colonized lands were reconstructed, with "savages" exhibited in their "natural habitat." At the end of the 20th century, historians dubbed these living dioramas for what they were: nothing less than "human zoos."

What makes Denić's work a palimpsest is not only the title but also the dialogue it creates with the architecture of the former Pavilion of Yugoslavia and current Serbian Pavilion. This architecture, designed by the Venetian architect Brenno del Guidice, is a striking mixture that defies easy classification. It bears witness to the evolution of Venetian architecture from the Renaissance to modern times. It has always managed to create a dialogue with what preceded it while subtly renewing itself. It is not wrong to say that the architecture of Venice itself is a palimpsest.

"Exposition Coloniale" begins at the entrance of the Pavilion. Denić has created a kiosk with Art Deco overtones that fits perfectly into the oval of the Pavilion's immense entrance door. With this simple kiosk, Denić reveals the tensions and geopolitical realities that have shaped the history of the venerable Venice Biennale. The diversity of architectures of the different national pavilions in the Giardini is a striking indicator. Architecture is a battlefield. Since its inception in the late 19th century, the Venice Biennale has been a place where the backdrop has always been the political and cultural conflicts of the moment. It is the privileged witness to the porosity between art and history, for better or for worse.

Once past the first airlock, this kiosk where one takes the entrance ticket, we enter an extremely scenographic space composed of multiple installations or modules in which visitors become actors. With "Exposition Coloniale", Denić seems to combine the means of Antonin Artaud's Theatre of Cruelty with the content of Samuel Beckett or Harold Pinter's Theatre of the Absurd. The abolition of the boundary between stage and audience, dear to Antonin Artaud, is complete. The absurdity of the human condition is experienced in a narrative that unfolds as one moves from one space to another. In a baroque tangle, each module, each architecture is a visual creation whose profusion of details is not accidental. Some of these details seem familiar to us, while others are completely foreign. But upon closer inspection, it doesn't matter what nature the detail is; it is only valuable through its integration into a whole. The totality of the work "Exposition Coloniale" has a materiality that demands movement from us. In addition to the visual dimension of the work, there is also an equally important sound dimension. Each sound produced contributes to the narrative. The sum of the parts is not equal to the whole in Denić's work. "Exposition Coloniale" is a polyphonic architecture that projects us into the contemporary history of Europe in its contradictory and absurd dimensions. It is the cursed part of Europe that emerges at the heart of "Exposition Coloniale". Denić's narrative, with its polyphonic dimension, is reminiscent of Patrik Ouředník's book "Europeana – A Brief History of the 20th Century." Both are characterized by an economy of words and metaphors that express the truth of our time. Their narrative devices are elliptical, rapidly chaining together apparently incongruous connections. This incongruity acts as a revealer of what hides behind the collective amnesias specific to the *Society of the Spectacle*, to borrow Guy Debord's expression. *The Society of the Spectacle* is defined as "the distancing from reality through its representation." It makes us strangers to our own existence. The alienation here is defined by the experience of being dispossessed of reality. In a reversal of terms, Denić brings us closer to reality through its representation.

Denić's message resonates aptly with the title of this 60th edition of the Venice Art Biennale, "Foreigners Everywhere," proposed by Adriano Pedrosa, the curator of the international exhibition. Denić reminds us that the global and unified narrative of human destinies through merchandise is a simulacrum that expropriates us from our own existences; we are strangers to ourselves. As Guy Debord writes, "in a world turned upside down, the true is a moment of the false." Denić hacks

the simulacrum to invite us, like Alice, to step through the looking glass. Each installation in "Exposition Coloniale" reproduces familiar places whose character we perceive as sometimes anachronistic, sometimes artificial. The photo booth or telephone booth appear to us as relics of a lingering past, while the barrack or canteen appear to us as the commonplaces of acculturation. At the heart of "Colonial Exhibition," we begin as citizens of an *Absurdistan*, a non-place, an *atopie*, to become the subjects of our history and discover a heterotopia of which we become co-creators.

A central element of Denić's installation is a massive, isolated acronym that can only be read correctly through a rearview mirror. We read EUROPE™. Reading it this way in the mirror reveals the polysemy and polyphony of the word EUROPE. Neither dream nor nightmare, dystopia nor utopia, EUROPE escapes all fixity, all definition, resists all *trademarking*. It is up to us to understand ourselves as strangers to our condition in order to once again become subjects of history. Denić's work invites us to step into reality, which will always be shifting, trembling, alive. The artist is an exile. He is one who understands himself

as a stranger everywhere, who knows the uncertain and transitory nature of every society. We are invited to decenter ourselves to enter reality. Only a palimpsest can reveal the simulacrum of a present without past and future. The artist is one who knows himself to be a stranger everywhere. This is how I understand Hugues Saint-Victor's words: "he is perfect to whom the entire world is as a foreign land." The exile is the opposite of the nihilist. He speaks of the transitory nature of reality, not its negation. The exile has a voice that belongs only to himself. He does not claim to speak for others. He leaves time and space for each one.

Denić is an artist because he invests the real as an exile from reality. He has perfectly understood that a work of art can invite us to become subjects of history, in the sense understood by Guy Debord: "The subject of history can only be the living producing himself, becoming master and possessor of his world which is history, and existing as consciousness of his game." Denić invites us through the immersive experience offered by "Exposition Coloniale" to physically, sensorially, materially, through movement, experience that we can be subjects of history and not alienated from the present.

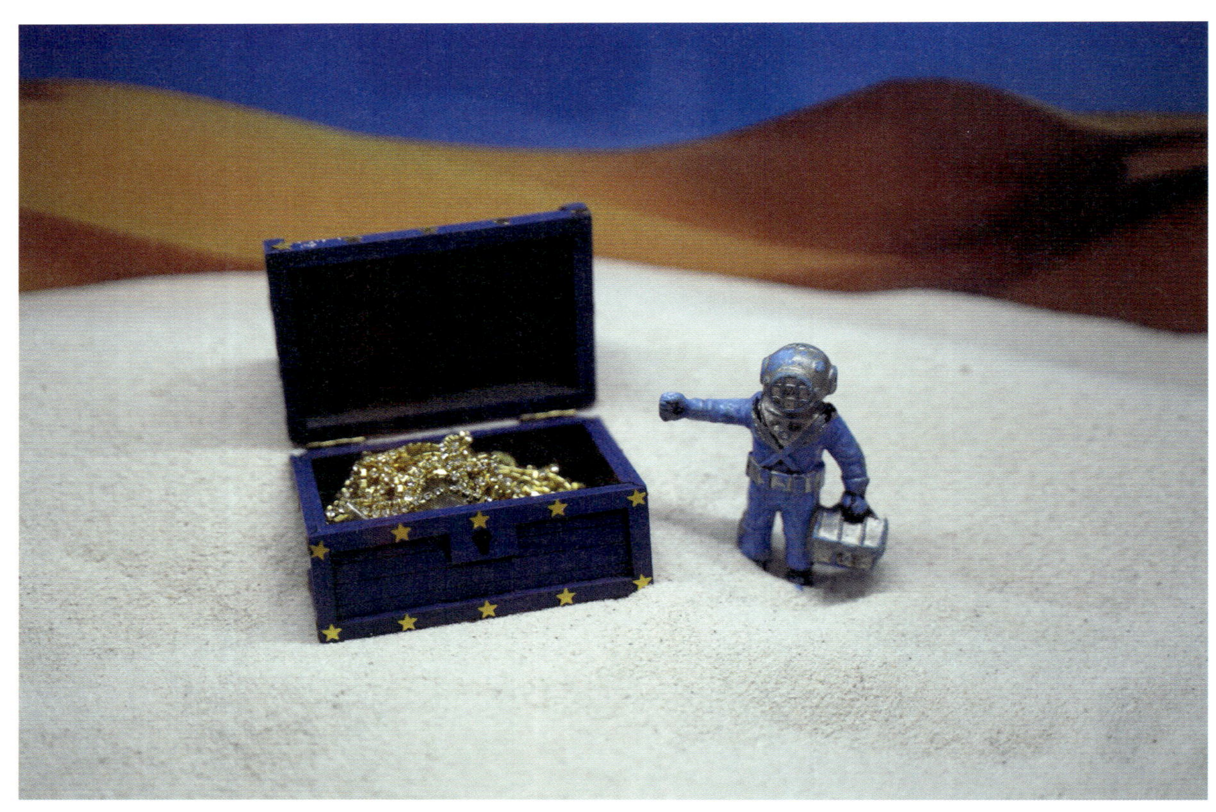

Kristofer Igdre

Evropa, Evropa!
Gde simulakrum postaje palimpsest

„Čovek kome je domovina slatka još je nežni početnik; onaj kome je svako tlo kao rodno, već je jak; ali savršen je onaj kome je ceo svet tuđina. Nežna duša učvrstila je svoju ljubav na jednom mestu u svetu; jak čovek je proširio svoju ljubav na sva mesta; savršen čovek je ugasio svoju.”
Ig de Sen-Viktor u *Didaskalikonu (1135)*

Odvažno! To je reč koja mi je odmah pala na pamet kada sam otkrio projekat Aleksandra Denića za 60. izdanje Venecijanskog bijenala. Odvažnost je kvalitet u umetnosti, a Denić je poseduje u izobilju. Imao sam privilegiju da unapred u Beogradu, decembra 2023. godine, u pratnji umetnice i kustoskinje Ksenije Samardžije, doživim sveobuhvatan i impresivan rad *Exposition Coloniale*, koji će biti predstavljen tokom sedam meseci, od aprila do novembra 2024. godine, u nekadašnjem Paviljonu Jugoslavije (krajem 20. veka postao Srpski paviljon) u Venecijanskom Đardiniju. Delo mi je predstavljeno u vidu makete, planova i skica. Otkriće ovih jednostavnih elemenata izazvalo je u meni osećaj uznemirenosti i nelagodnosti. Upravo to su emocije koje očekujem od umetničkog dela. Očekujem da će

predstavljati izazov za moja uverenja, moje misaone obrasce, moj komfor. Očekujem da će me uroniti u stanje vrtoglavice. Dugo ću pamtiti Denićev opis dela dok je stajao ispred svoje makete. Činilo se da je delo oživelo dok je on opisivao različite arhitektonske elemente instalacije i iskustva koja svaki od njih nosi. Malo je reći da me je delo *Exposition Coloniale* uznemirilo. Dok pišem ove redove, umetničko delo je u potpunosti realizovano u magacinu u predgrađu Beograda. Sada čeka prevoz do Venecije. U Parizu proučavam i gledam fotografije instalacije i gledam film u kojem se umetnik nečujno kreće kroz različite module *Exposition Coloniale*. Efekat je upečatljiv. Nešto što je postojalo kao plan sada postoji kao kompozitna arhitektura koja nudi stvarno, materijalno, fizičko, čulno iskustvo. Nemir i vrtoglavica se umnožavaju. Sada

željno čekam dolazak proleća da bih fizički ušao u *Exposition Coloniale* i postao jedan od aktera u hibridnom umetničkom delu, gde je svaki detalj značajan.

Razmatranje naslova otkriva pojedine naznake o iskustvu koje treba doživeti. On otkriva samu prirodu dela. To je palimpsest koji na površinu kolektivnog pamćenja izvlači činjenice koje su dugo potiskivane. Skoro jedan vek, od sredine 19. do sredine 20. veka, Evropljani su masovno putovali kako bi posetili kolonijalne izložbe. Ove izložbe su slavile osvajanja velikih kolonijalnih imperija, kao što su Ujedinjeno Kraljevstvo, Francuska, Belgija, Holandija, Portugal i Španija. Nije nebitan Denićev izbor da delu da naslov na francuskom. Francuska kolonijalna imperija je opravdavala potčinjavanje kolonizovanih naroda u ime univerzalnih principa nasleđenih iz prosvetiteljstva i Francuske revolucije. U ime ovih „civilizacijskih vrlina" Francuska je legitimisala kolonizaciju, vojne ekspedicije, oduzimanje imovine, akulturaciju i masakre. Između 1889. i 1937, za manje od pedeset godina, Francuska je organizovala čak četrnaest kolonijalnih izložbi, privlačeći publiku iz cele Evrope. Pre pojave bioskopa, ove izložbe su bile jedna od prvih industrija masovne zabave. Najstrašnije je otkriti da su na ovim kolonijalnim izložbama rekonstruisana čitava sela iz kolonizovanih zemalja, sa „divljacima" izloženim u njihovom „prirodnom staništu". Krajem 20. veka, istoričari su nazvali ove žive diorame njihovim pravim imenom: u najmanju ruku, to su bili „ljudski zoološki vrtovi".

Ono što Denićevo delo čini palimpsestom nije samo naslov, već i dijalog koji stvara sa arhitekturom nekadašnjeg Paviljona Jugoslavije i sadašnjeg Paviljona Srbije. Ovo zdanje, koje je projektovao venecijanski arhitekt Breno del Gvidiče, predstavlja upečatljivu mešavinu koja prkosi jednostavnoj klasifikaciji. Ono svedoči o evoluciji venecijanske arhitekture od renesanse do modernog doba. Ova arhitektura je uspevala da stvori dija-

log sa onim što joj je prethodilo dok se suptilno obnavljala. Nije pogrešno reći da je sama arhitektura Venecije palimpsest.

Exposition Coloniale počinje na ulazu u Paviljon. Denić je napravio kiosk sa prizvukom art dekoa koji se savršeno uklapa u oval ogromnih ulaznih vrata Paviljona. Ovim jednostavnim kioskom, Denić otkriva tenzije i geopolitičke realnosti koje su oblikovale istoriju renomiranog Venecijanskog bijenala. Raznovrsnost arhitektura različitih nacionalnih paviljona u Đardiniju je, u tom smislu, upečatljiv pokazatelj. Arhitektura je bojno polje. Od svog nastanka krajem 19. veka, Venecijansko bijenale je mesto gde su pozadinu uvek činili aktuelni politički i kulturni sukobi. Ono je privilegovani svedok poroznosti između umetnosti i istorije, u dobru i u zlu.

Kada prođemo prvu vazdušnu komoru, kiosk gde se uzima ulaznica, ulazimo u izuzetan scenografski prostor sastavljen od više instalacija ili modula u kojima posetioci postaju glumci. Sa *Exposition Coloniale* Denić kao da spaja sredstva Teatra surovosti Antonena Artoa sa sadržajem Semjuela Beketa ili Teatra apsurda Harolda Pintera. Time je završeno ukidanje granice između scene i

publike, toliko drage Antonenu Artou. Apsurd ljudskog stanja doživljava se u narativu koji se odvija dok se krećemo iz jednog prostora u drugi. U baroknom spletu, svaki modul, svaka arhitektura je vizuelna tvorevina čije obilje detalja nije slučajno. Neki od ovih detalja nam deluju poznato, dok su drugi potpuno strani. Ali nakon detaljnijeg pregleda, nije važno kakve je prirode detalj; njegova vrednost dolazi do izražaja samo integracijom u širu celinu. Celokupnost dela *Exposition Coloniale* poseduje materijalnost koja od nas zahteva kretanje. Pored vizuelne, postoji i podjednako važna zvučna dimenzija dela. Svaki proizvedeni zvuk doprinosi naraciji. Zbir delova nije jednak celini u Denićevom delu. *Exposition Coloniale* je polifona arhitektura koja nas projektuje u savremenu istoriju Evrope u njenim kontradiktornim i apsurdnim dimenzijama. To je prokleti deo Evrope koji se pojavljuje u srcu *Exposition Coloniale*. Denićev narativ svojom polifonom dimenzijom podseća na knjigu Patrika Orednika *Europeana – kratka istorija 20. veka*. Obe karakteriše ekonomičnost reči i metafora koje izražavaju istinu našeg vremena. Njihovi narativni uređaji su eliptični i brzo spajaju naizgled neskladne veze. Ova nepodudarnost deluje kao otkrivač onoga što se krije iza kolektivne amnezije karakteristične za *Društvo spektakla*, da pozajmimo izraz Gi Debora. *Društvo spektakla* se definiše kao „udaljavanje od stvarnosti kroz njeno predstavljanje". To nas čini strancima sopstvenog postojanja. Otuđenje je ovde determinisano iskustvom lišavanja stvarnosti. U preokretu pojmova, Denić nas kroz njenu reprezentaciju približava stvarnosti.

Denićeva poruka dobro rezonuje sa naslovom ovog 60. izdanja Venecijanskog bijenala umetnosti, čiji je naslov, *Stranci svuda*, predložio kustos međunarodne izložbe, Adriano Pedrosa. Denić podseća da je globalni i jedinstveni narativ ljudskih sudbina kroz robu simulakrum koji nas ekspropriše iz sopstvenih egzistencija; mi smo sami sebi stranci. Kao što piše Gi Debor, „u svetu okrenutom naglavačke, istina je samo trenutak laži". Denić hakuje simulakrum da nas, poput Alise, pozove da zakoračimo u ogledalo. Svaka instalacija u *Exposition Coloniale* reprodukuje poznata mesta čiji karakter ponekad doživljavamo kao anahron, a ponekad kao veštački. Foto kabina ili telefonska govornica nam se pojavljuju kao relikti davne prošlosti, dok nam se baraka ili kantina pojavljuju kao opšte mesto akulturacije. U srcu *Kolonijalne izložbe*, kao građani *apsurdistana*, ne-mesta, *atopije*, postajemo subjekti naše istorije i otkrivamo heterotopiju čiji smo kokreatori.

Centralni element Denićeve instalacije je masivni, izolovani akronim koji se može ispravno pročitati samo kroz retrovizor. Čitamo EVROPA™. Ovako čitanje u ogledalu otkriva polisemiju i polifoniju reči EVROPA. Ni san ni noćna mora, ni distopija ni utopija, EVROPA izmiče svakoj fiksnosti, svakoj definiciji, opire se svim *zaštitnim znakovima*. Na nama je da sebe shvatimo kao strance u odnosu na sebe same da bismo ponovo postali subjekti istorije. Denićevo delo nas poziva da zakoračimo u stvarnost, koja će uvek biti u stanju pomeranja, drhtanja, živosti. Umetnik je izgnanik. On je taj koji sebe svuda shvata kao stranca, koji poznaje neizvesnu i prolaznu prirodu svakog društva. Pozvani smo da se udaljimo od centra kako bismo ušli u stvarnost. Samo palimpsest može otkriti simulakrum sadašnjosti bez prošlosti i budućnosti. Umetnik je taj koji zna da je svuda stranac. Ovako razumem reči Iga Sen Viktora: „savršen je onaj kome je ceo svet tuđina". Izgnanstvo je suprotnost nihilizmu. Ono govori o prolaznosti stvarnosti, a ne o njenoj negaciji. Izgnanik ima glas koji pripada samo njemu. On ne tvrdi da govori u ime drugih. Svakome ostavlja sopstveno vreme i prostor.

Denić je umetnik jer ulaže stvarno kao izgnanik iz stvarnosti. On je savršeno shvatio da nas umetničko delo može pozvati da postanemo subjekti istorije, po shvatanju Gi Debora: „Subjekat istorije može biti samo živi koji proizvodi sebe, postaje gospodar i posednik svog sveta, koji predstavlja istoriju, a postoji kao svest o svojoj igri". Denić nas kroz imerzivno iskustvo koje nudi *Exposition Coloniale* poziva da fizički, čulno, materijalno, kroz pokret, doživimo mogućnost da budemo subjekti istorije, a ne otuđenici od sadašnjosti.

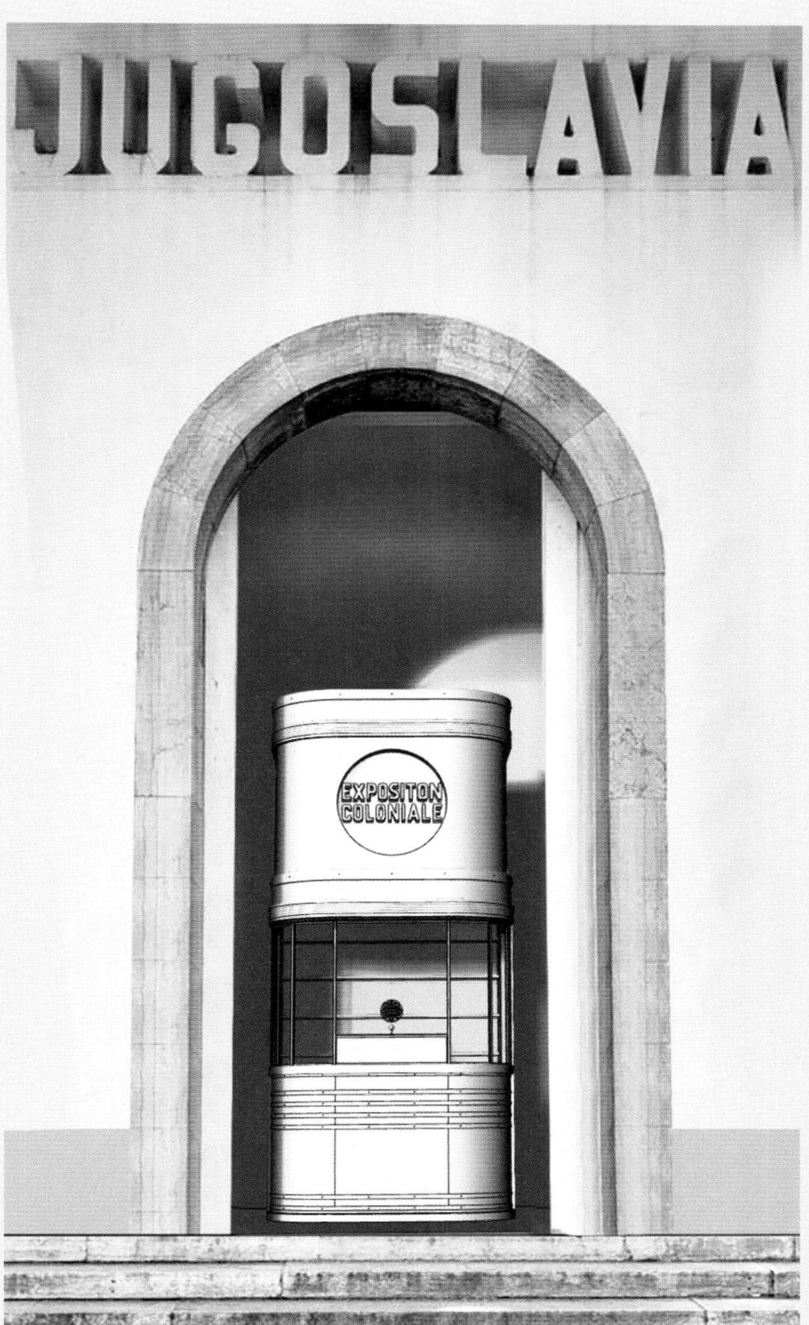

JUGOSLAVIA
EXPOSITON
COLONIALE

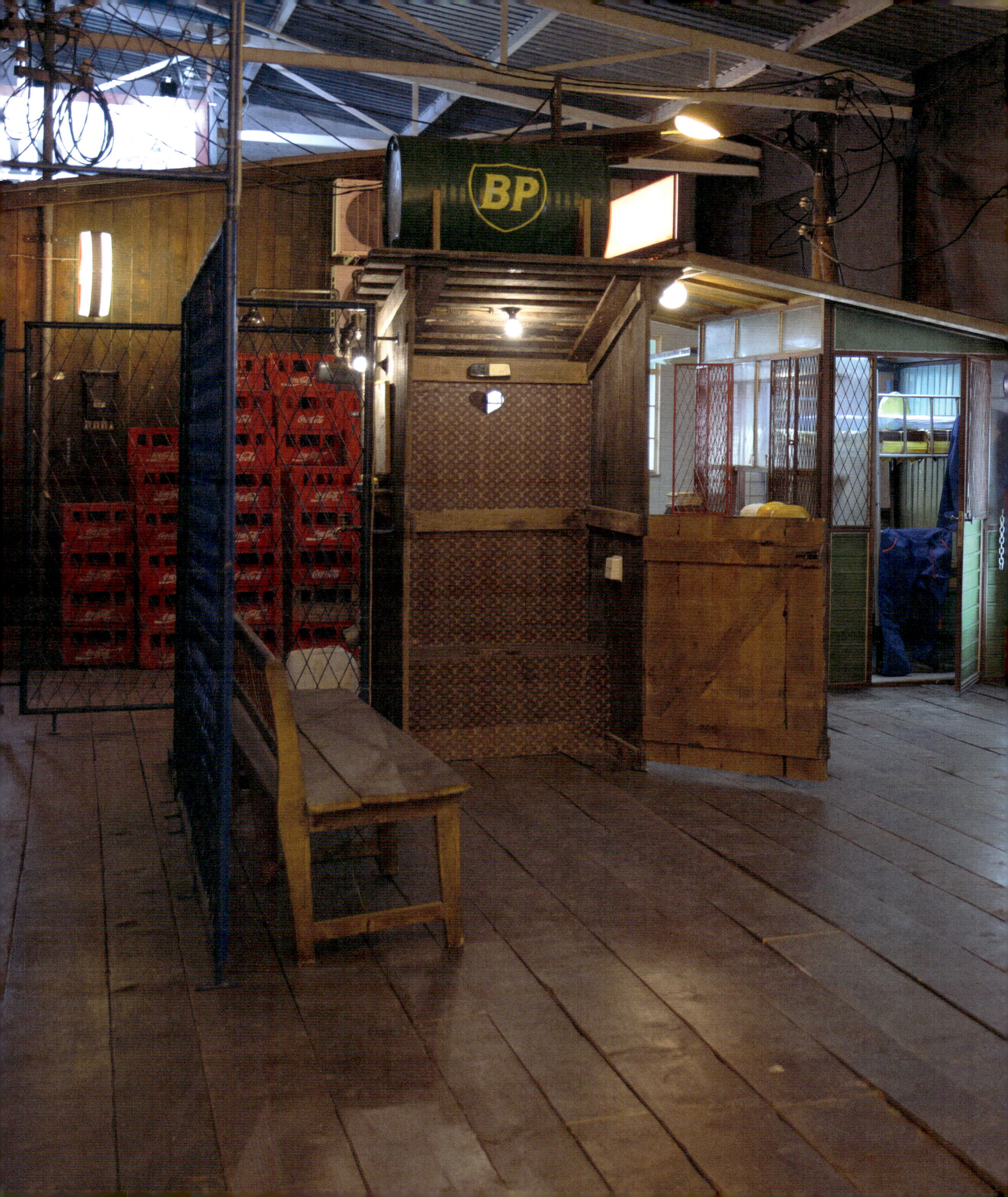

BP

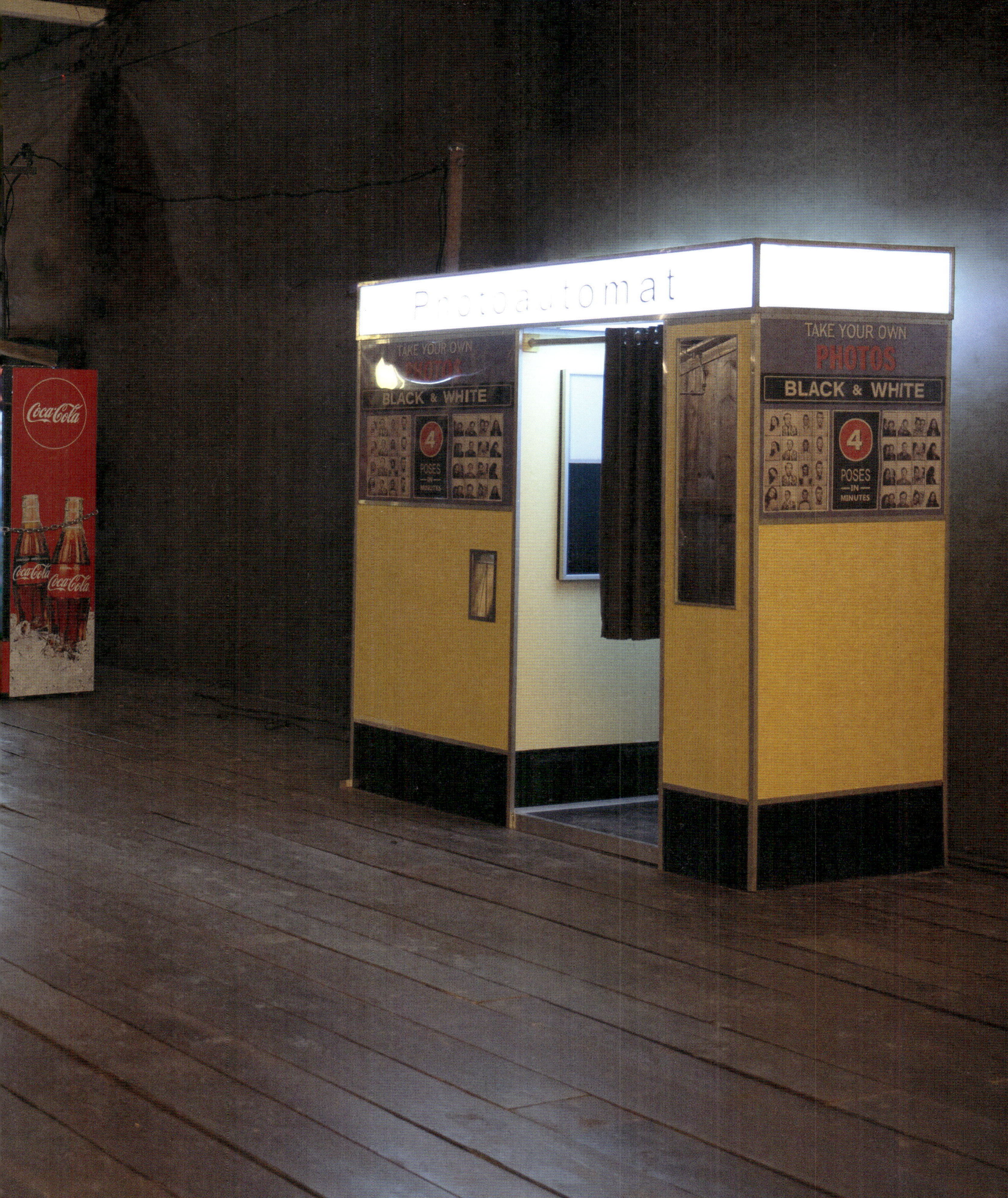
Photoautomat
TAKE YOUR OWN
PHOTOS
BLACK & WHITE
4
POSES
IN
MINUTES
TAKE YOUR OWN
PHOTOS
BLACK & WHITE
4
POSES
IN
MINUTES
Coca-Cola
Coca-Cola
Coca-Cola

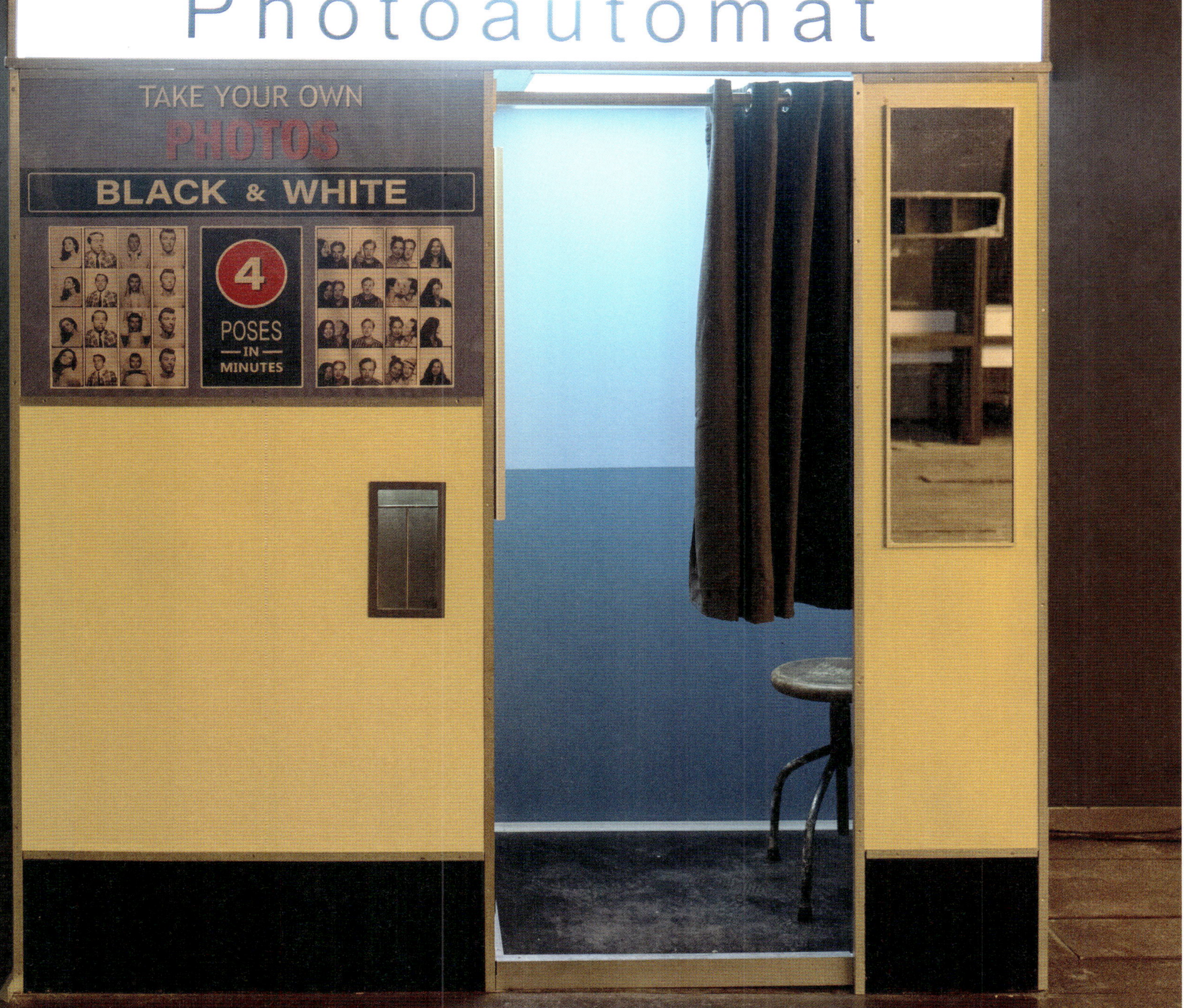
Photoautomat
TAKE YOUR OWN
PHOTOS
BLACK & WHITE
4
POSES
IN
MINUTES

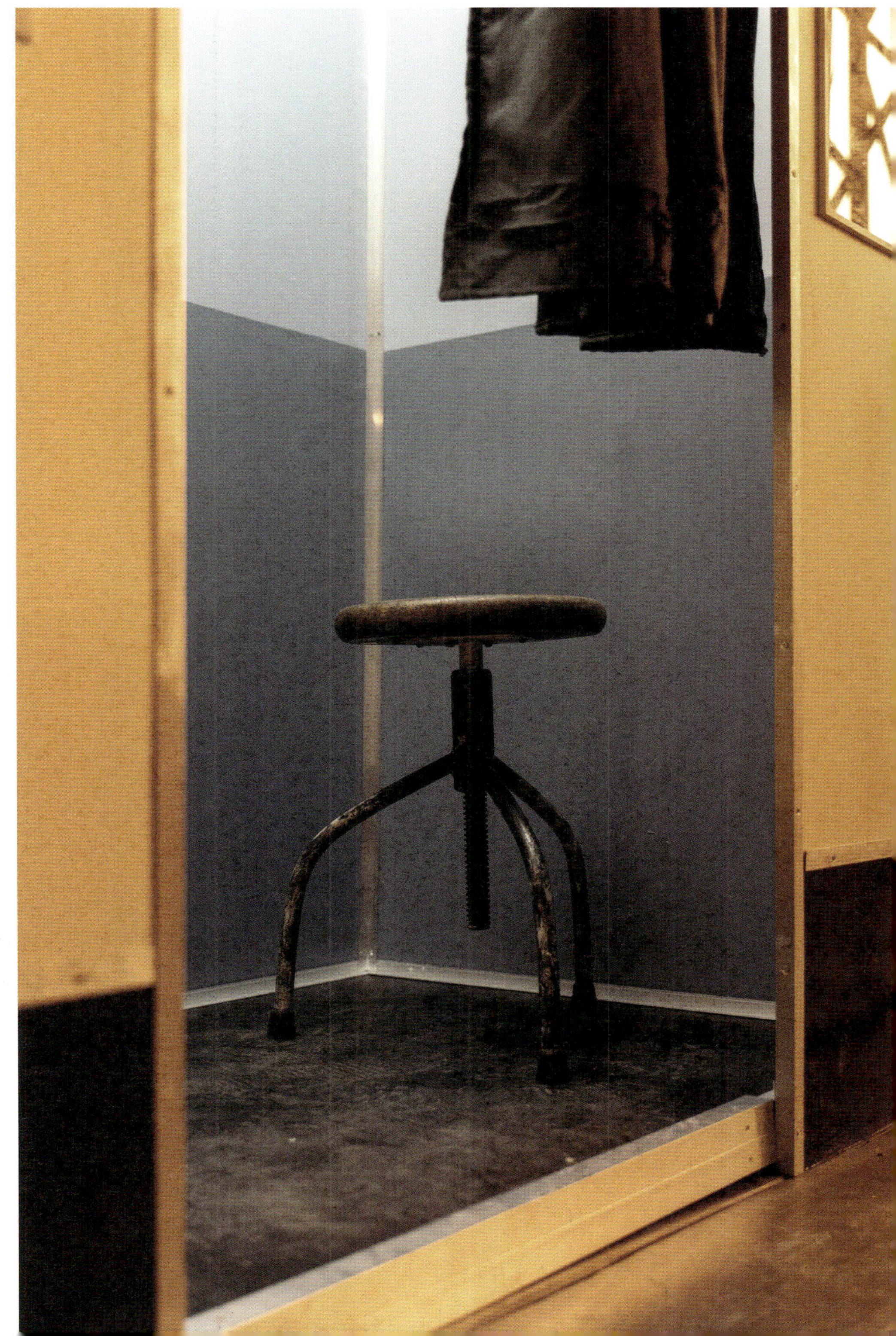

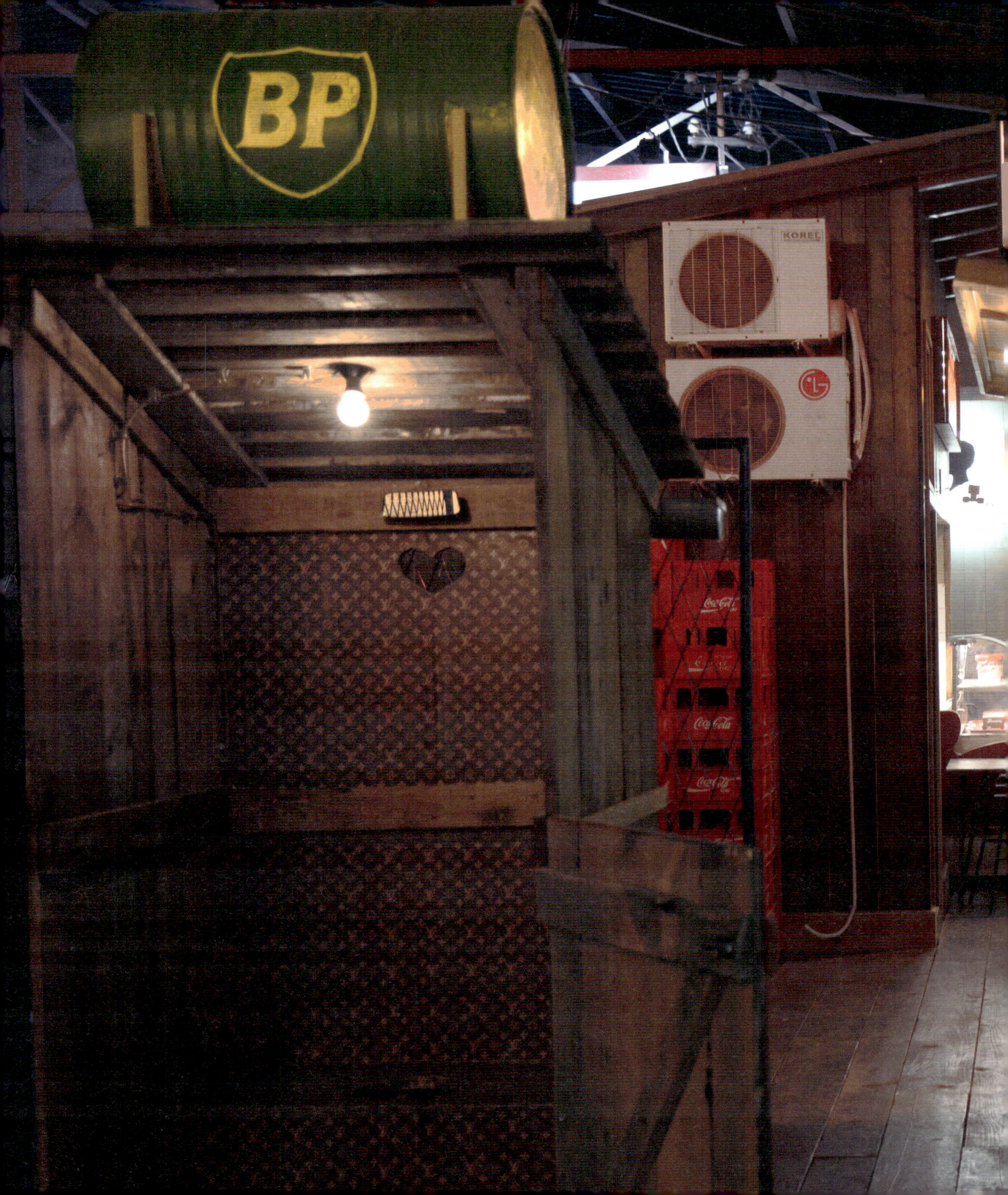
BP
KOREL
LG
Coca-Cola
Coca-Cola
Coca-Cola

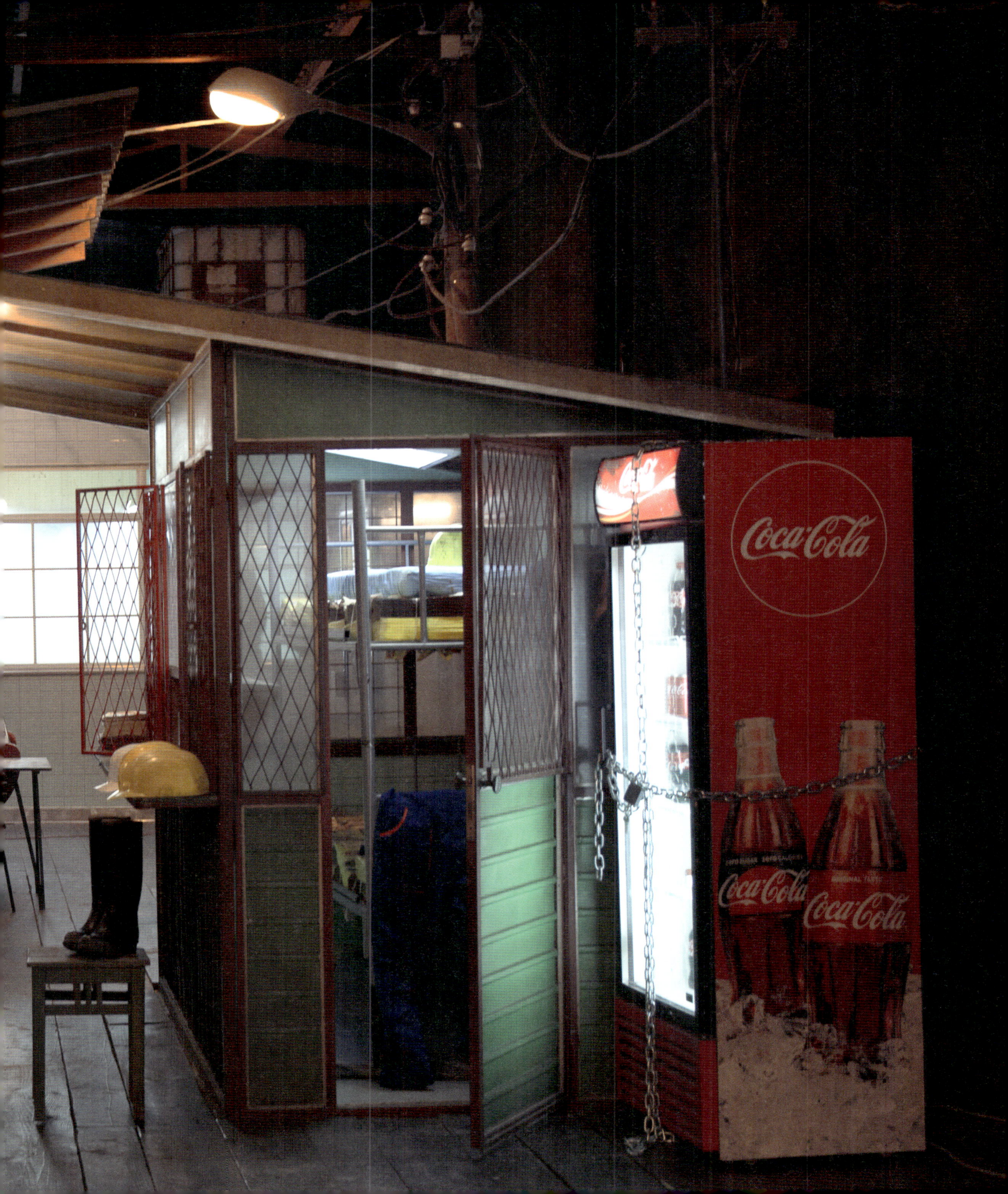
Coca-Cola
Coca-Cola
Coca-Cola

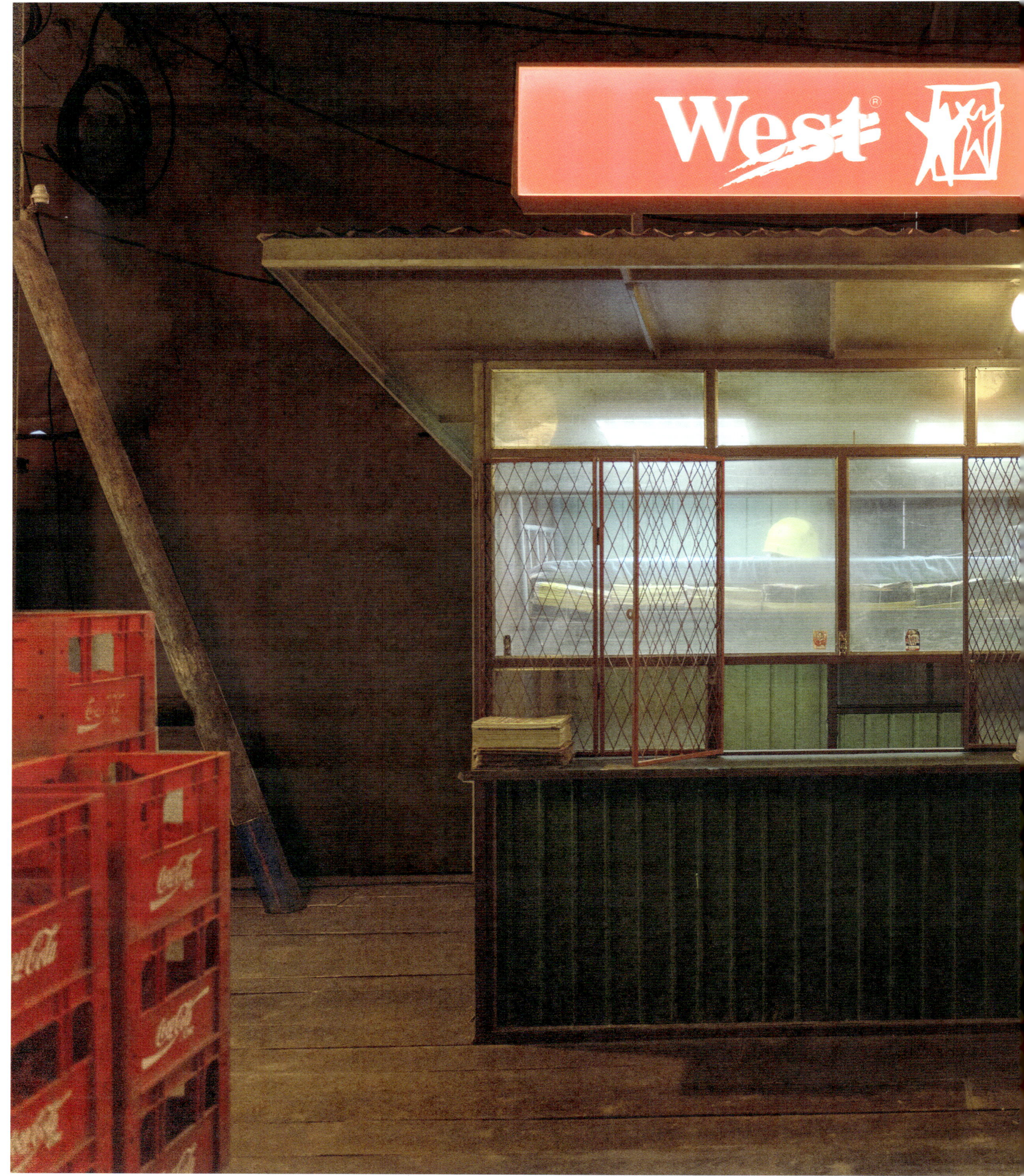

West

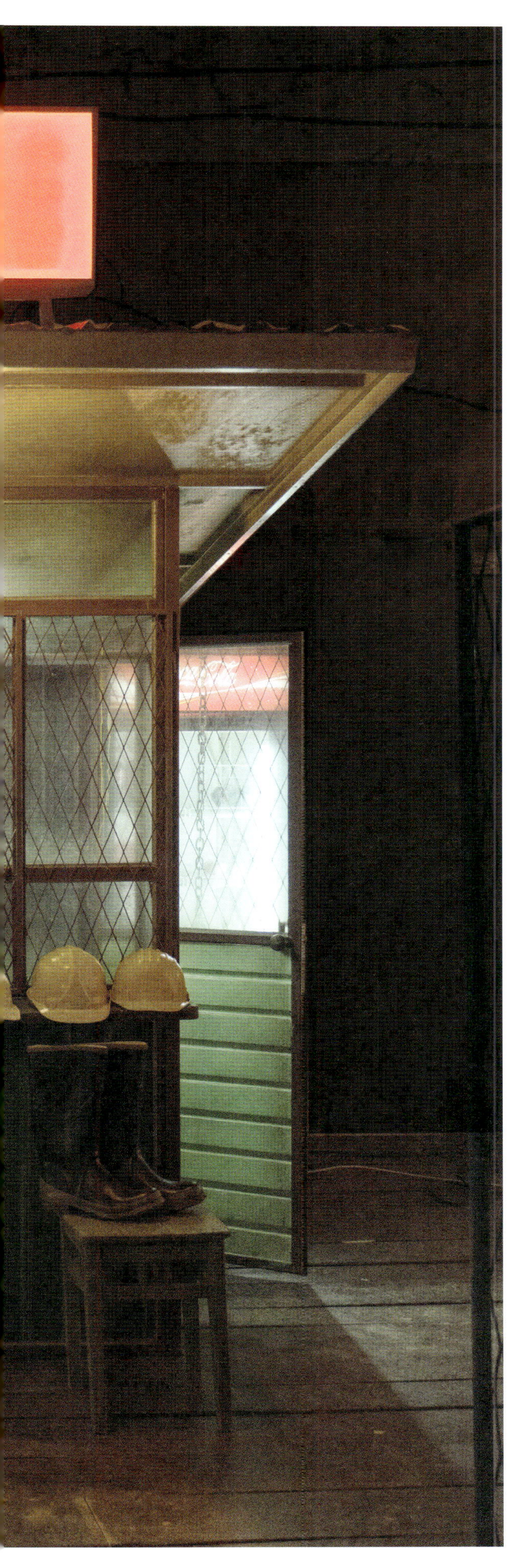

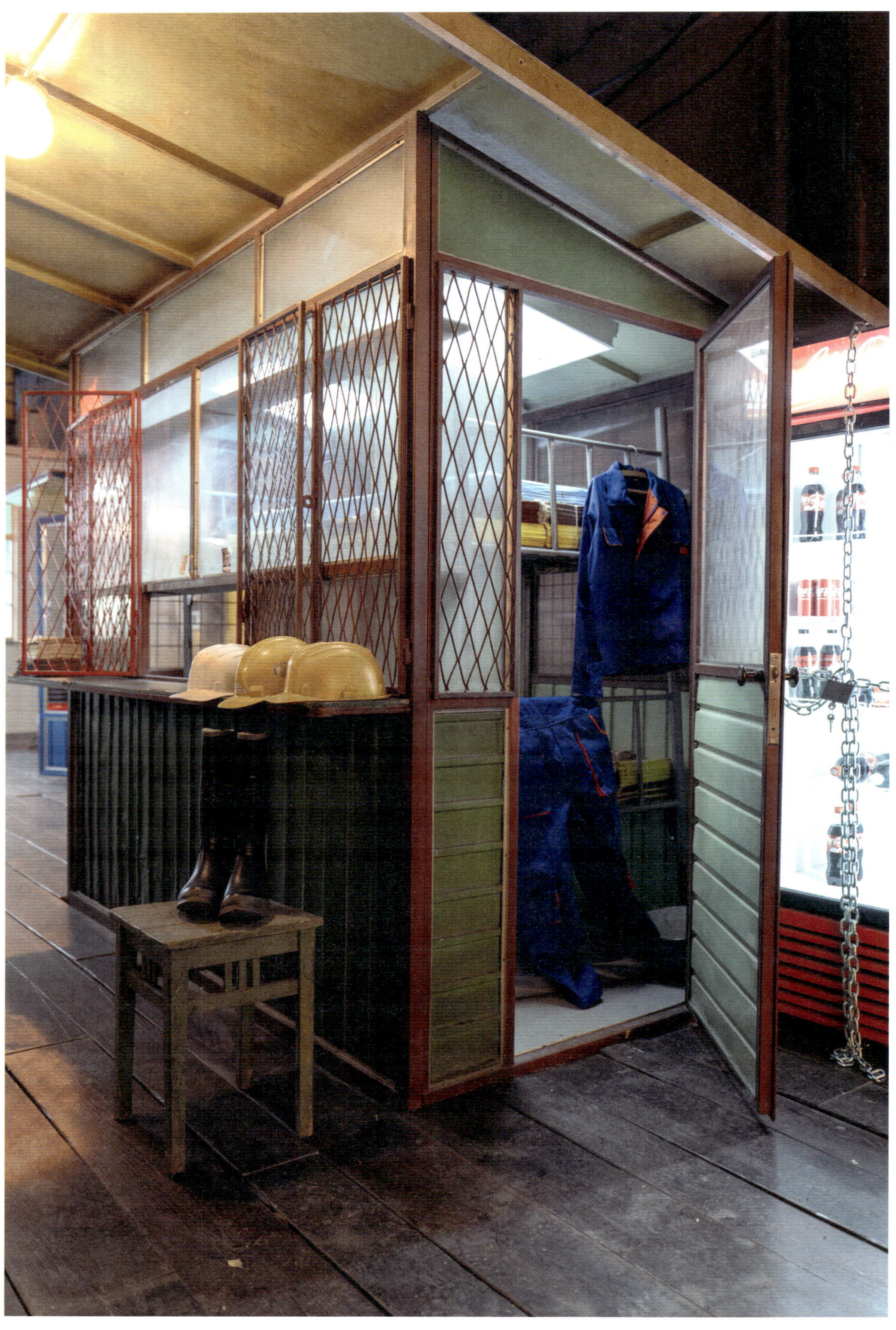

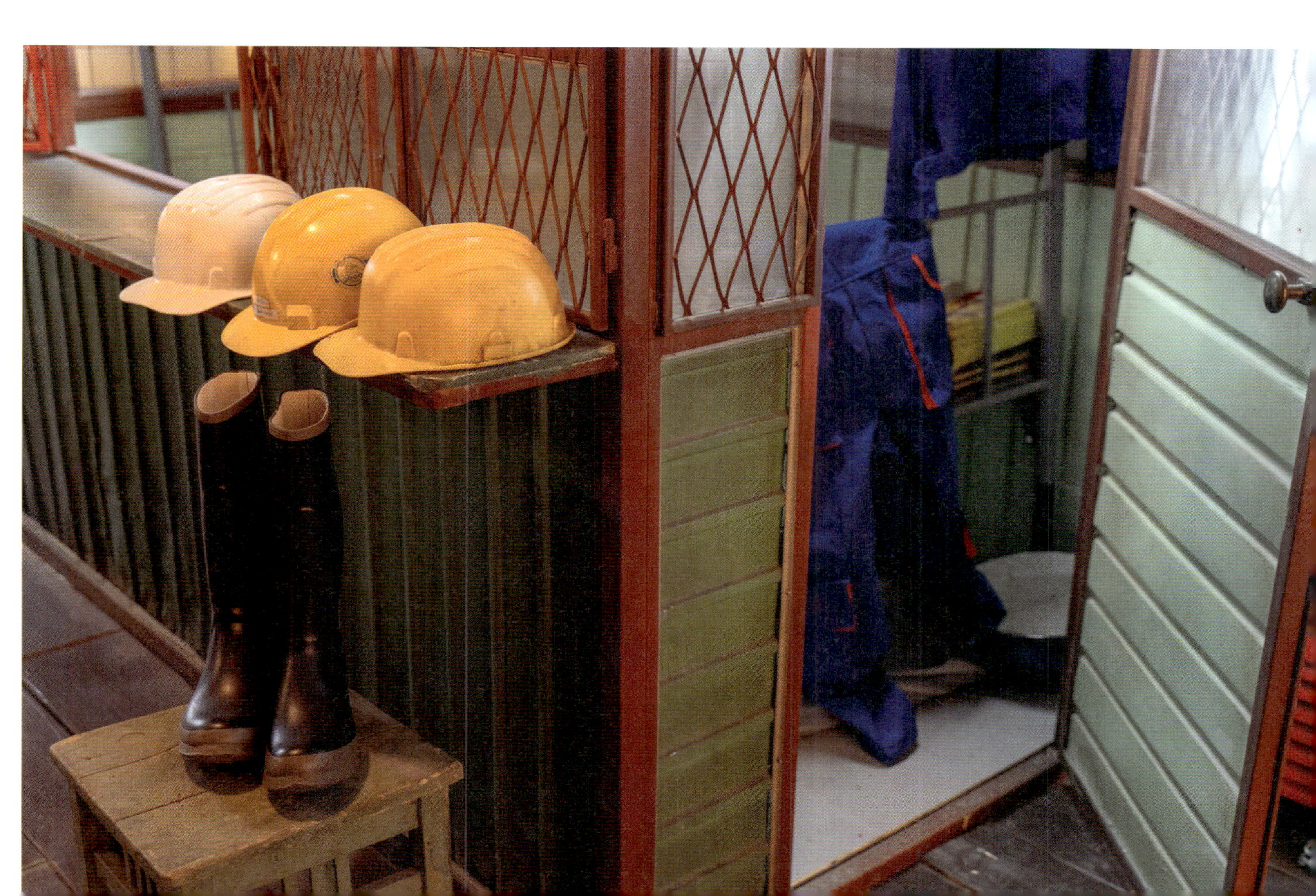

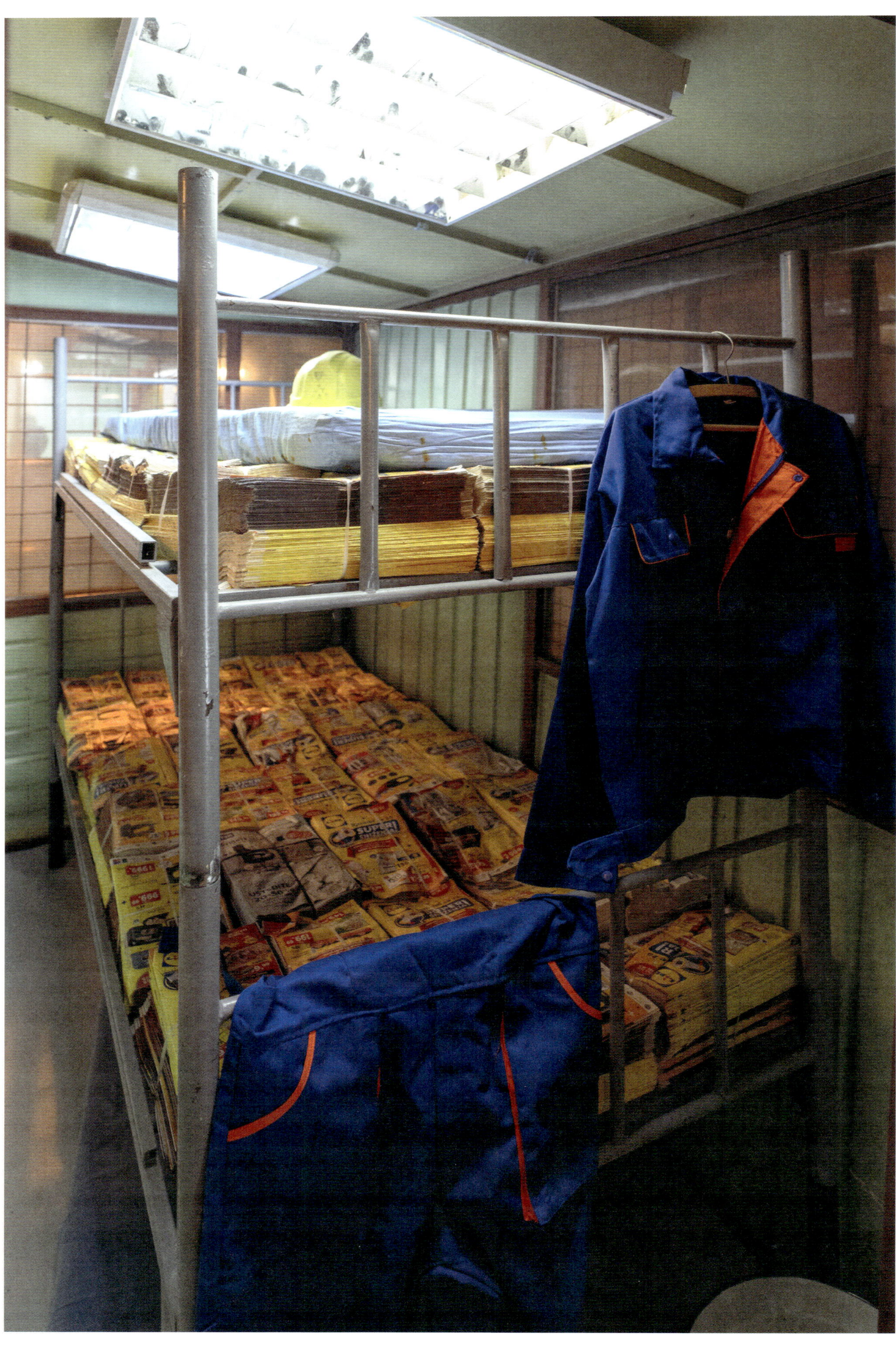

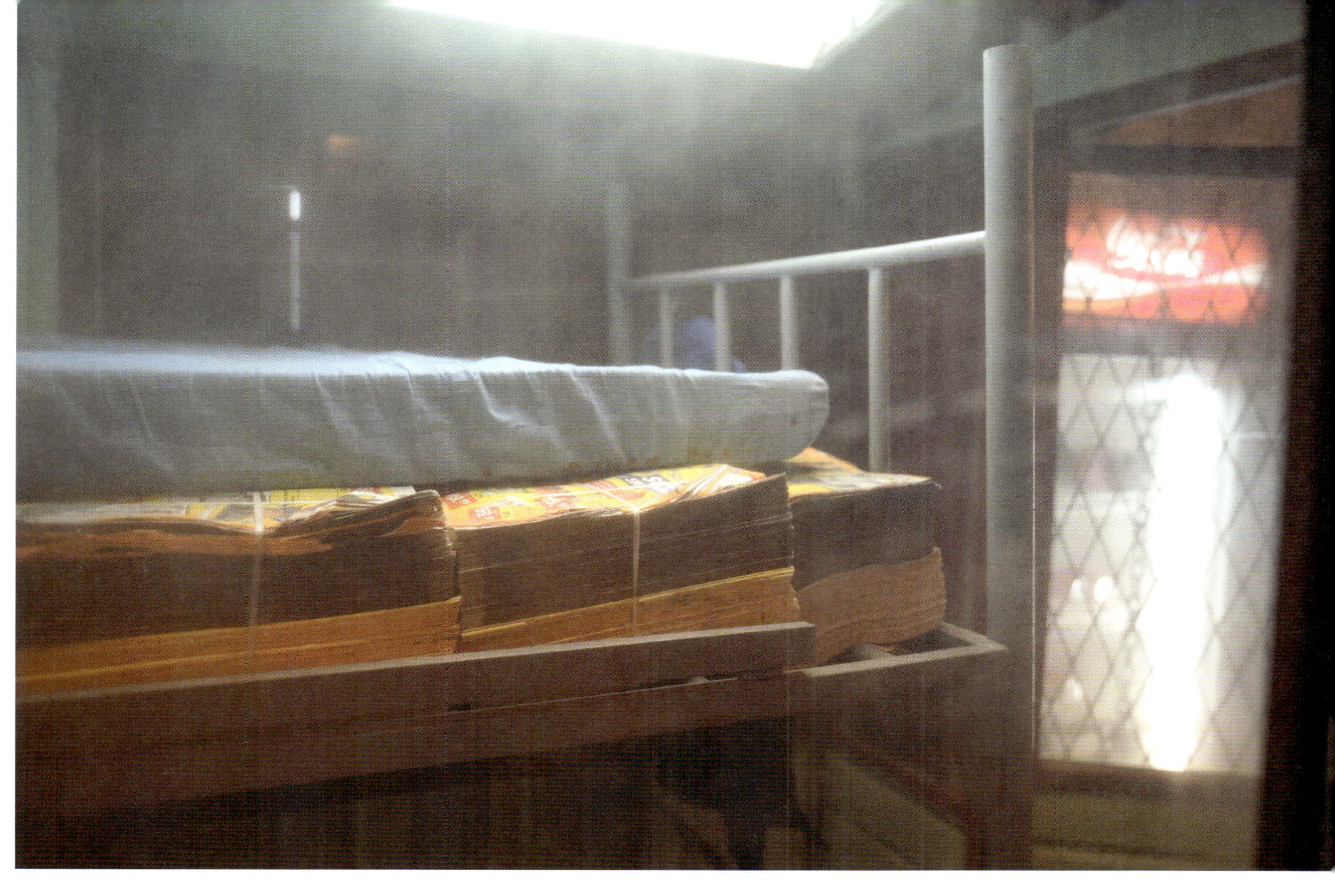

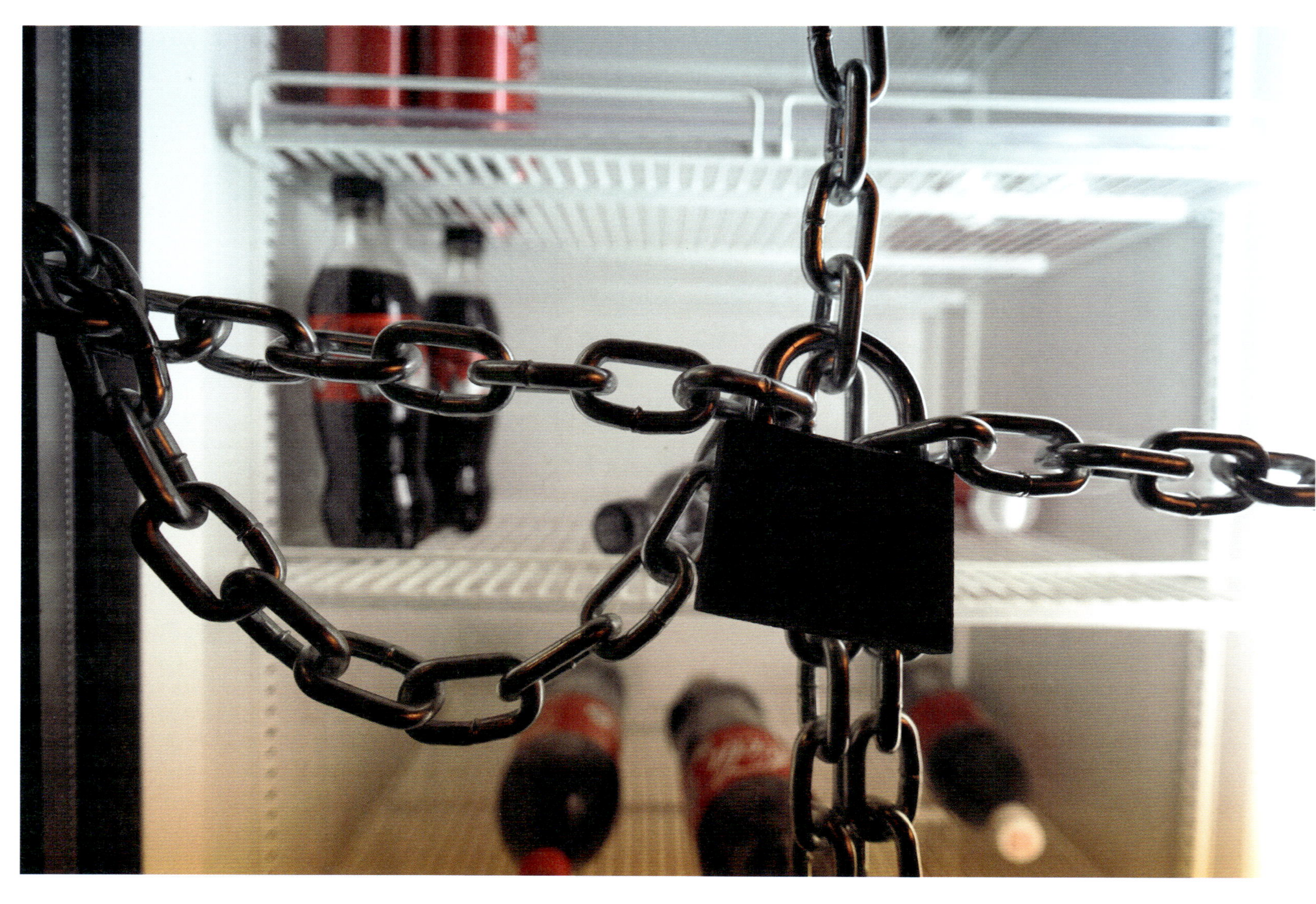

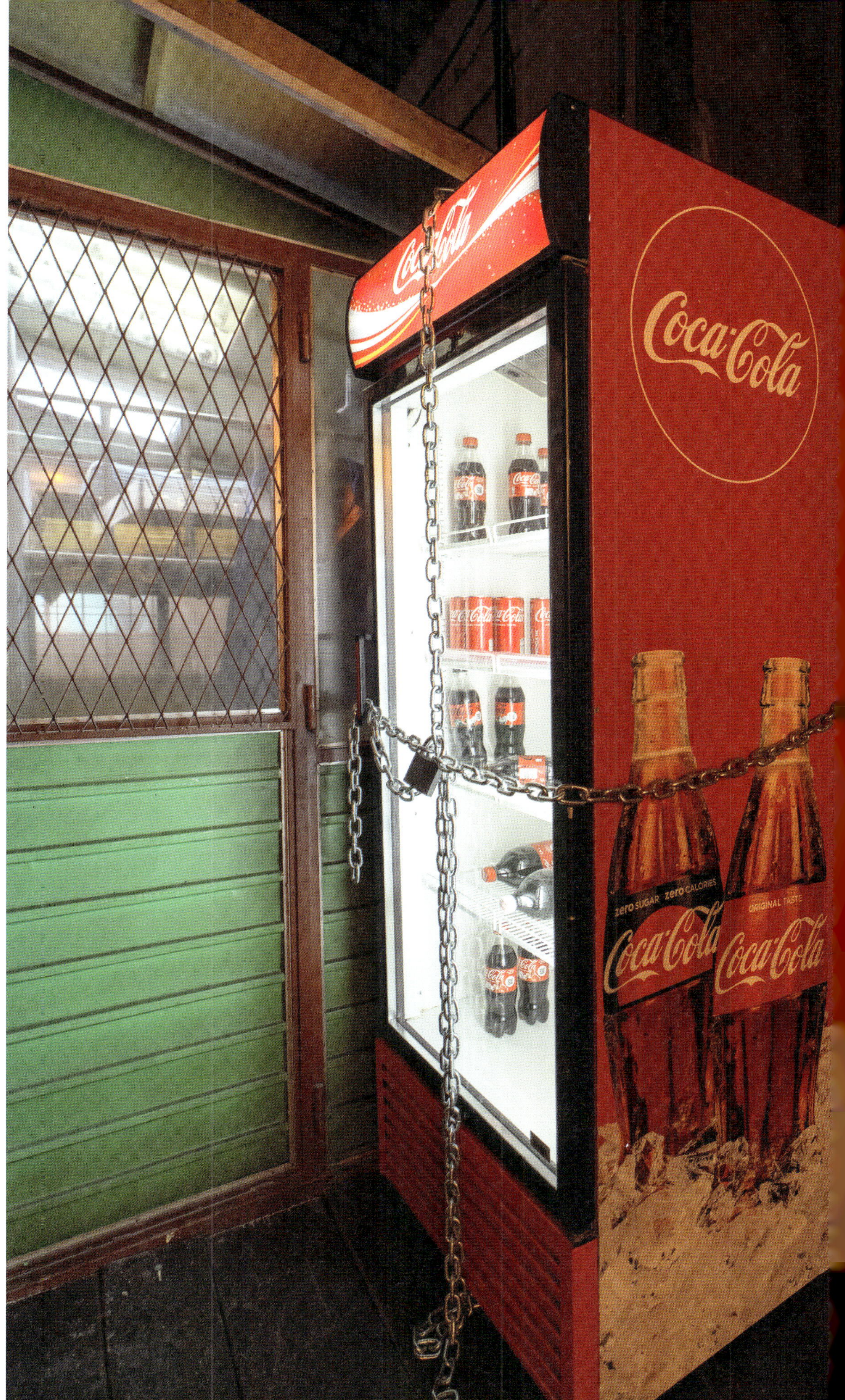
Coca-Cola
Coca-Cola
zero SUGAR zero CALORIES
Coca-Cola
ORIGINAL TASTE
Coca-Cola

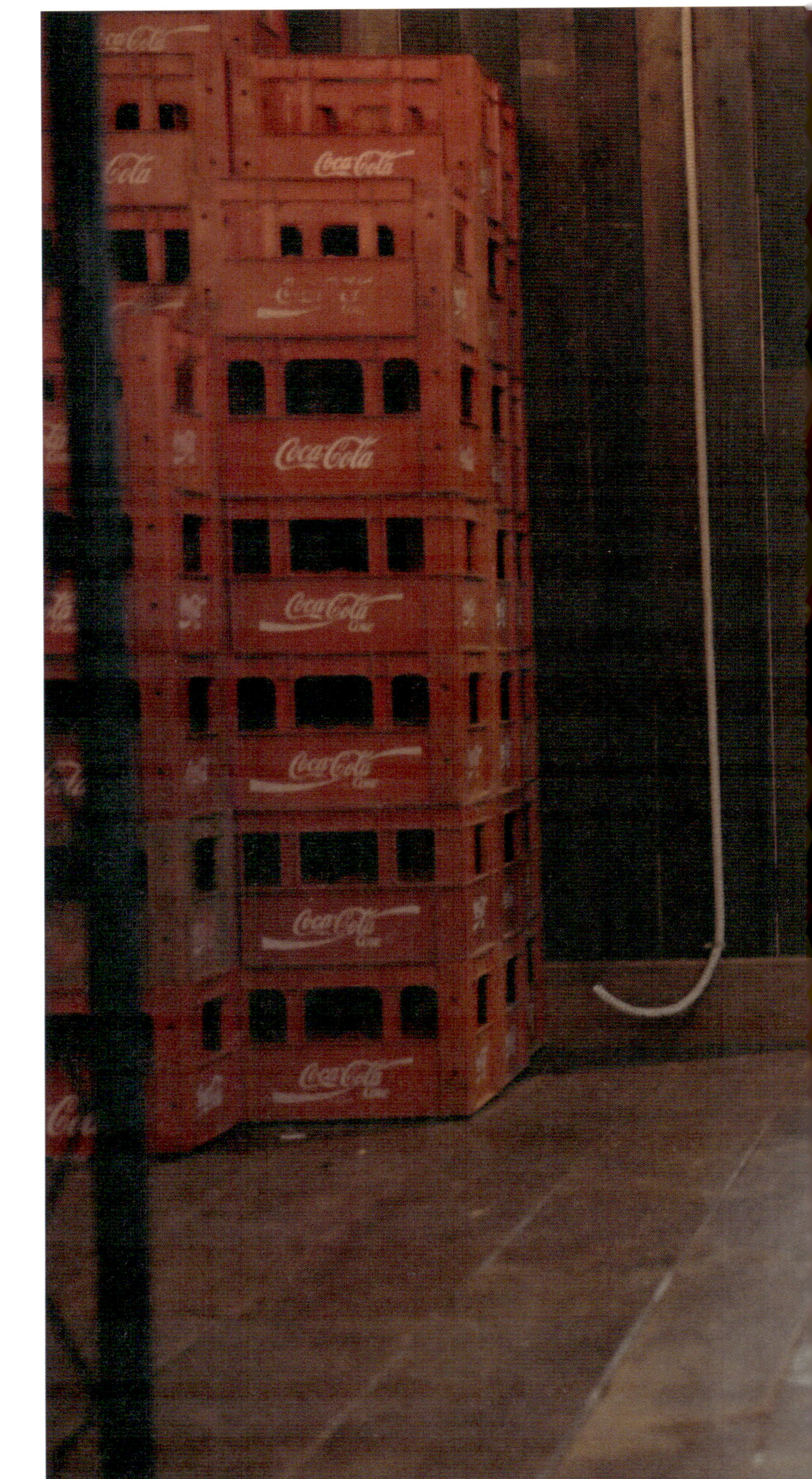

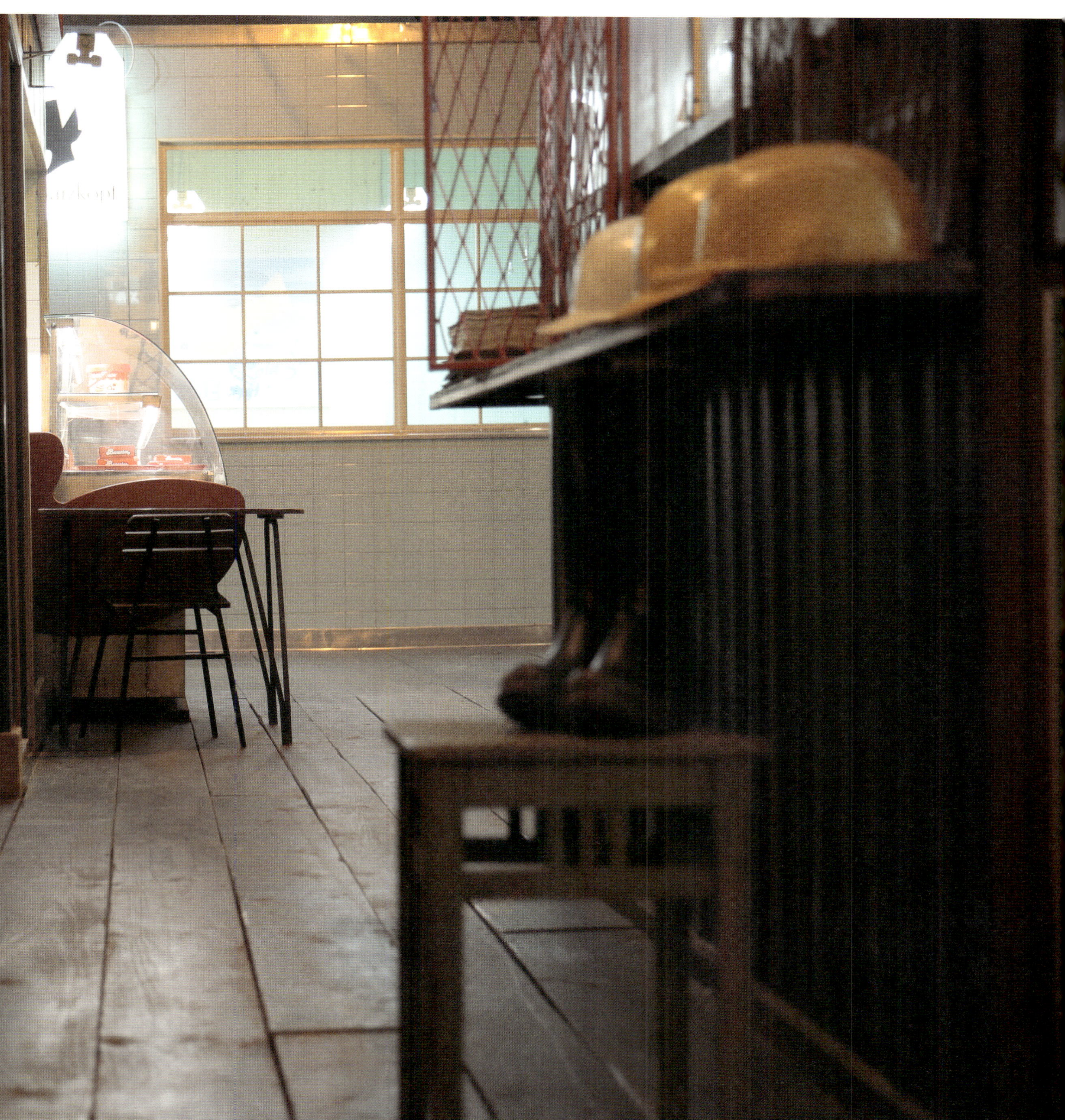

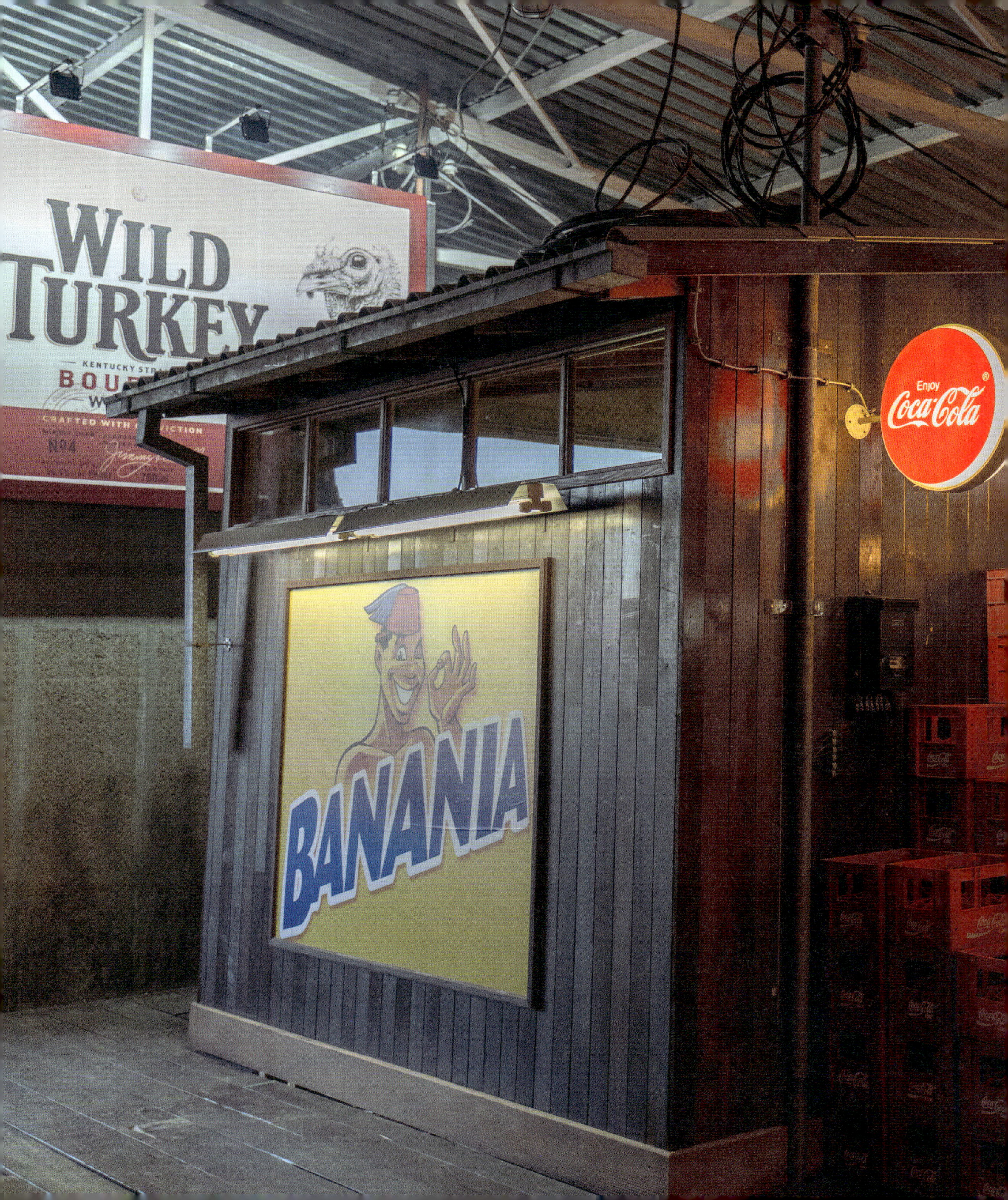

WILD TURKEY
KENTUCKY STRAIGHT
BOURBON
CRAFTED WITH CONVICTION
N°4
BANANIA
Enjoy
Coca-Cola

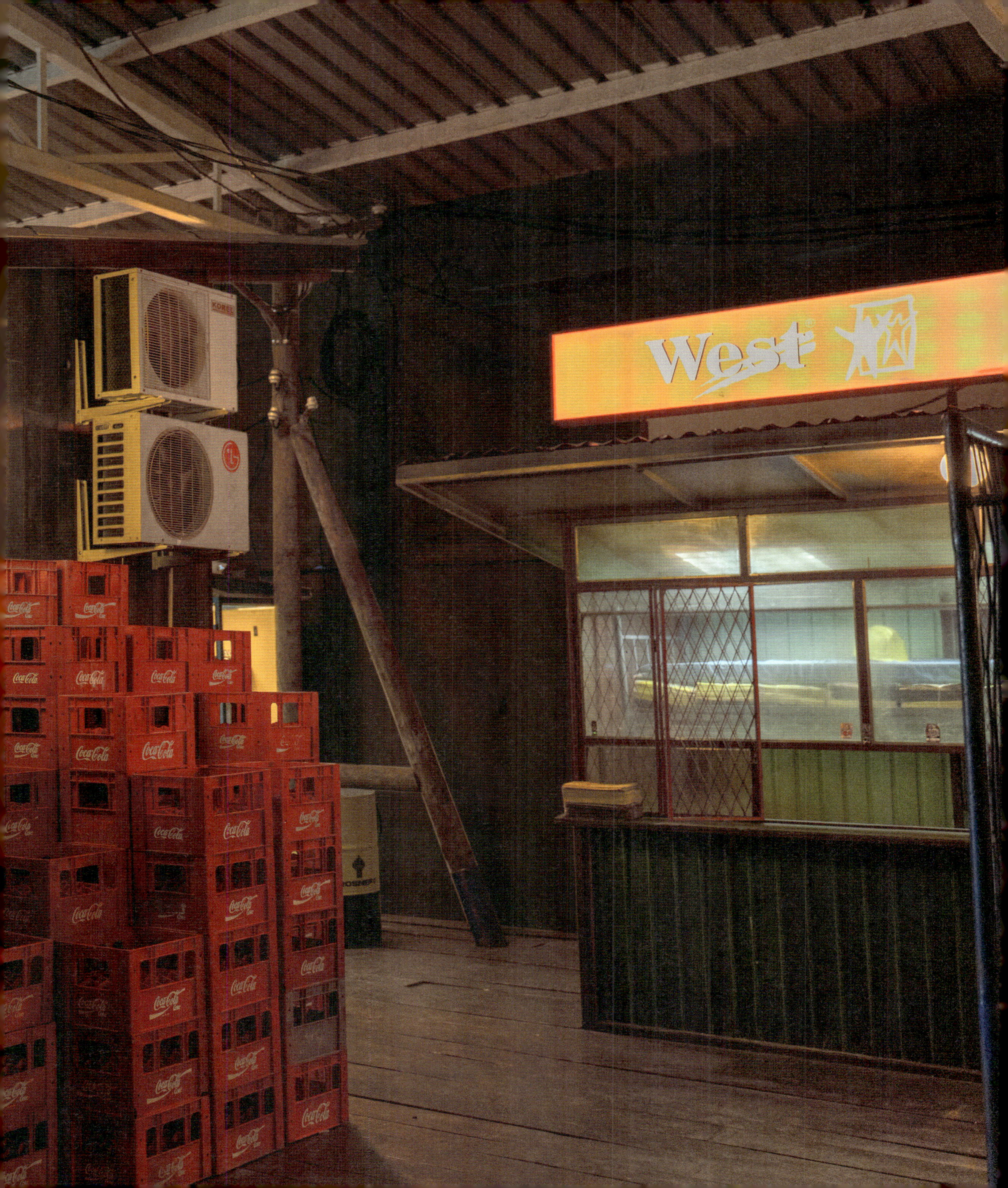

West
Coca Cola
KOREL
LG

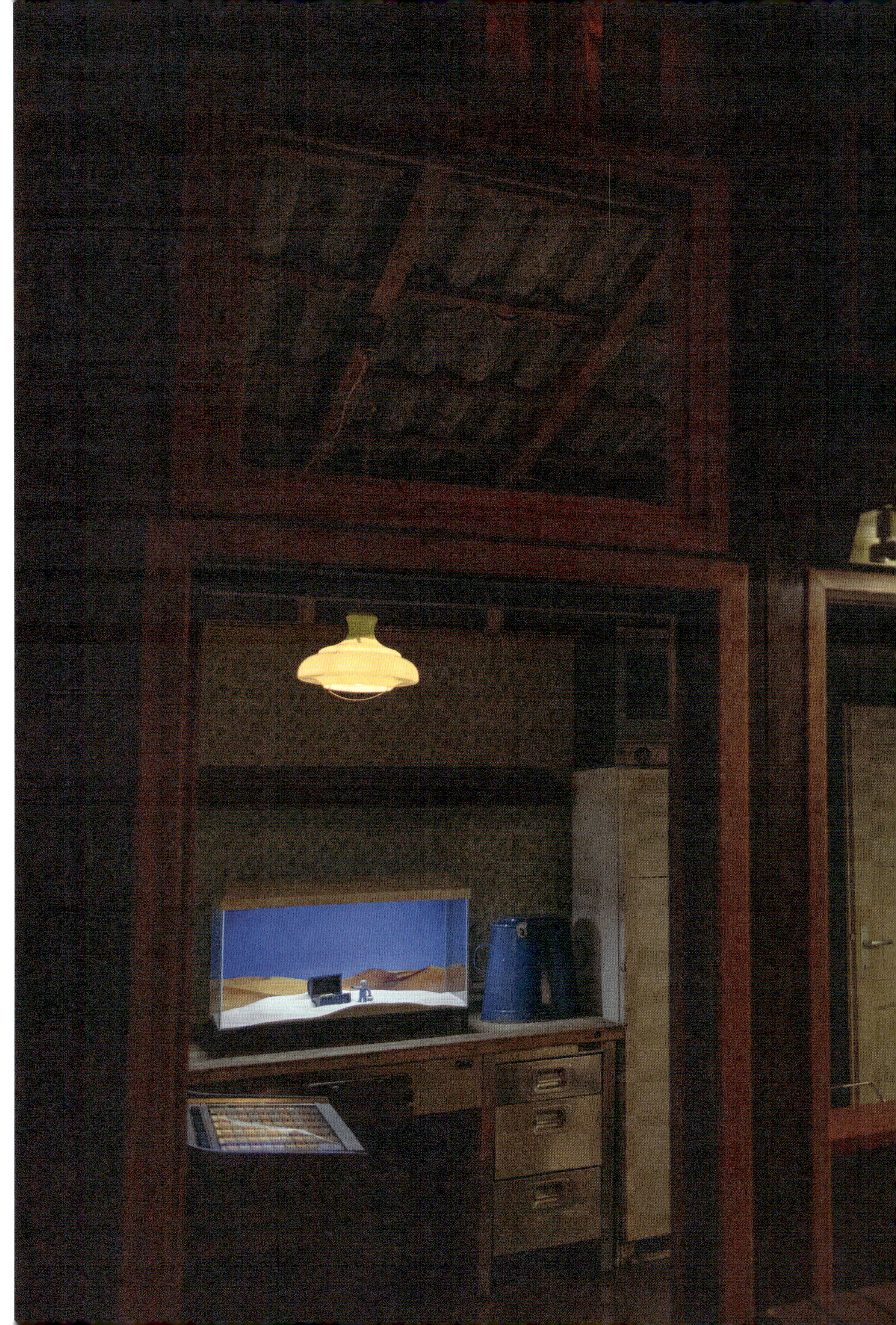

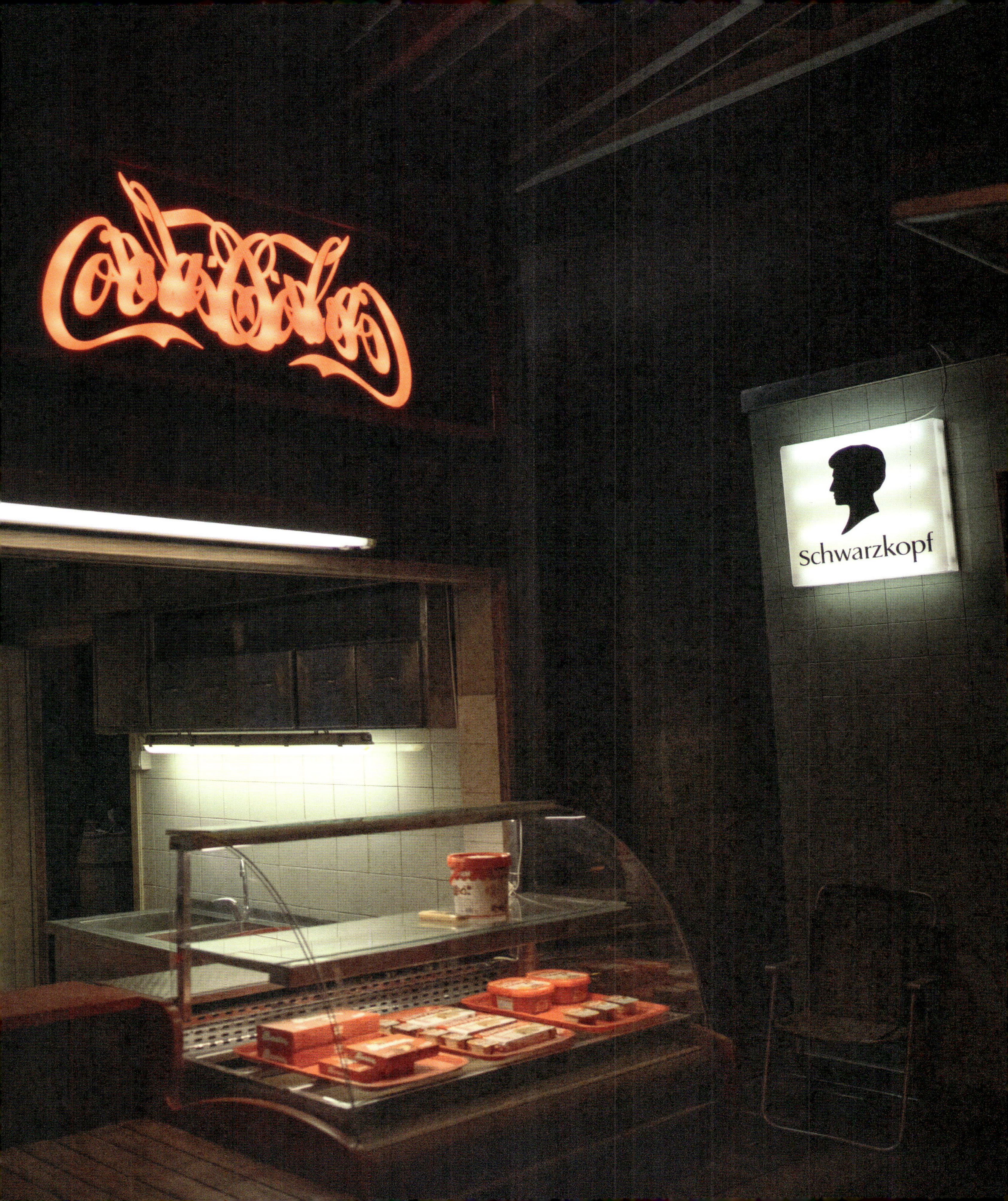
Schwarzkopf

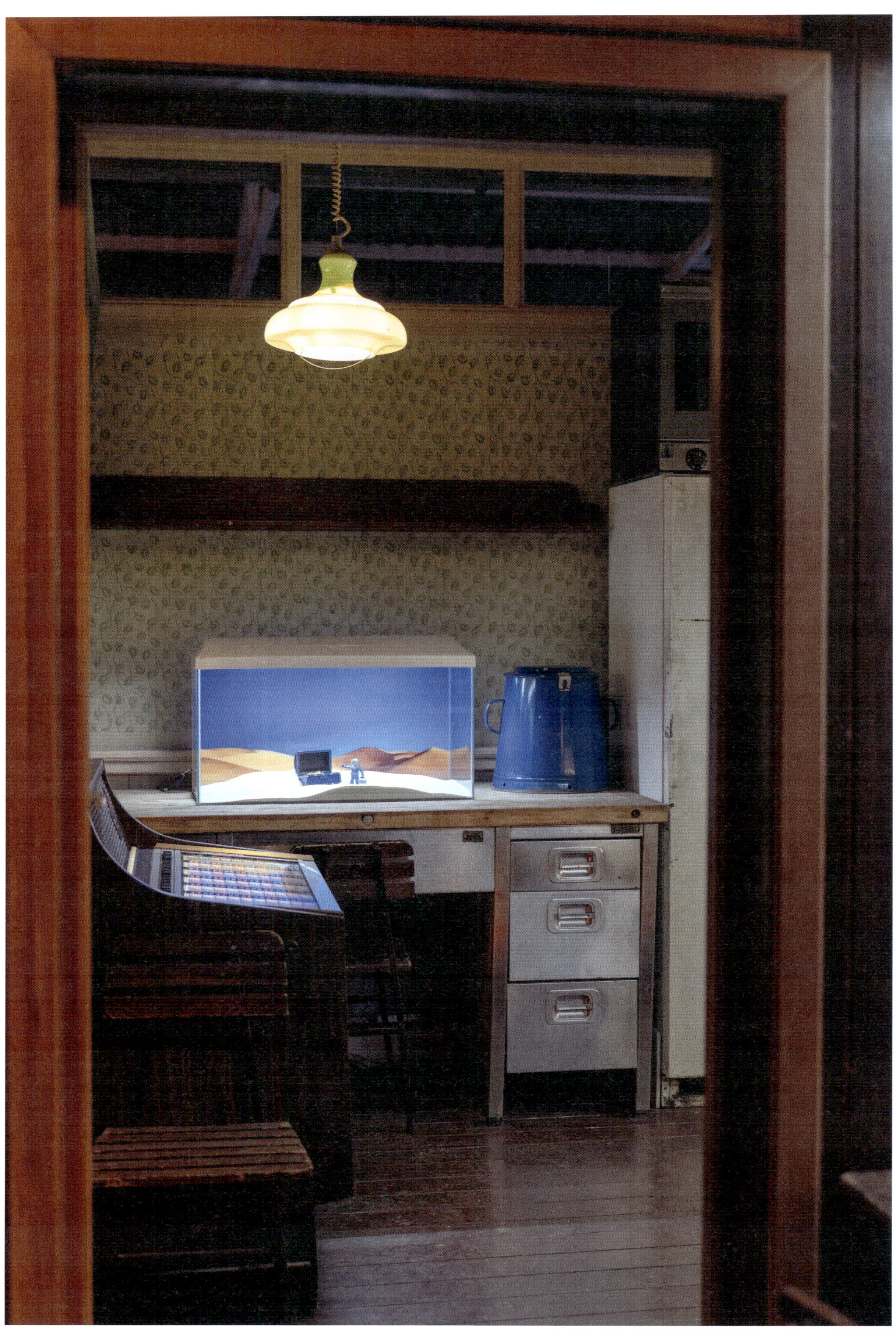

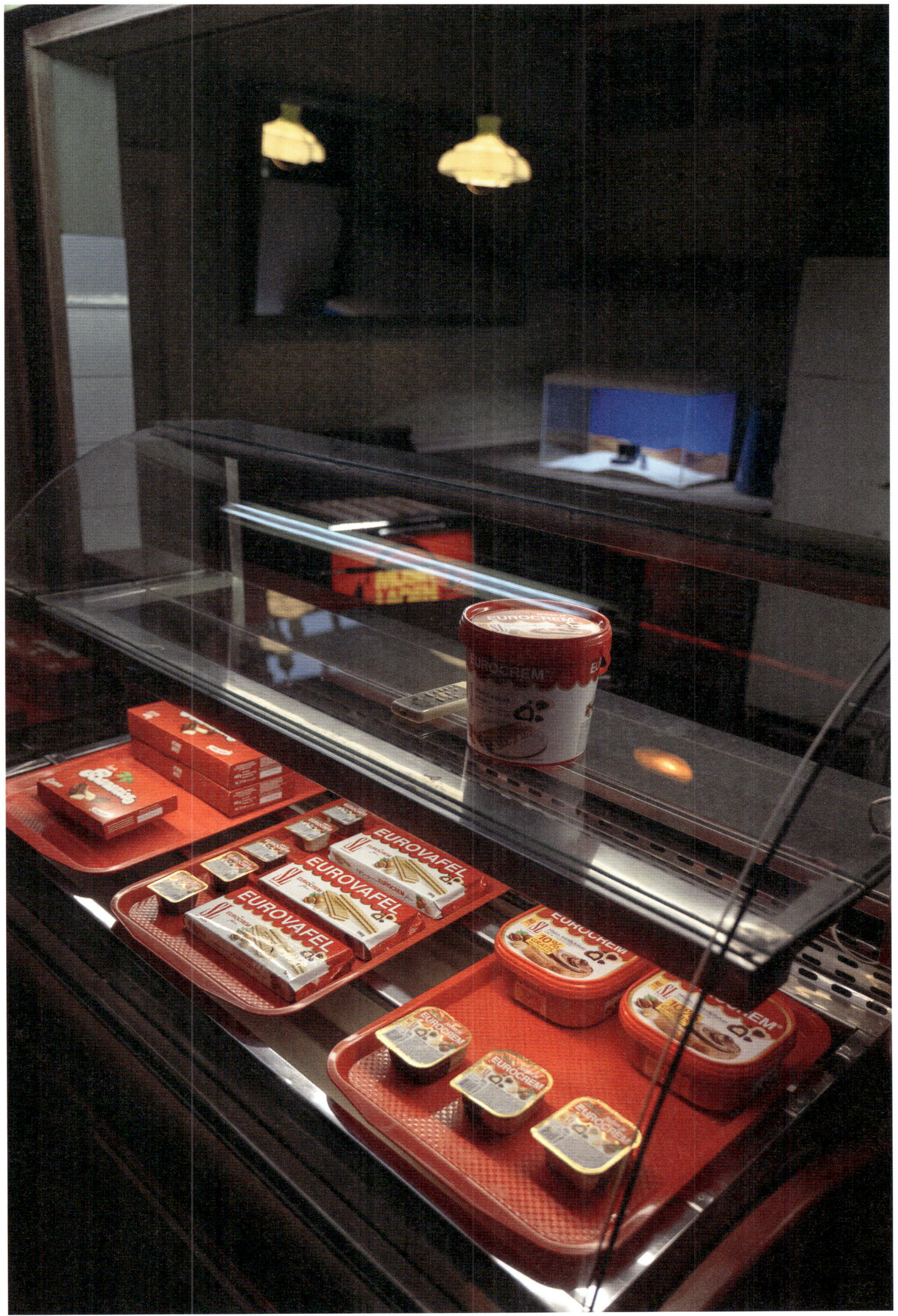

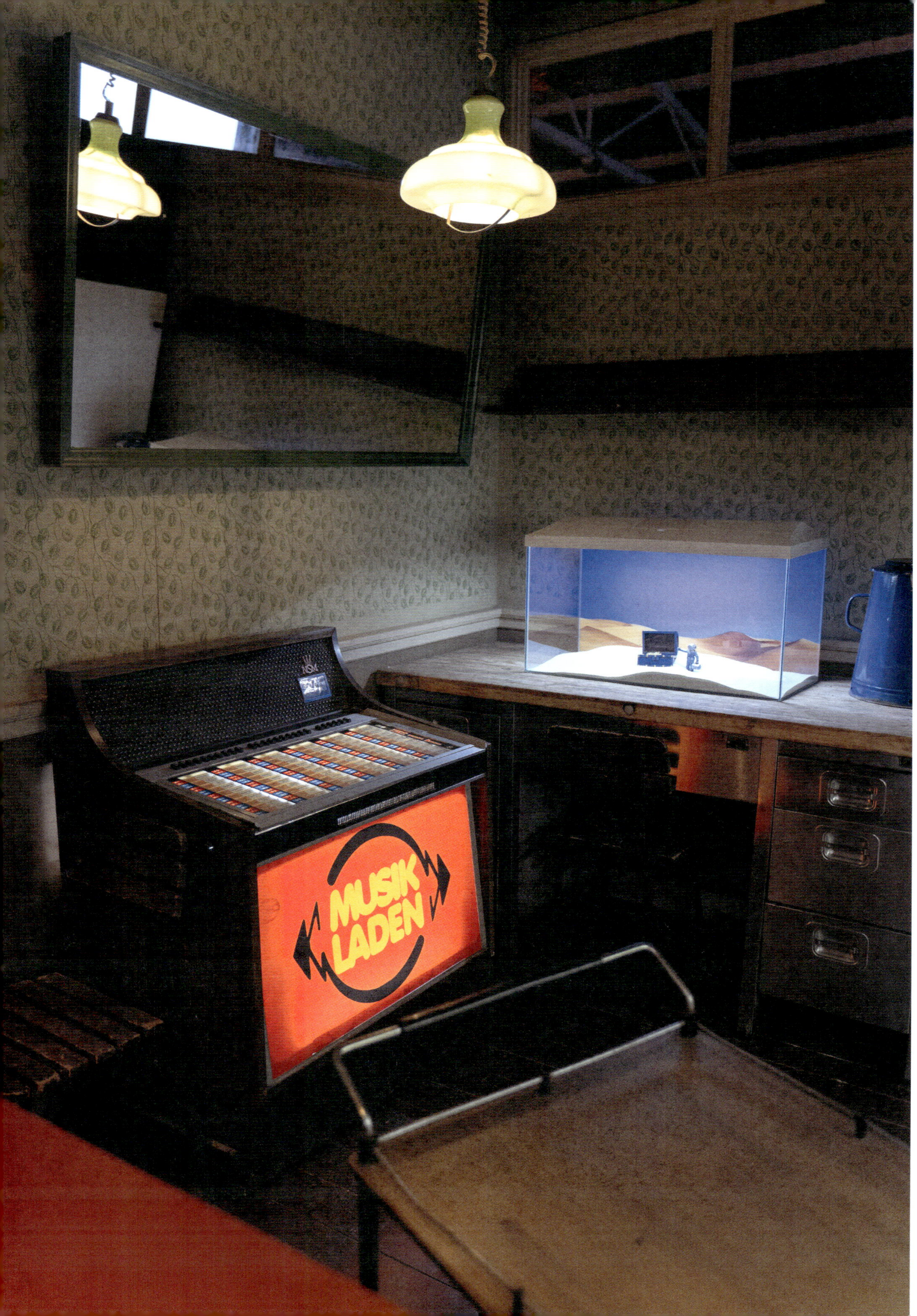

MUSIK
LADEN

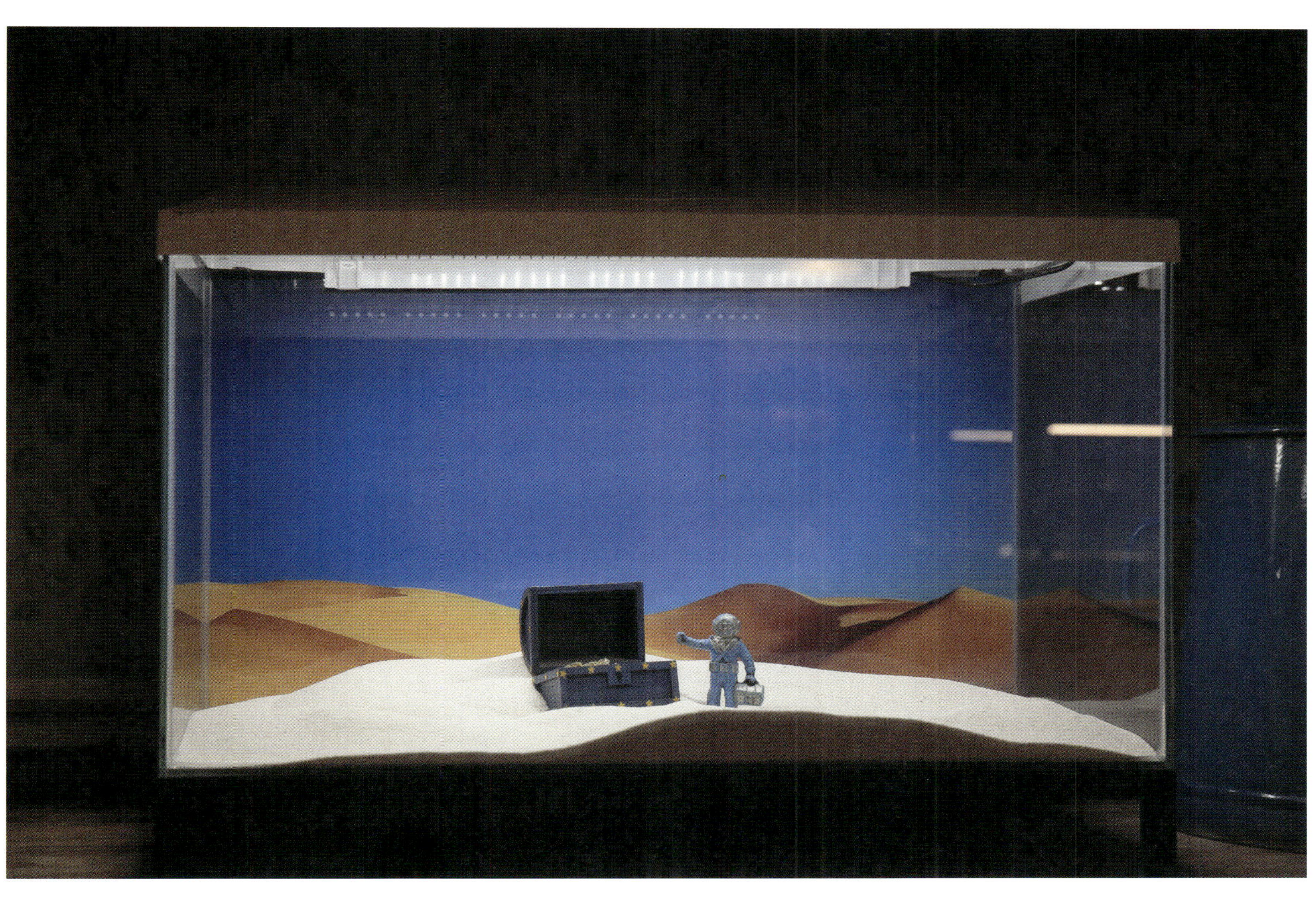

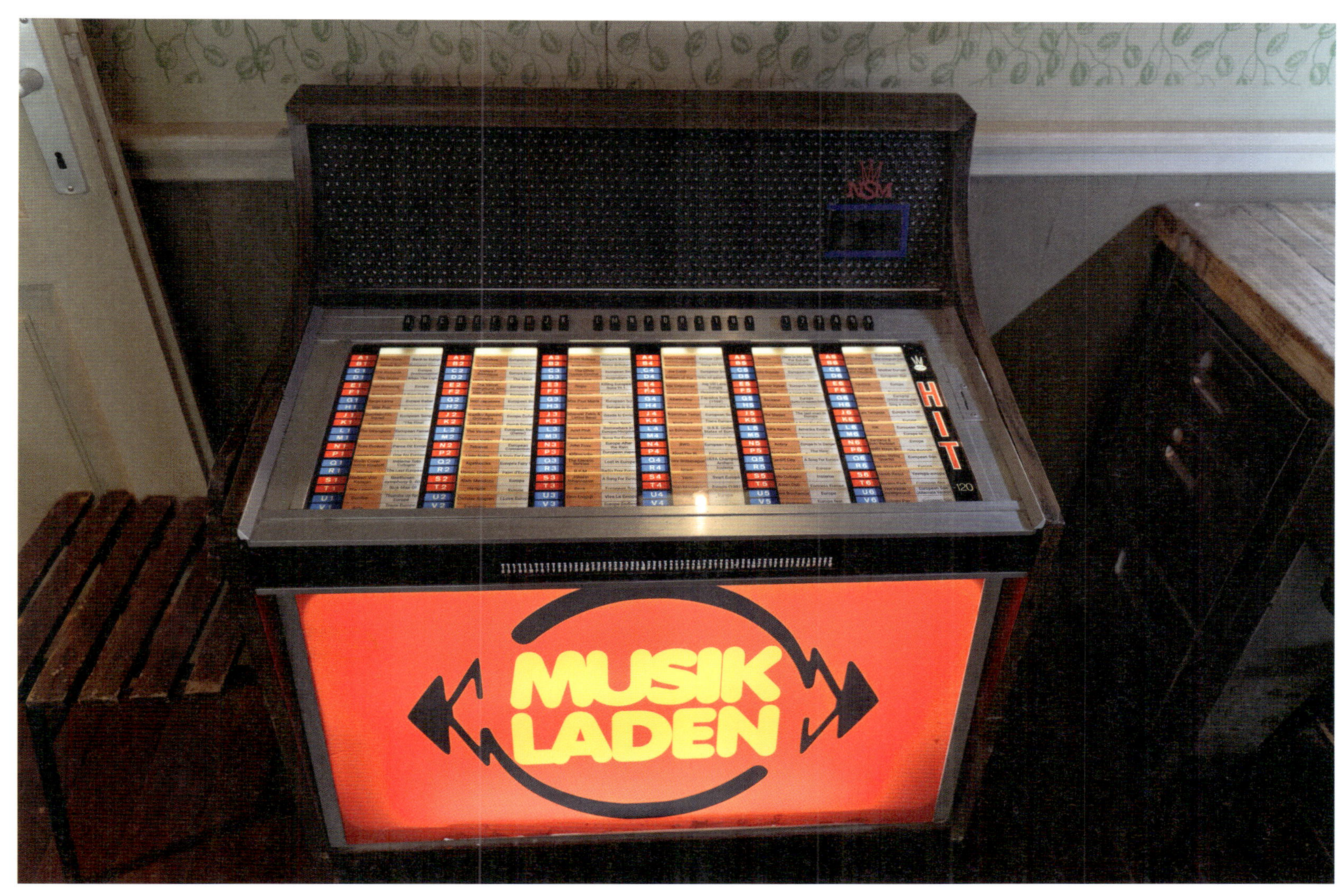

NSM
HIT
120
MUSIK
LADEN

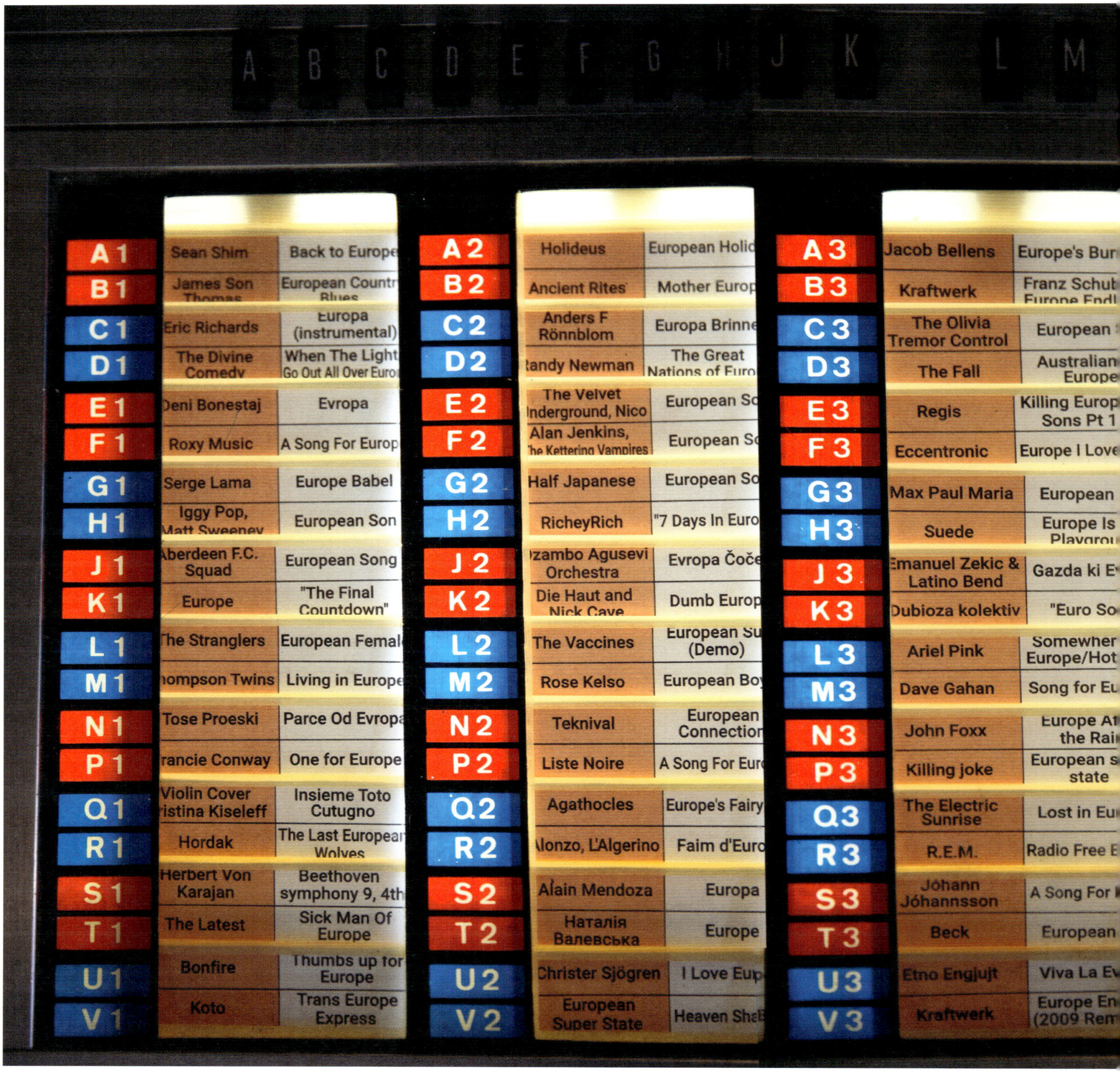

A B C D E F G H J K L M

Code	Artist	Title
A 1	Sean Shim	Back to Europe
B 1	James Son Thomas	European Country Blues
C 1	Eric Richards	Europa (instrumental)
D 1	The Divine Comedy	When The Light Go Out All Over Europe
E 1	Deni Bonestaj	Evropa
F 1	Roxy Music	A Song For Europe
G 1	Serge Lama	Europe Babel
H 1	Iggy Pop, Matt Sweeney	European Son
J 1	Aberdeen F.C. Squad	European Song
K 1	Europe	"The Final Countdown"
L 1	The Stranglers	European Female
M 1	Thompson Twins	Living in Europe
N 1	Tose Proeski	Parce Od Evropa
P 1	Francie Conway	One for Europe
Q 1	Violin Cover Cristina Kiseleff	Insieme Toto Cutugno
R 1	Hordak	The Last European Wolves
S 1	Herbert Von Karajan	Beethoven symphony 9, 4th
T 1	The Latest	Sick Man Of Europe
U 1	Bonfire	Thumbs up for Europe
V 1	Koto	Trans Europe Express

Code	Artist	Title
A 2	Holideus	European Holiday
B 2	Ancient Rites	Mother Europe
C 2	Anders F Rönnblom	Europa Brinner
D 2	Randy Newman	The Great Nations of Europe
E 2	The Velvet Underground, Nico	European Son
F 2	Alan Jenkins, The Kettering Vampires	European So…
G 2	Half Japanese	European So…
H 2	RicheyRich	"7 Days In Euro…
J 2	Dzambo Agusevi Orchestra	Evropa Čoče
K 2	Die Haut and Nick Cave	Dumb Europe
L 2	The Vaccines	European Su… (Demo)
M 2	Rose Kelso	European Boy
N 2	Teknival	European Connection
P 2	Liste Noire	A Song For Euro…
Q 2	Agathocles	Europe's Fairy…
R 2	Alonzo, L'Algerino	Faim d'Euro…
S 2	Alain Mendoza	Europa
T 2	Наталія Валевська	Europe
U 2	Christer Sjögren	I Love Eur…
V 2	European Super State	Heaven Sha…

Code	Artist	Title
A 3	Jacob Bellens	Europe's Bur…
B 3	Kraftwerk	Franz Schub… Europe Endl…
C 3	The Olivia Tremor Control	European…
D 3	The Fall	Australians in Europe
E 3	Regis	Killing Europe Sons Pt 1
F 3	Eccentronic	Europe I Love…
G 3	Max Paul Maria	European…
H 3	Suede	Europe Is Our Playground
J 3	Emanuel Zekic & Latino Bend	Gazda ki Ev…
K 3	Dubioza kolektiv	"Euro So…
L 3	Ariel Pink	Somewhere in Europe/Hot…
M 3	Dave Gahan	Song for Eu…
N 3	John Foxx	Europe After the Rain
P 3	Killing joke	European s… state
Q 3	The Electric Sunrise	Lost in Eu…
R 3	R.E.M.	Radio Free E…
S 3	Jóhann Jóhannsson	A Song For…
T 3	Beck	European…
U 3	Etno Engjujt	Viva La Ev…
V 3	Kraftwerk	Europe En… (2009 Rem…)

Code	Artist	Title
A 4	krem Mamutovic	Evropa (2015
B 4	bigniew Preisner	Song for the Unification of Eur
C 4	Joe Cahill	European So
D 4	Anthem of The European Union	"Ode ad gaudiu [Latin]
E 4	Arja Saijonmaa	Jag Vill Leva Europa
F 4	ropa Earth's Cry	Heaven's Smil 1 hour by Gato Barb
G 4	Atheist Rap	Zapadna Evrop (1998)
H 4	do Lindenberg	Americans In Europe
J 4	Mujercitas Terror	European So
K 4	Kraftwerk	Trans Europa Express (origina
L 4	an Böhmermann	U.S.E. United States of Euro
M 4	Matt Berninger	European So
N 4	BWO	European Psyc
P 4	ot Per W	European So
Q 4	ony Brittenague	UEFA Champio Anthem
R 4	Miani	Insieme (Radio Edit)
S 4	Yemi	Svart Europe
T 4	Boki Milosevic	Evropa (1987
U 4	Dr. Saxlove	Europa
V 4	Gruff Rhys	I Love EU

Code	Artist	Title
A 5	Denim	Here Is My Song For Europe
B 5	Kraftwerk	Trans-Europe Express
C 5	Solo Sounds	European Son
D 5	onica Naranjo	Europa
E 5	exander Rybak	"Europe's Skies"
F 5	Jóhann Jóhannsson	A Song For Europa
G 5	Santana	Europa (Earth's Cry Heaven's Smile
H 5	nir Kusturica & No Smoking Orchestra	Evropa
J 5	The Blades	The last man in Europe
K 5	ichaela Melián	A Song For Europe
L 5	PoPa SapKA	Amerika Evropa
M 5	Japan	European Son
N 5	Actiny	Europe Is In Danger
P 5	ilent Scream	The New European Son
Q 5	Cardiff City	A Song For Europe
R 5	eve Saucedo	Europe
S 5	Toto Cutugno	Insieme
T 5	Asian Dub Foundation	Fortress Europe
U 5	ien Bischerour	Europe
V 5	co Hemingway	Europa feat. Bedoes

Code	Artist	Title
A 6	Sonic Youth	European Son (Velvet Underground Cover
B 6	Elle Critch	Europe
C 6	iklos Varga & eslie Mandoki	Mother Europe
D 6	Greg Fenton	European Sun (Original Mix)
E 6	Santana	Europa
F 6	V-Sor,X	Euromantic
G 6	e Divine Comedy	Europop (2020 remaster)
H 6	Mary Carewe	Sing a song for Europe!
J 6	Kate Tempest	Europe Is Lost
K 6	Saga	Europe
L 6	IDK	European Skies
M 6	kshinder Shinda	Europe te UK Wangu
N 6	Santana & Gato Barbieri	Evropa
P 6	vedbi klape Sv. rai i orkestra HRM-a	Oda Radosti
Q 6	Vitamin String Quartet	European Son
R 6	XIII. STOLETÍ	Evropa
S 6	Janob Rasul	Yevropa-avropa
T 6	Maxïmo Park	European Son
U 6	The Velvet Underground	European Son (Alternate Version
V 6	Johnny Pav	European Sun

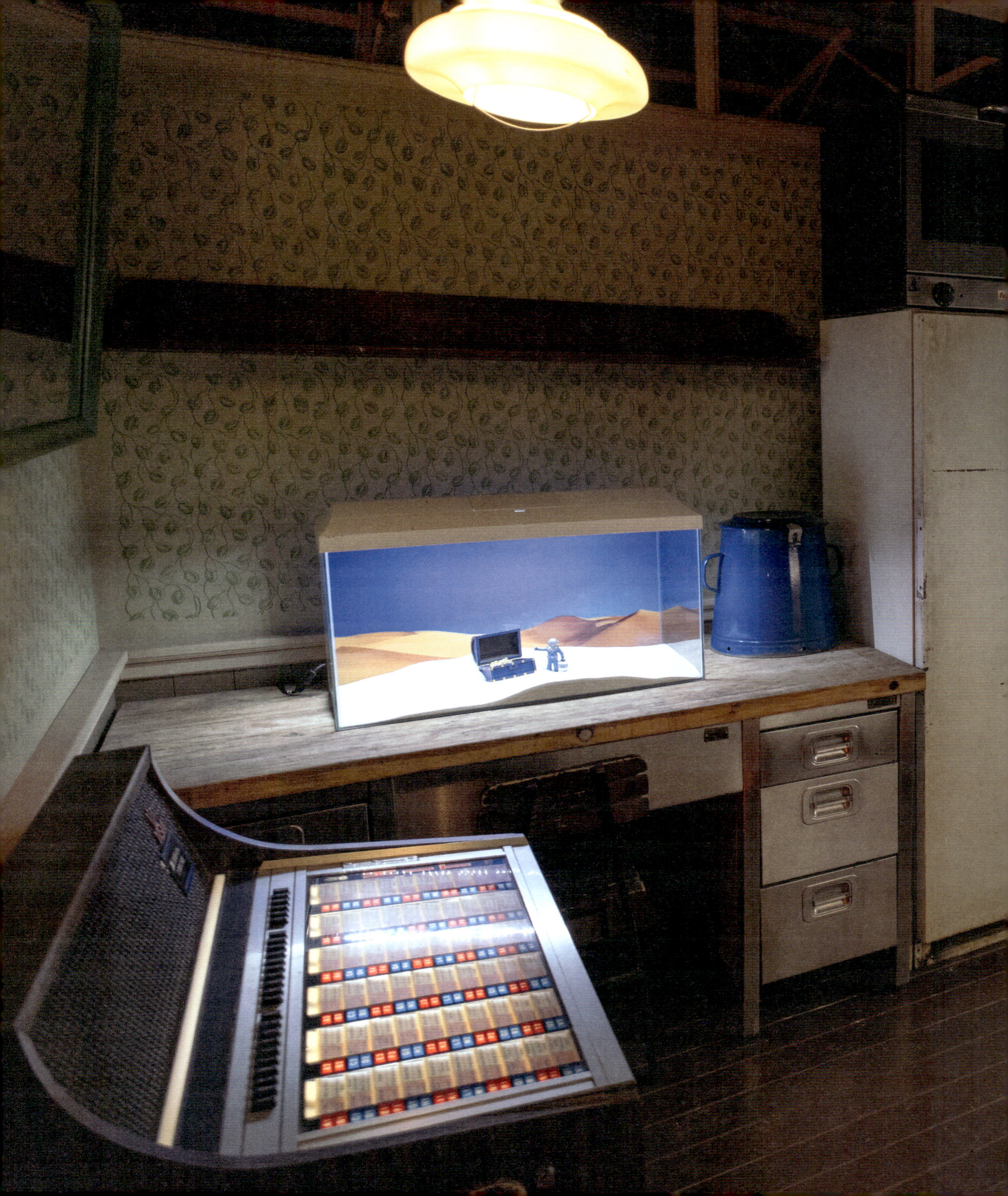

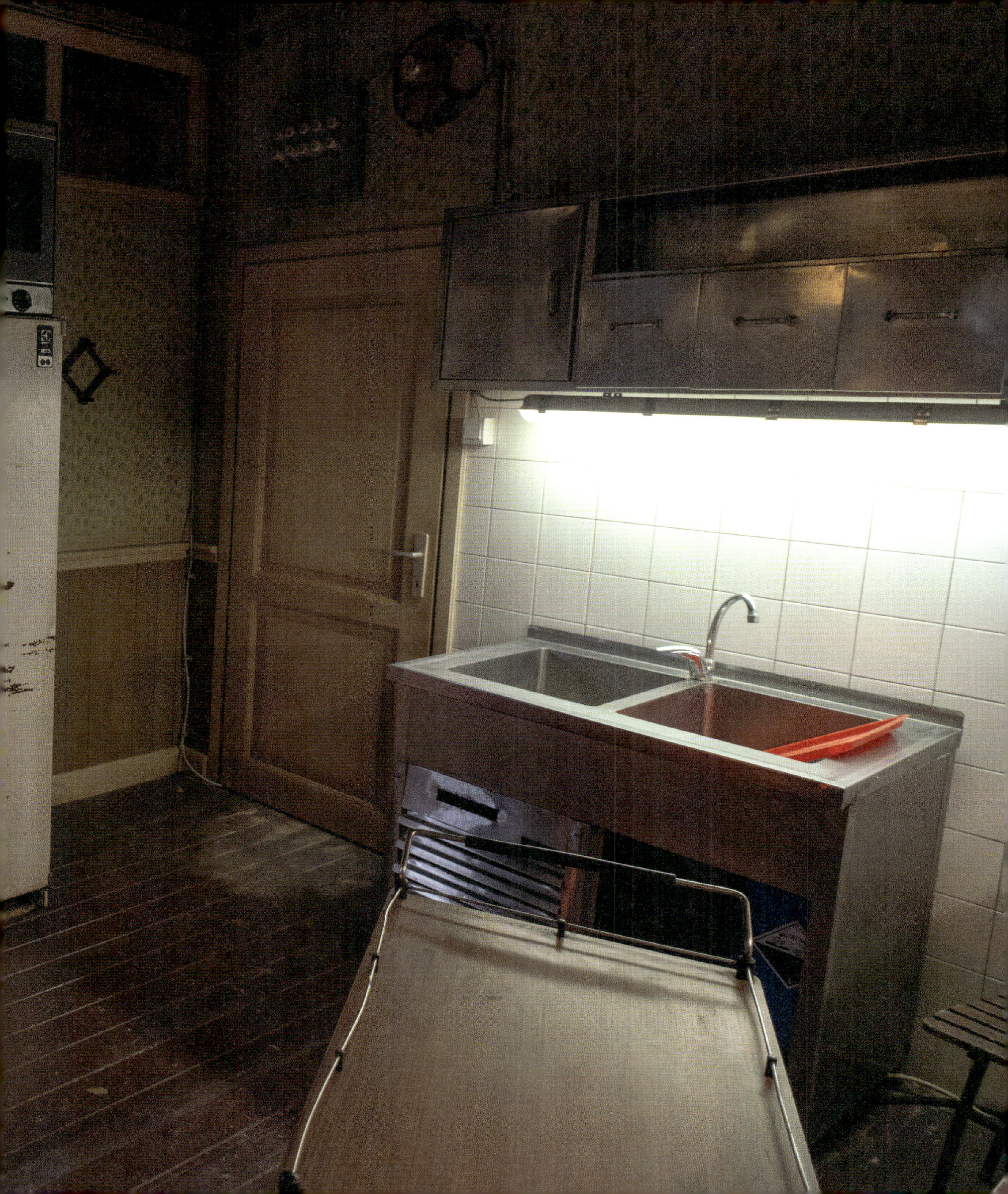

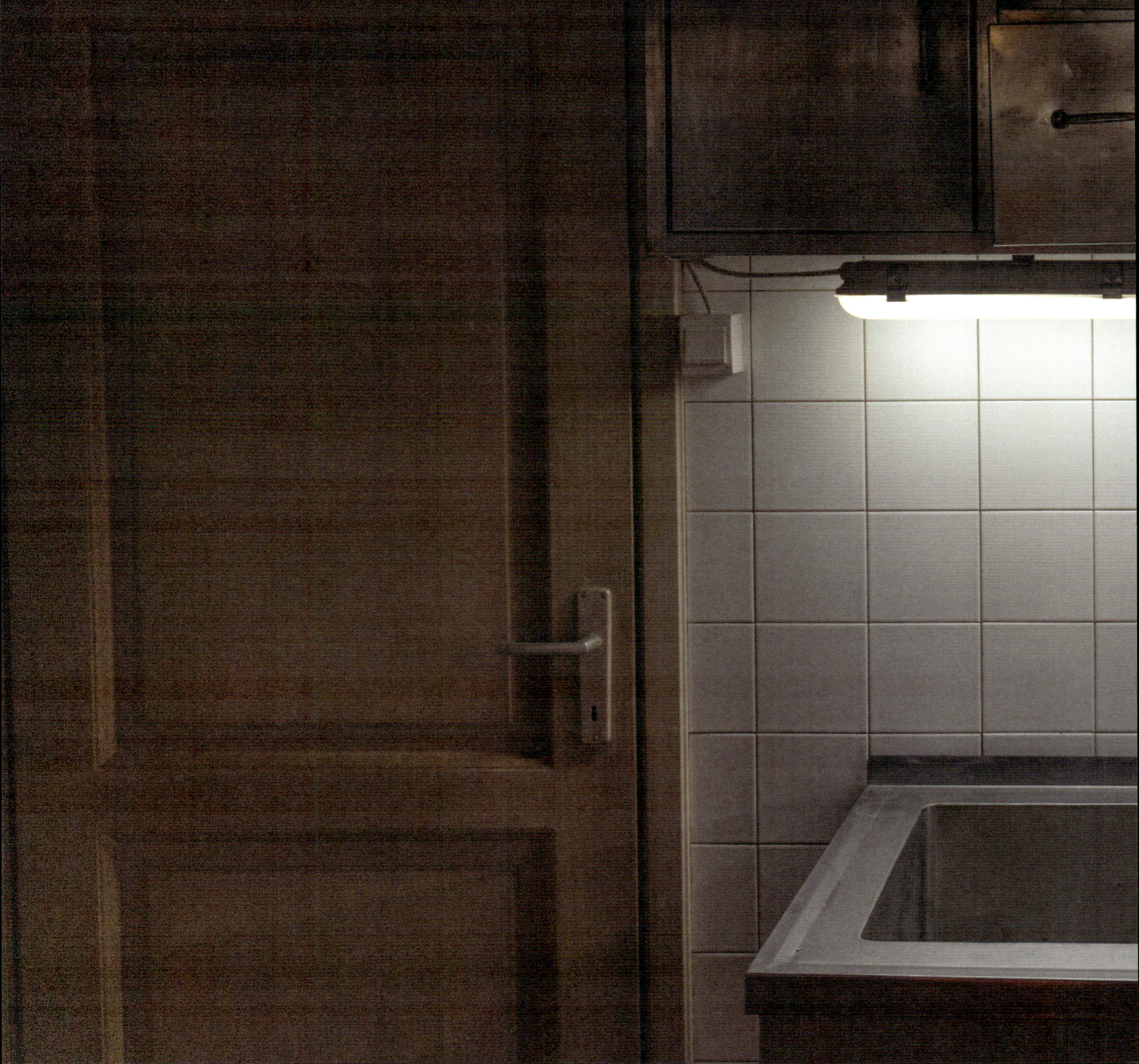

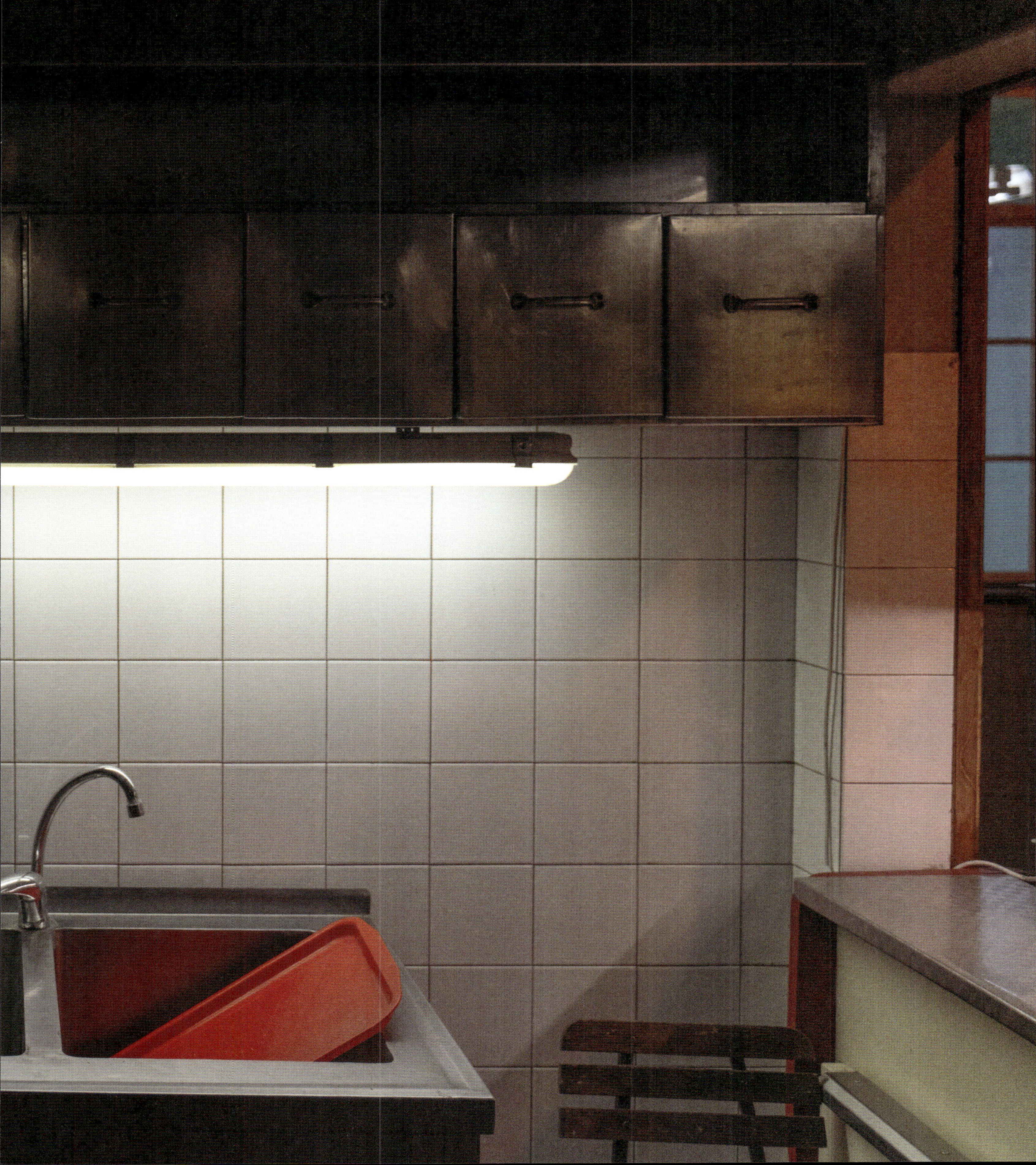

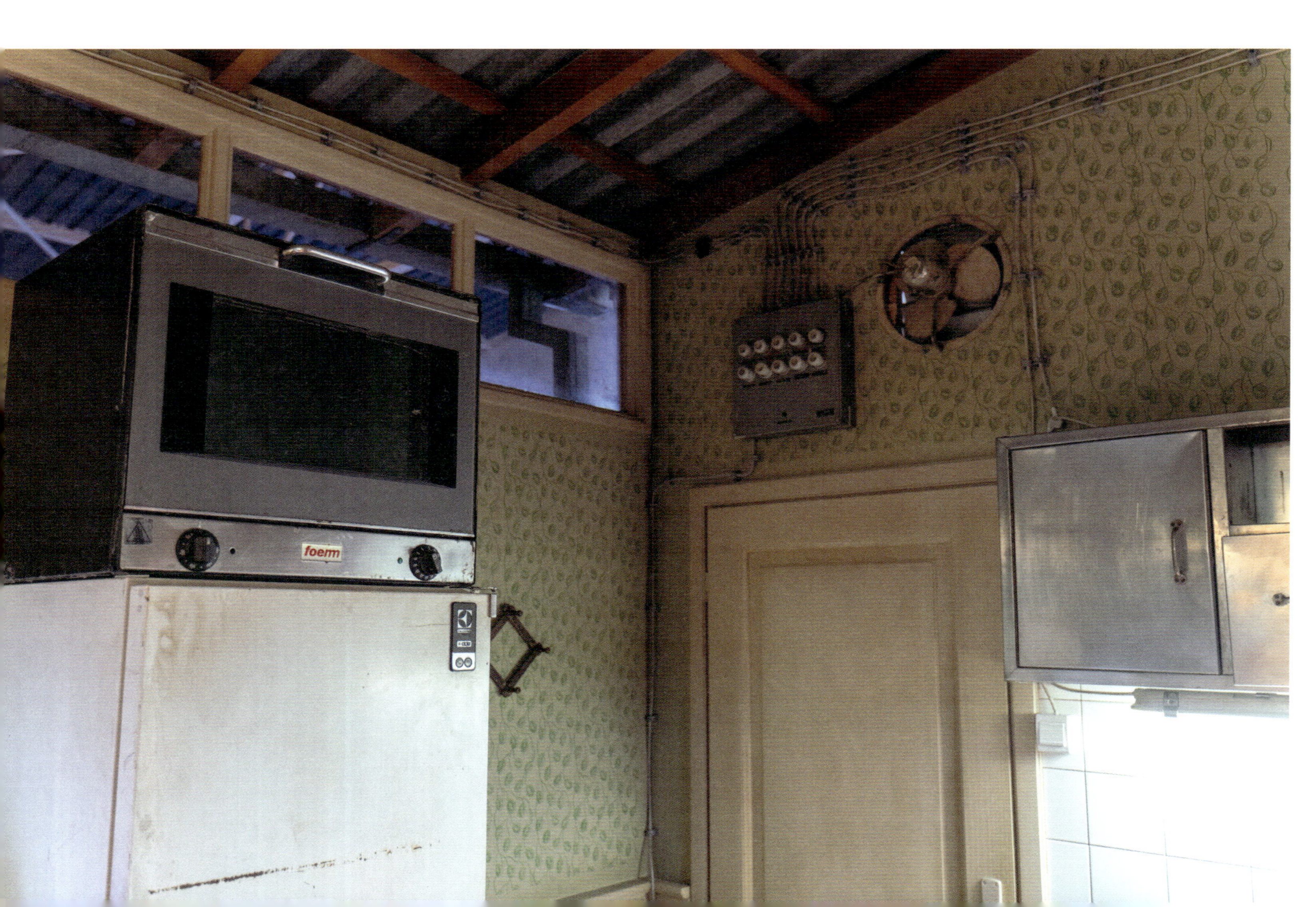

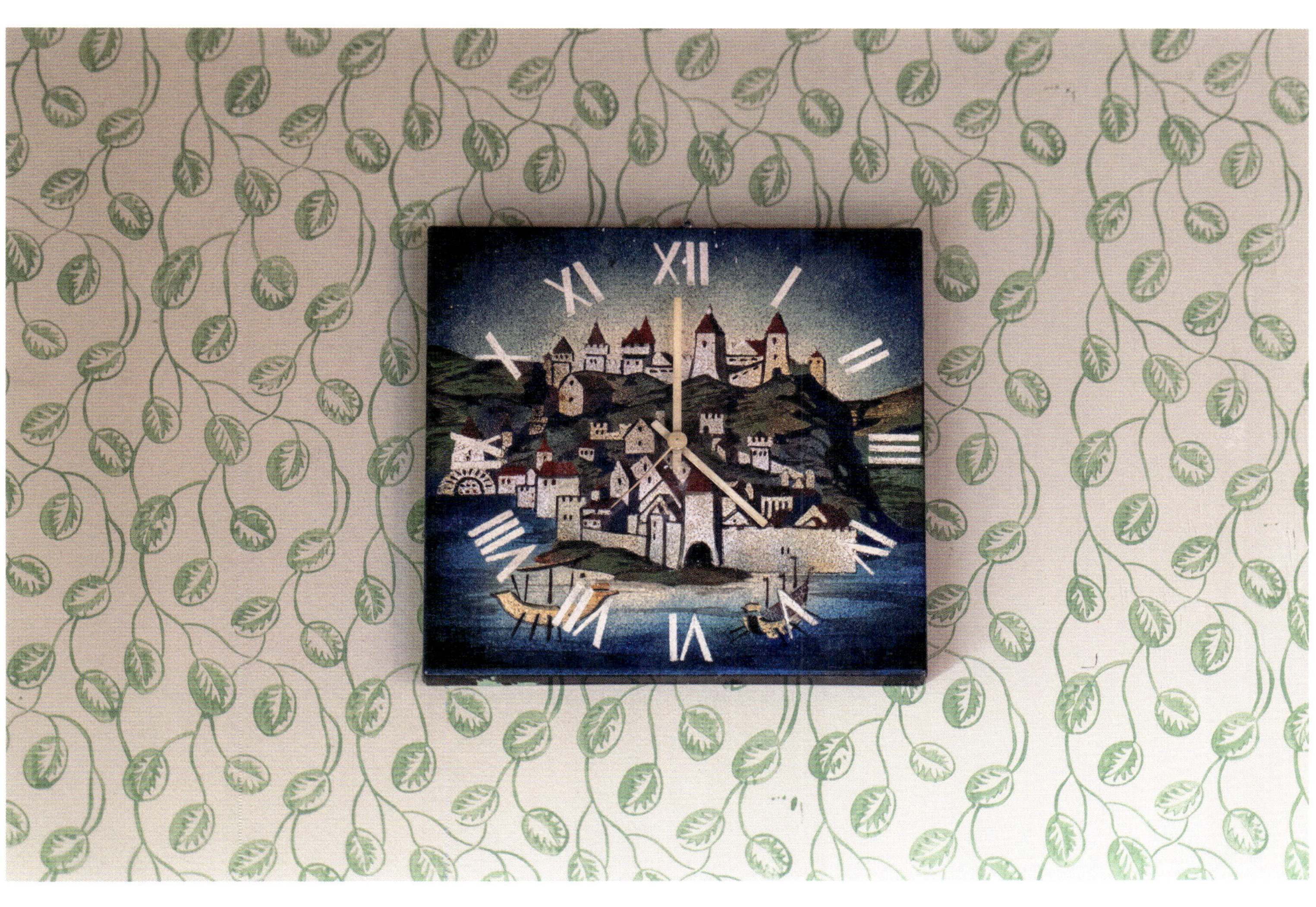

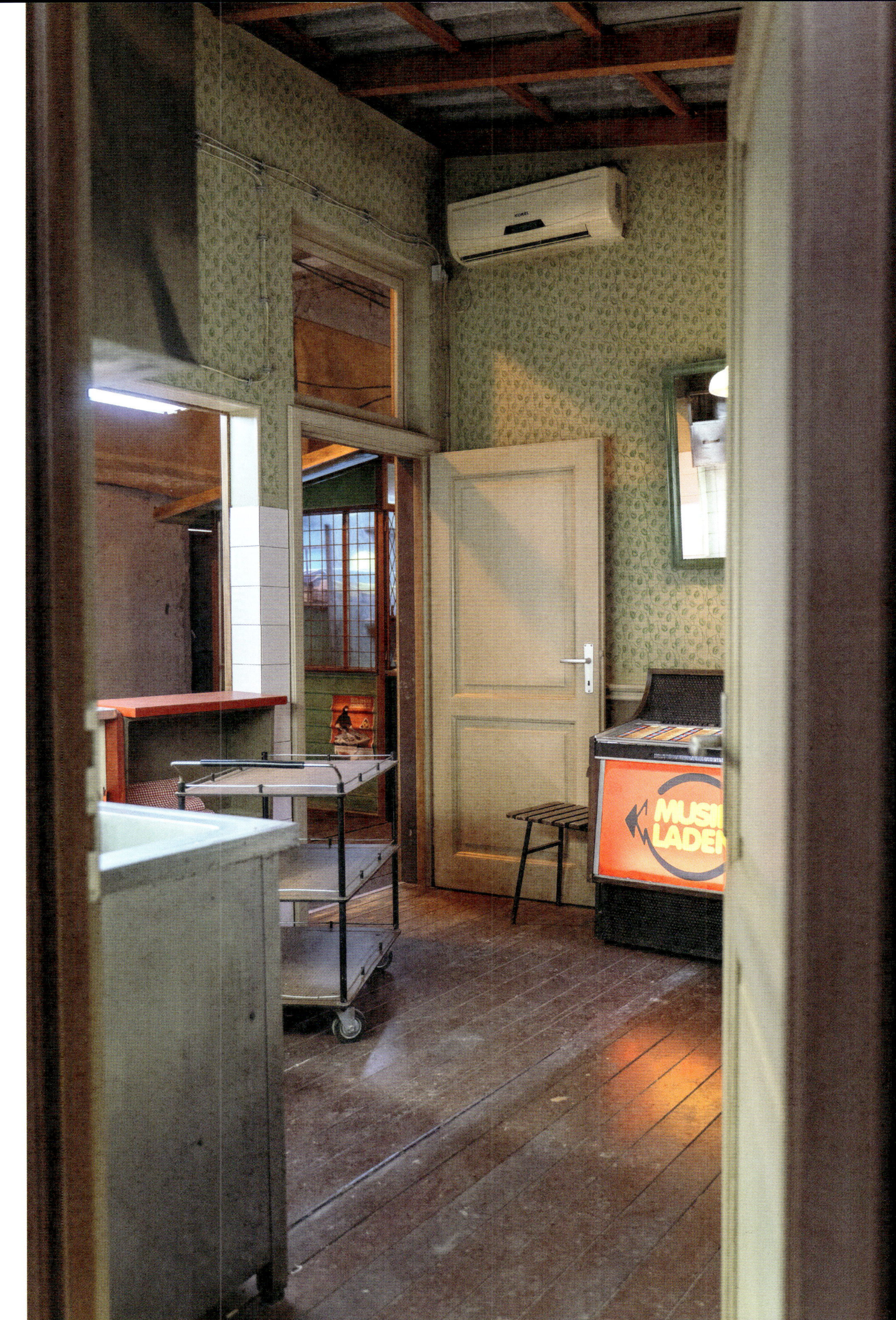
MUSIK
LADEN

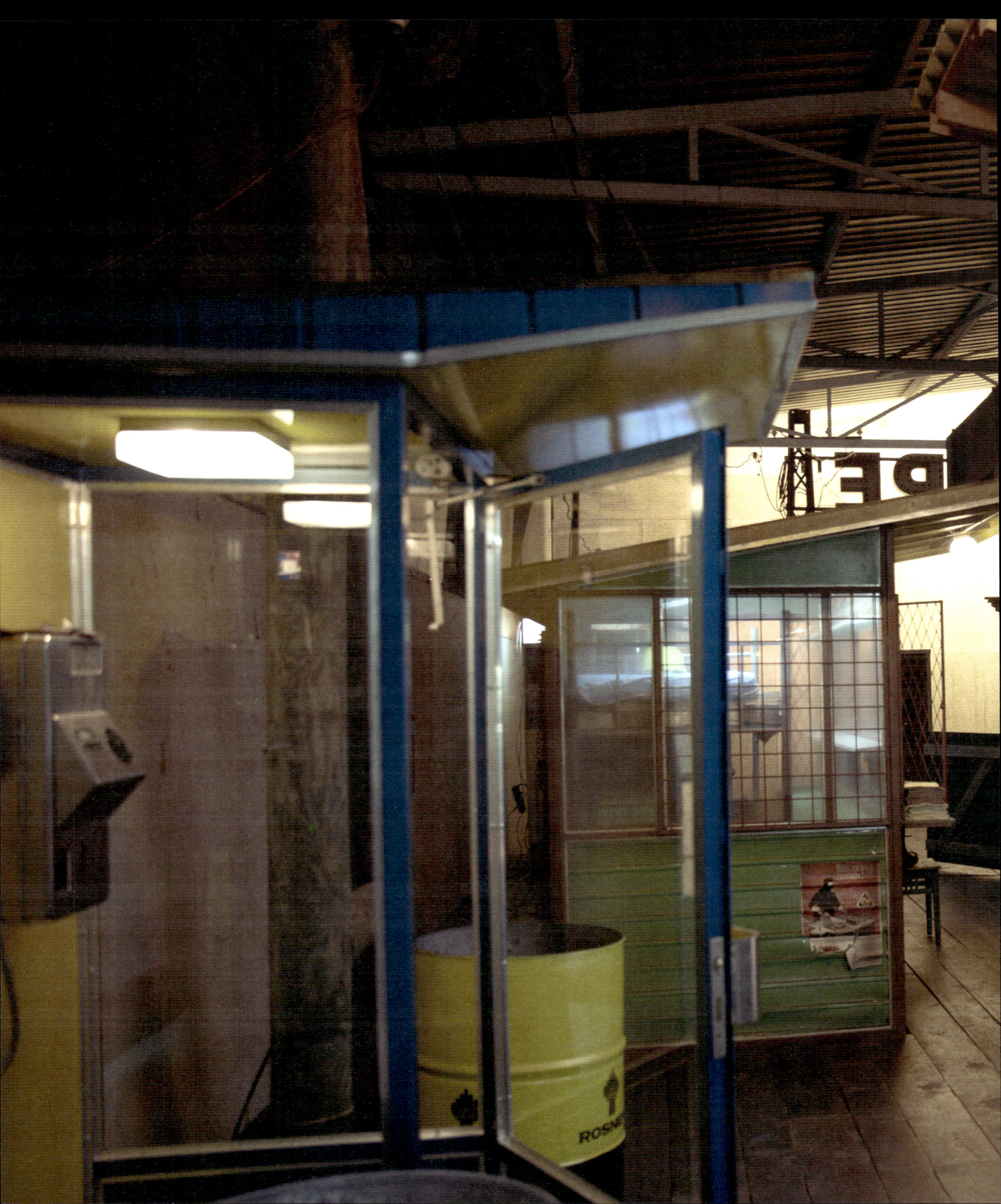
DIE
ROSN

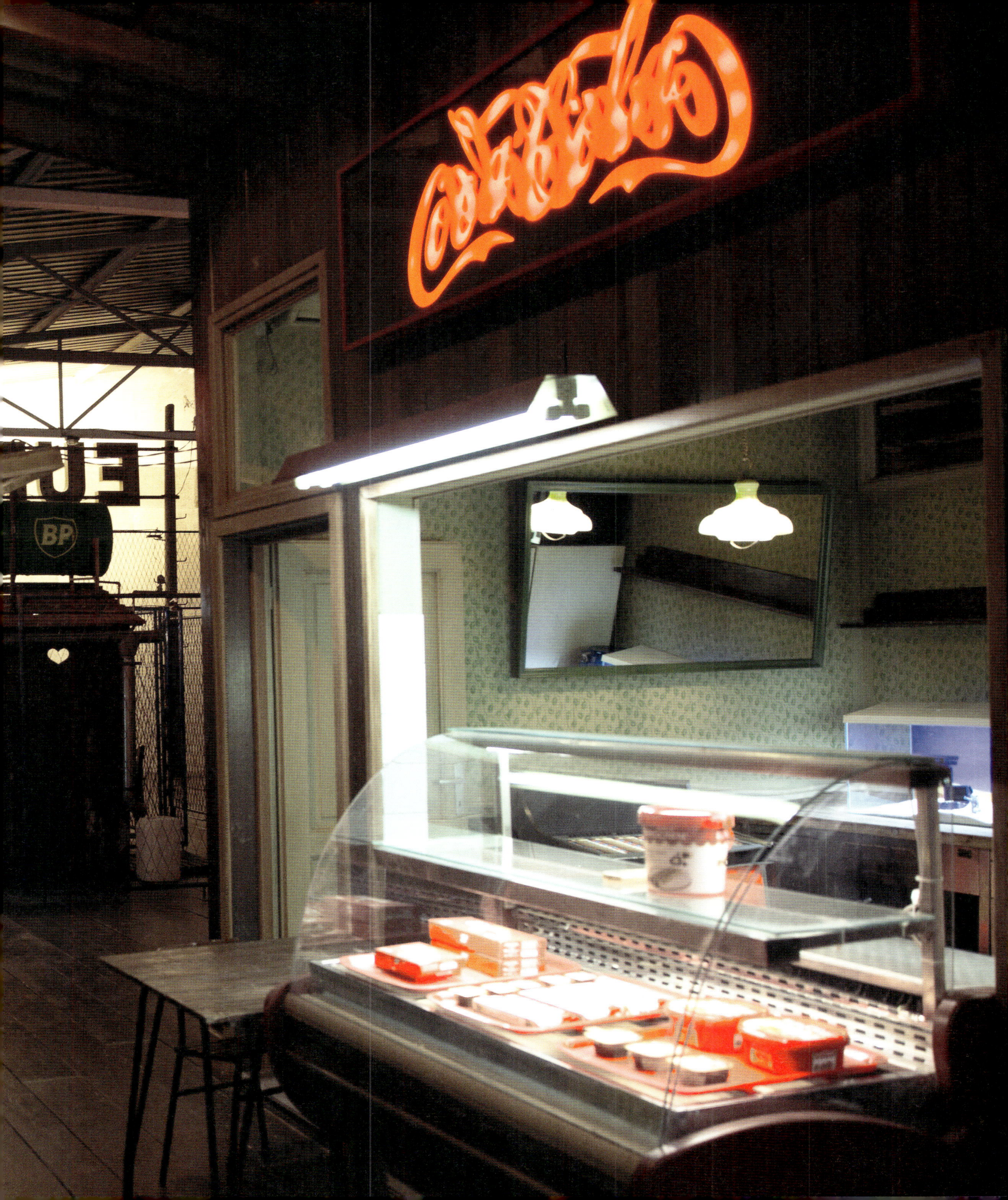
BP

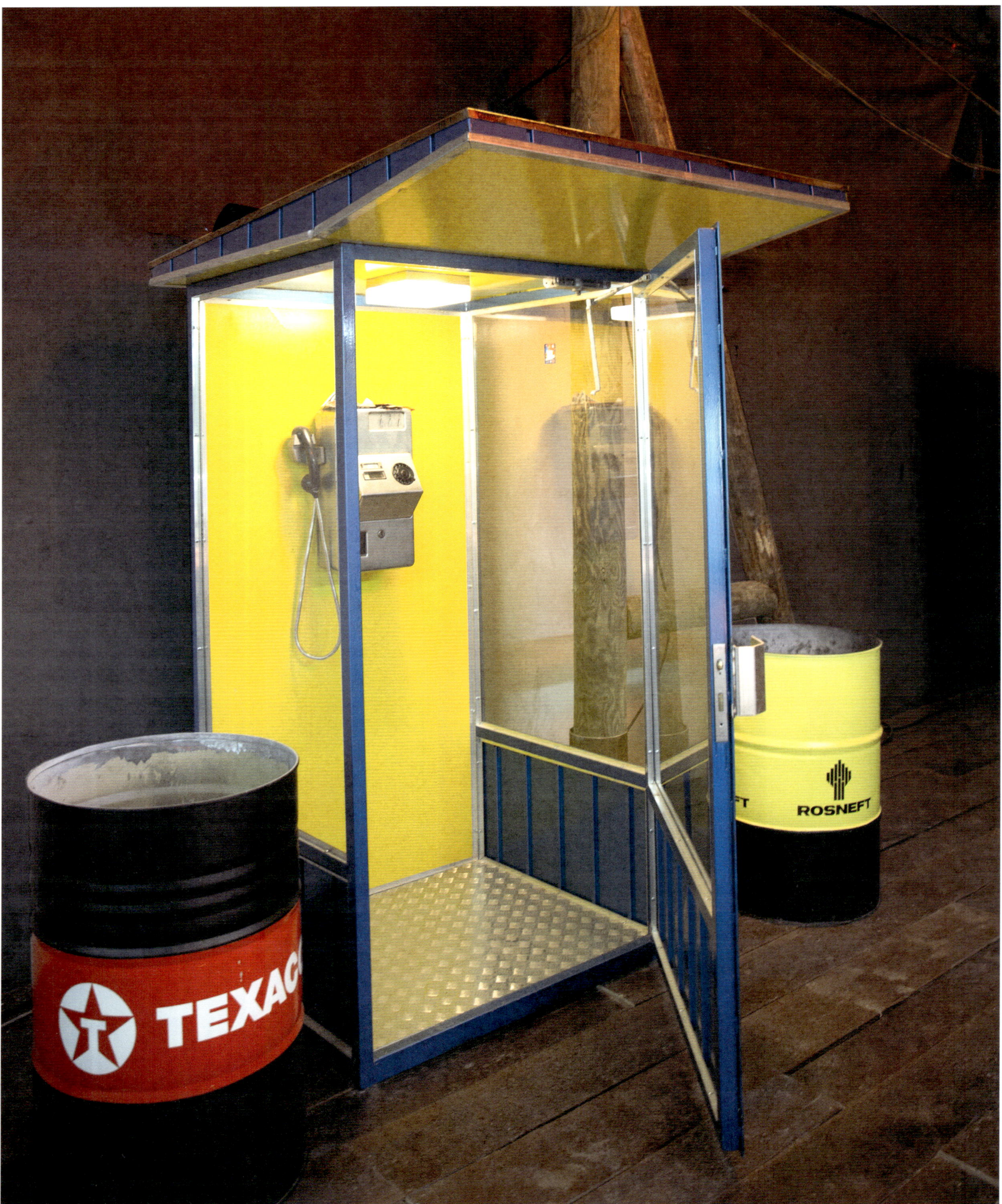

TEXACO
ROSNEFT

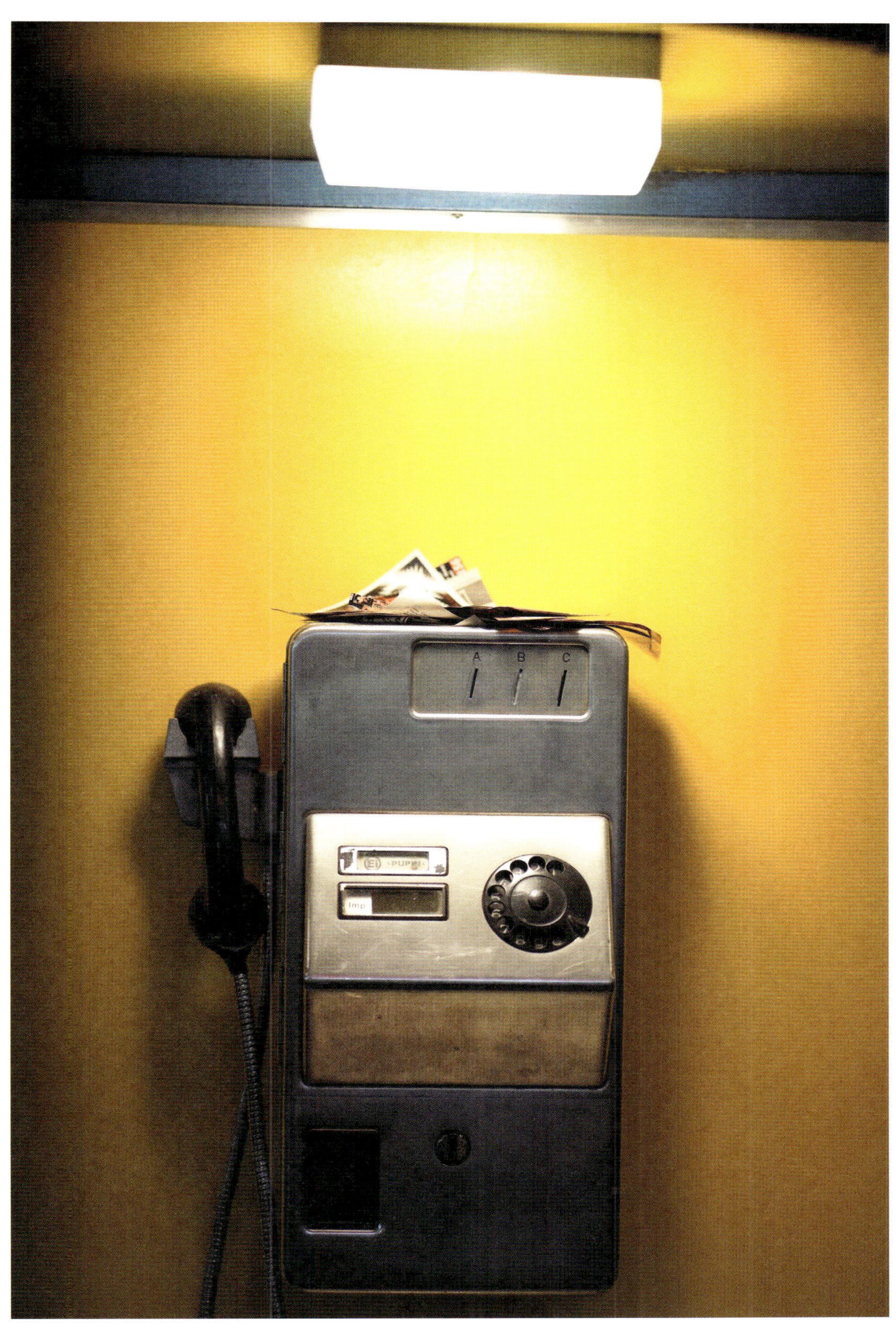

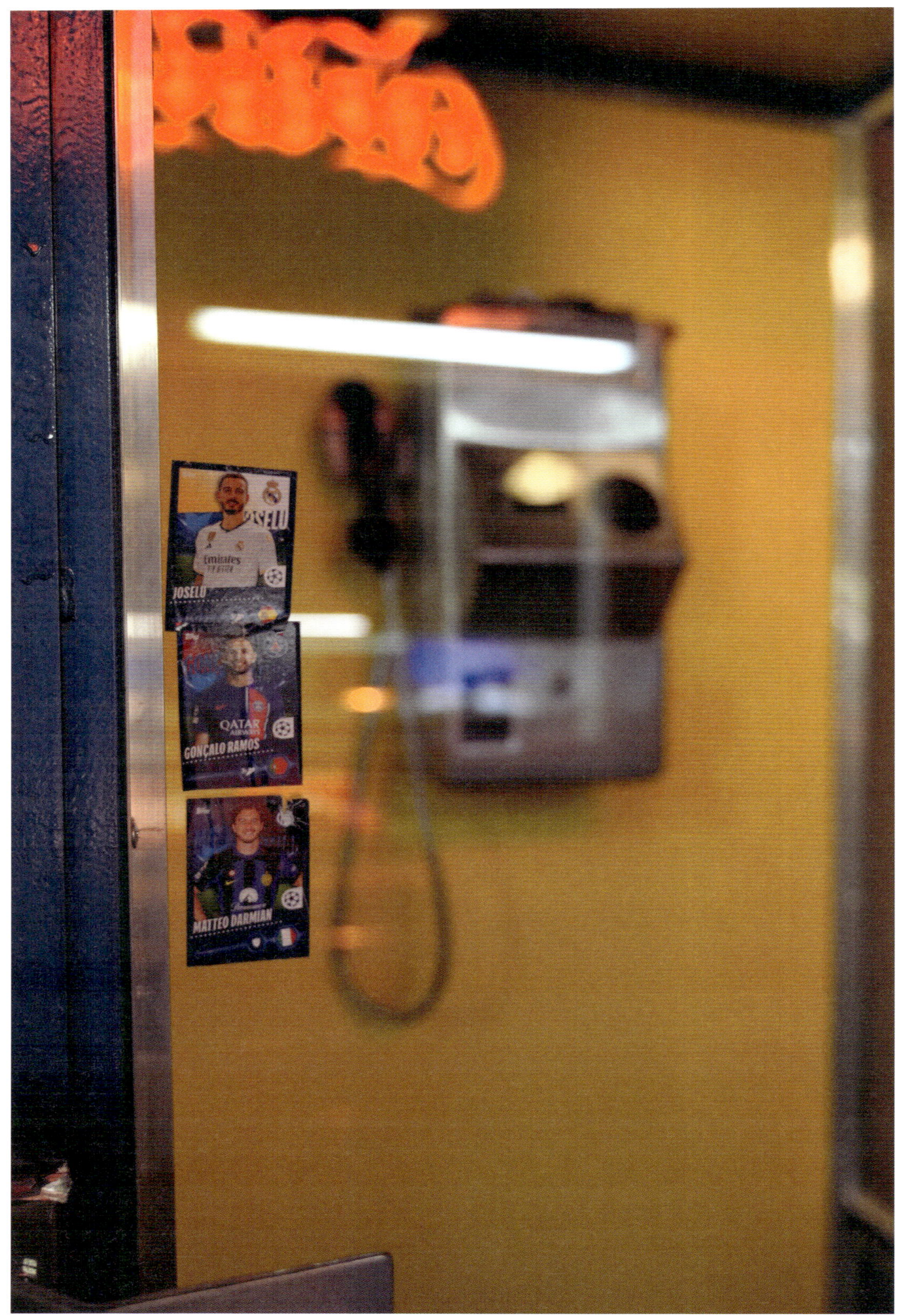
JOSELU
GONÇALO RAMOS
MATTEO DARMIAN

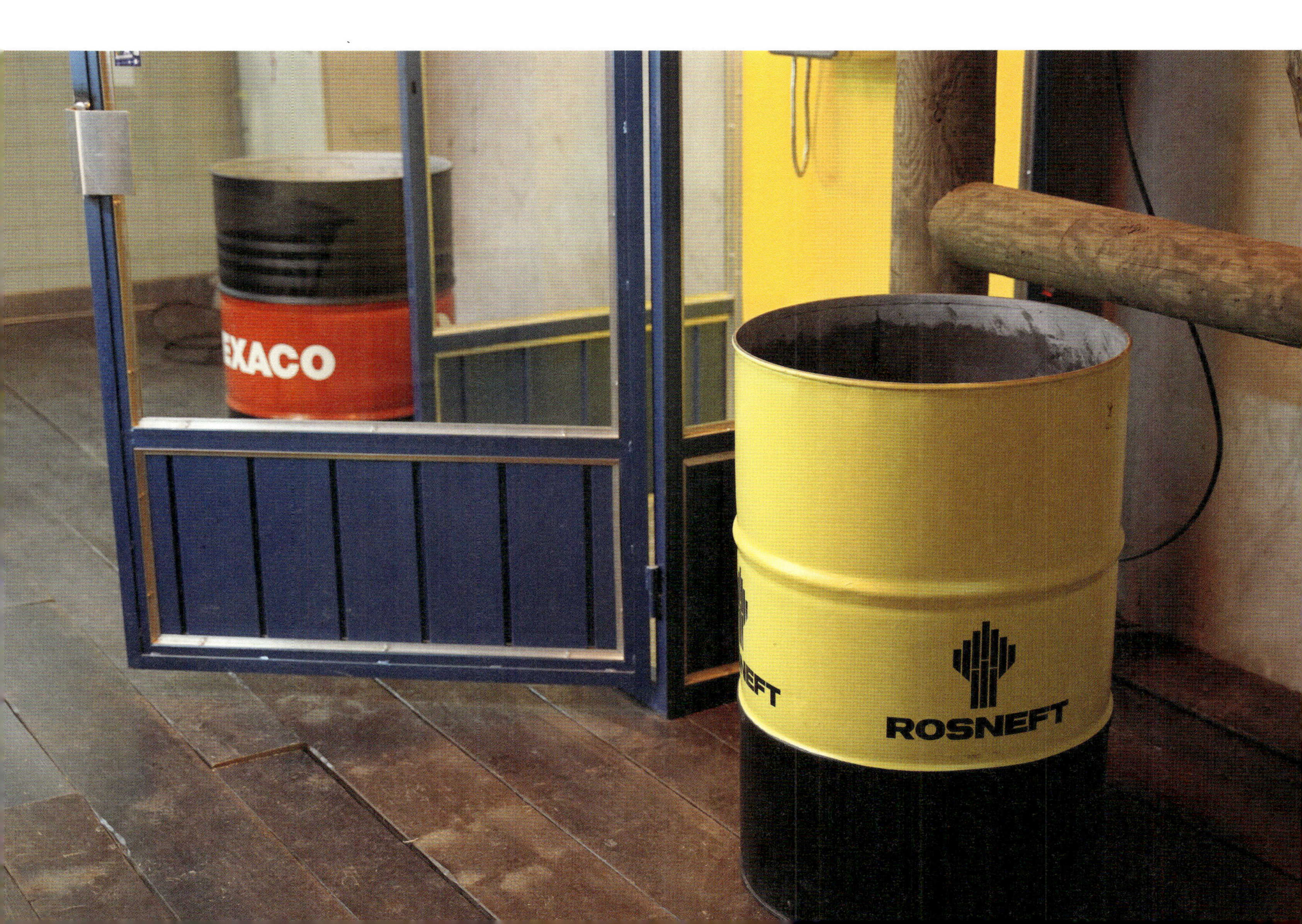
EXACO
ROSNEFT
NEFT

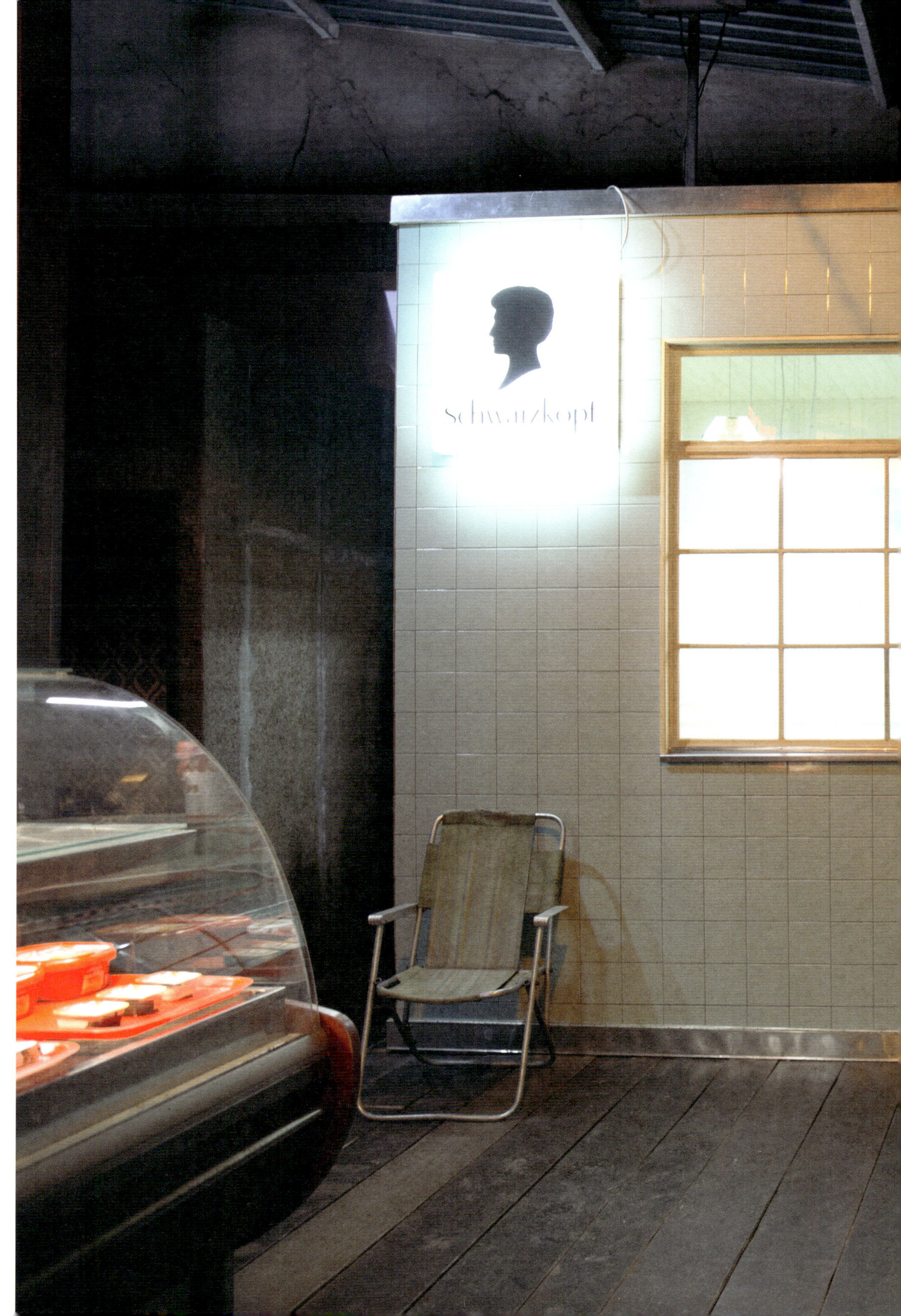
schwarzkopf

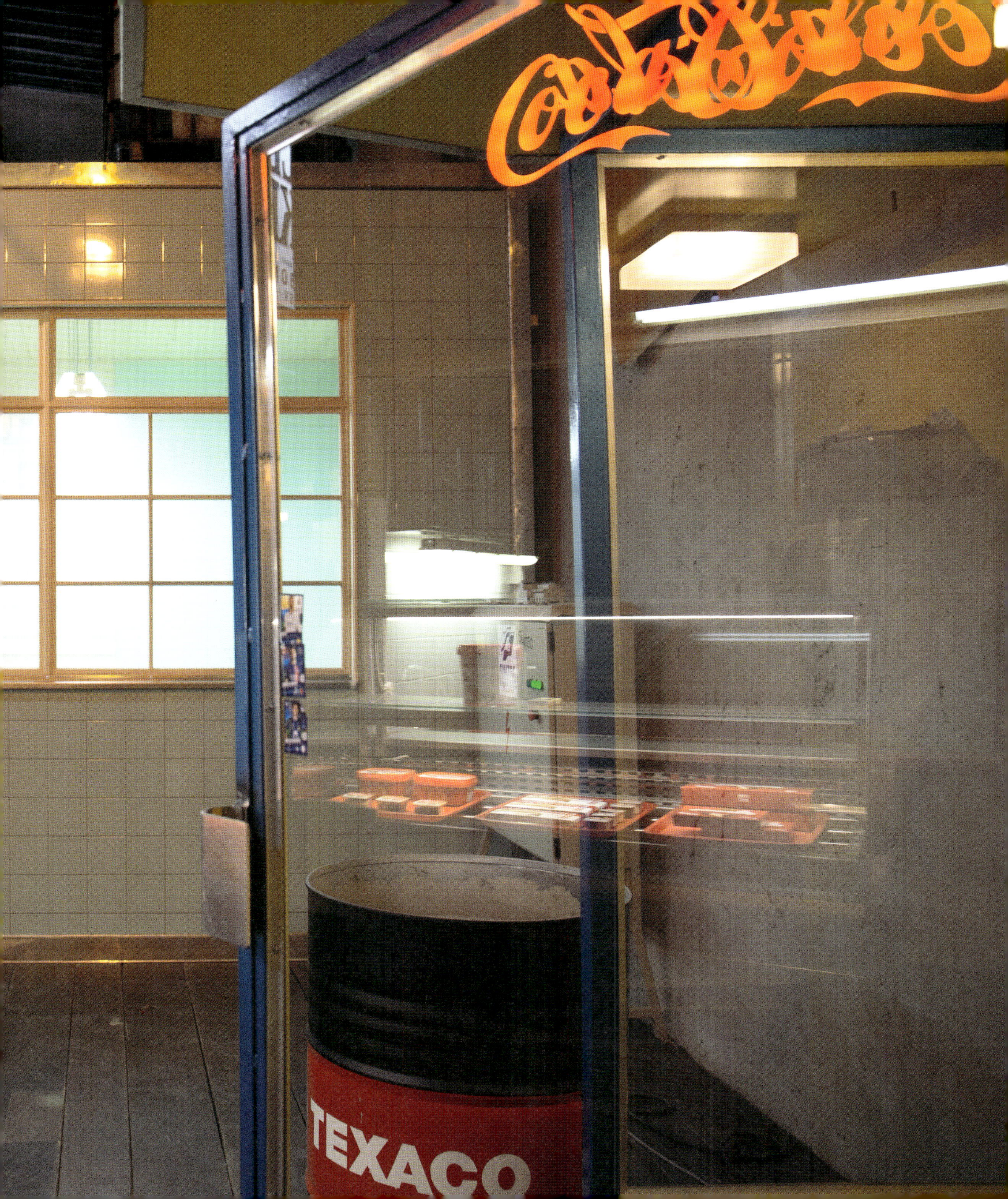

TEXACO

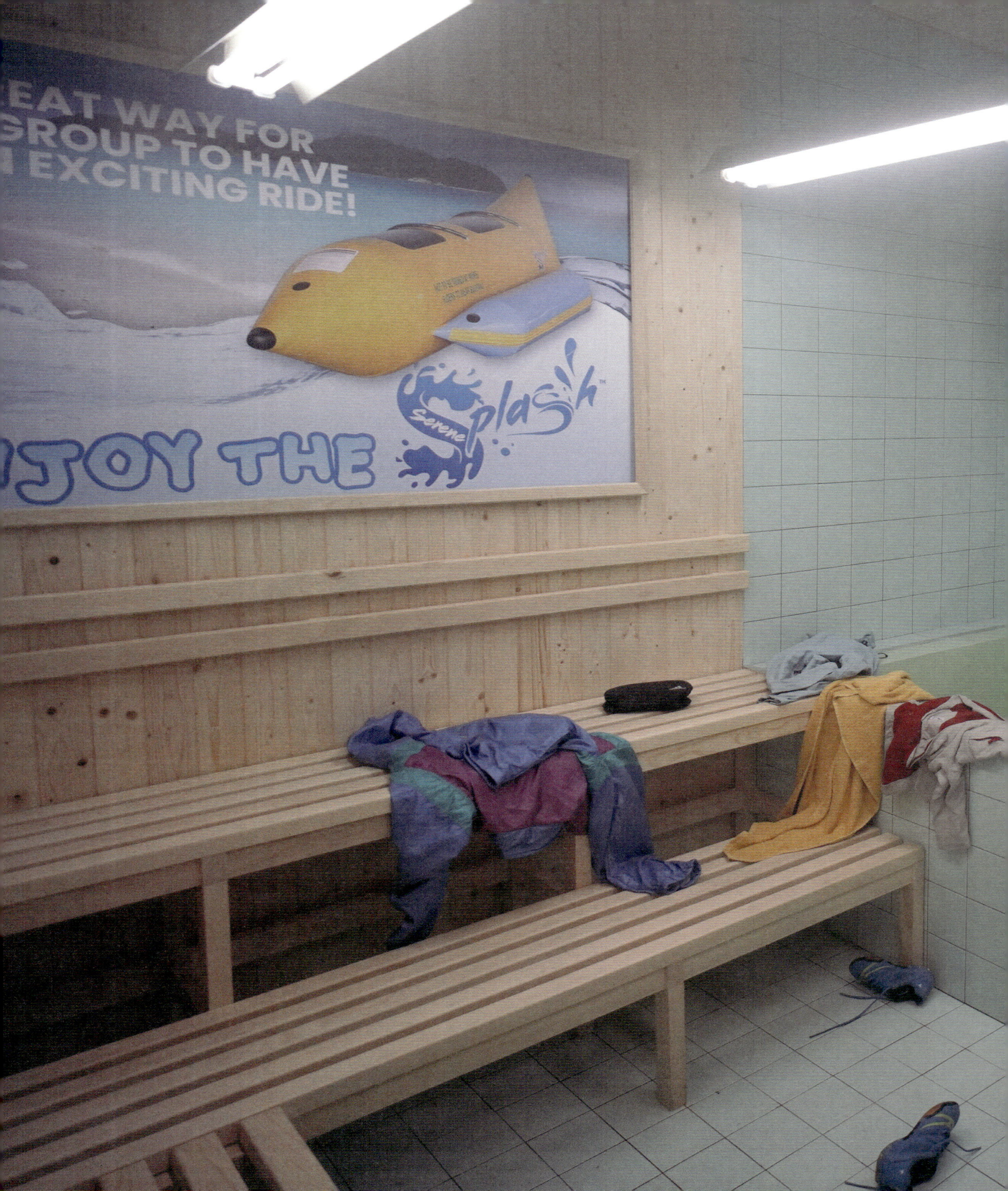
EAT WAY FOR
GROUP TO HAVE
EXCITING RIDE!
NJOY THE
serene
Splash

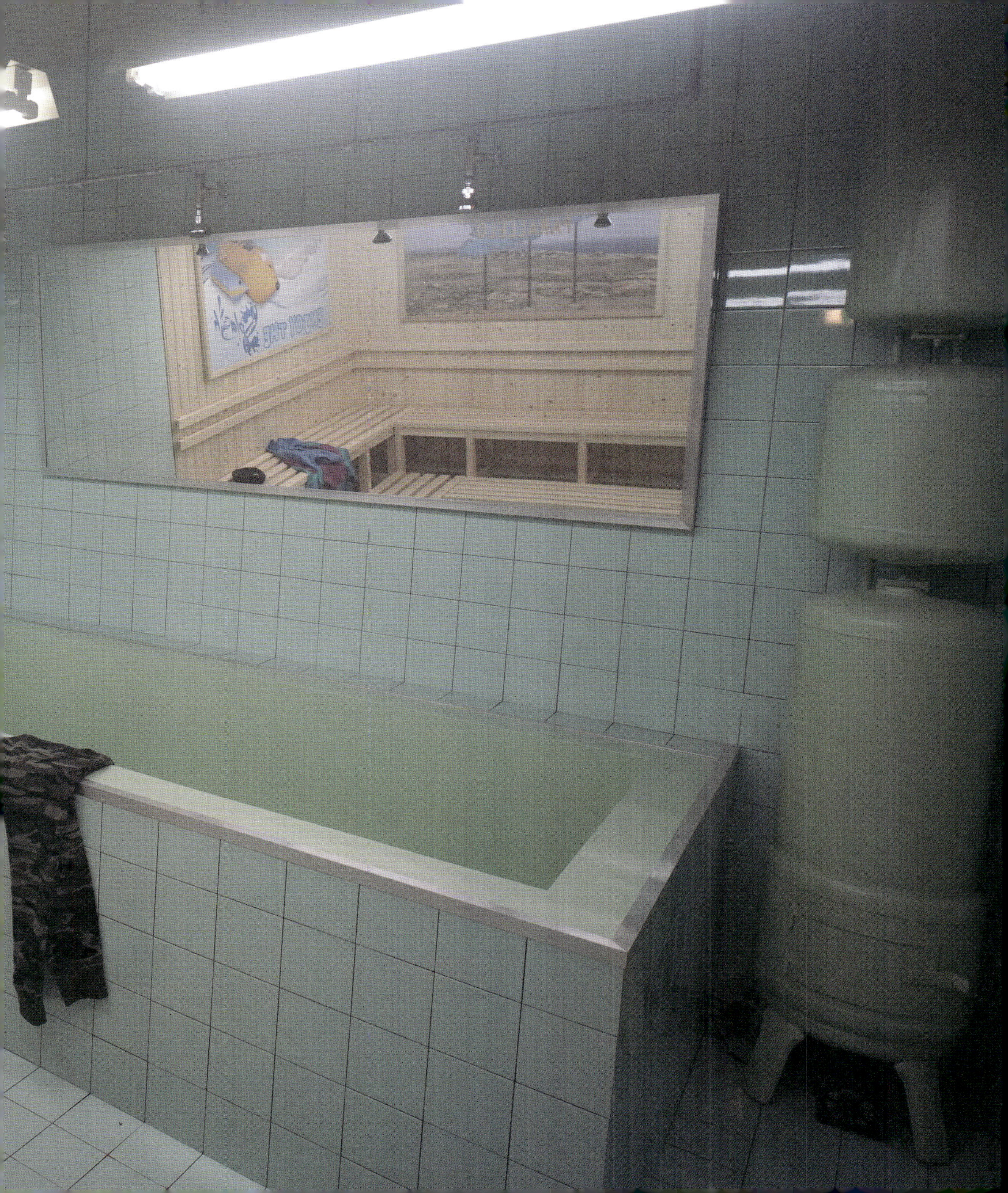

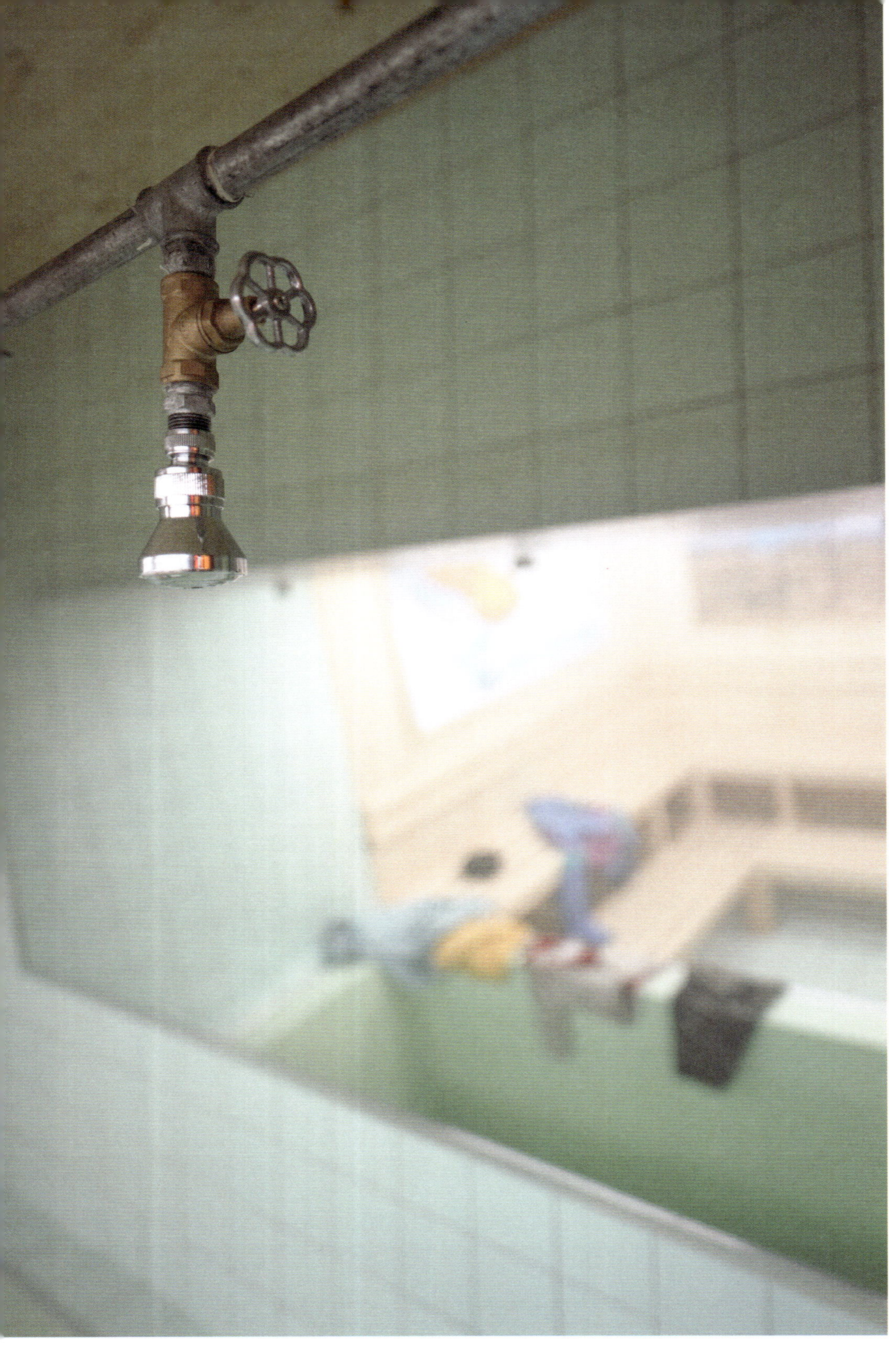

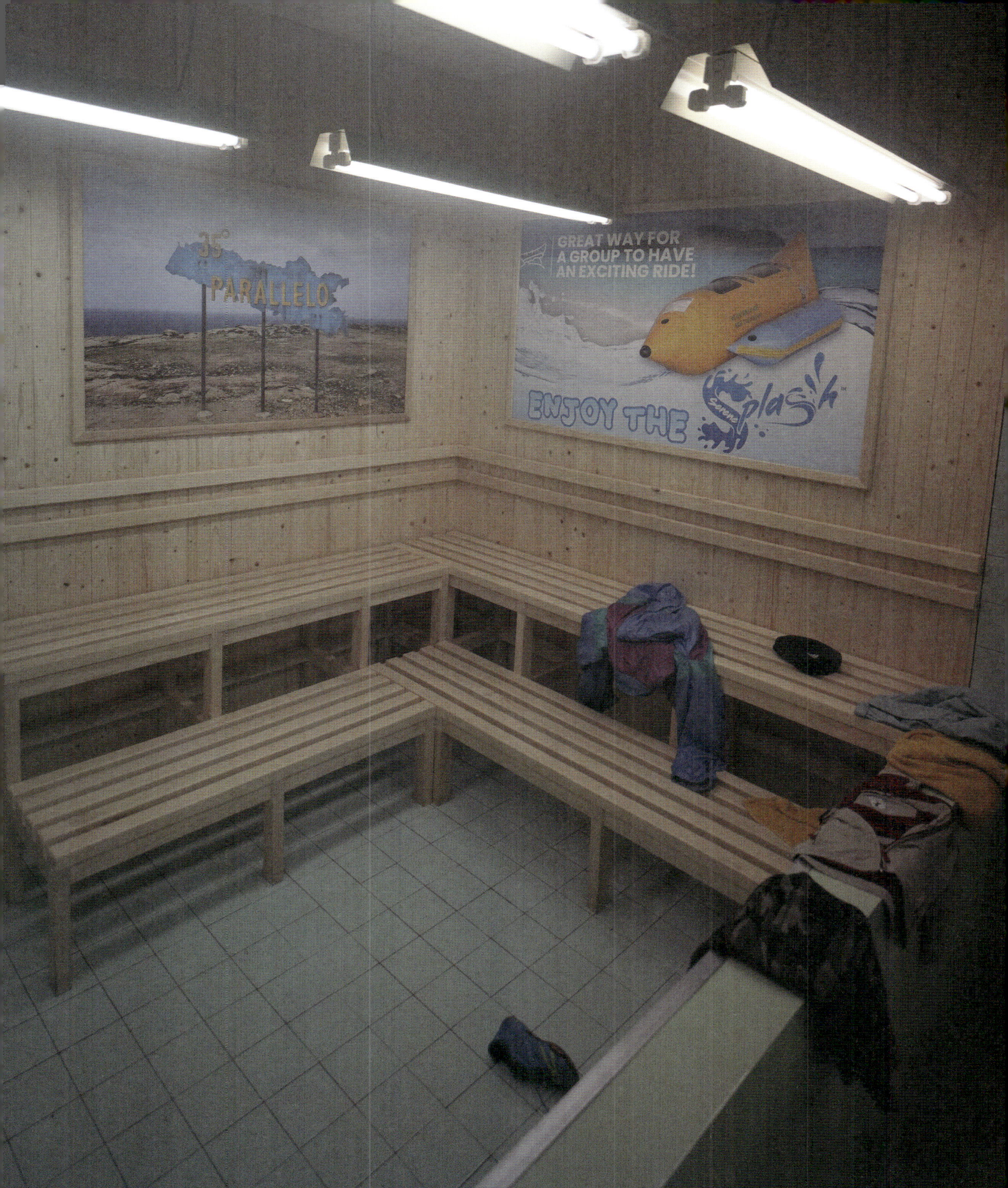
35°
PARALLELO
GREAT WAY FOR
A GROUP TO HAVE
AN EXCITING RIDE!
ENJOY THE
Splash

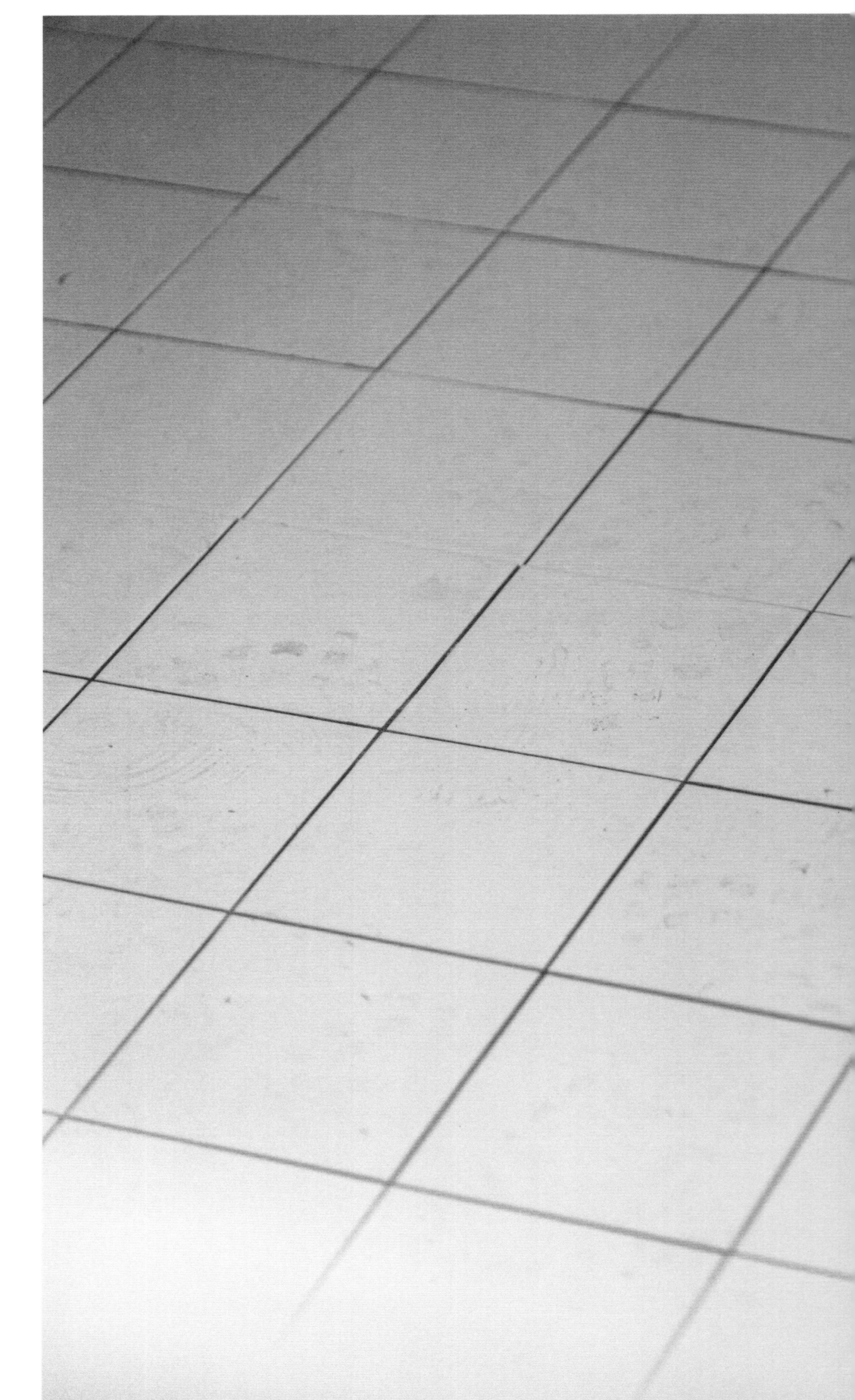

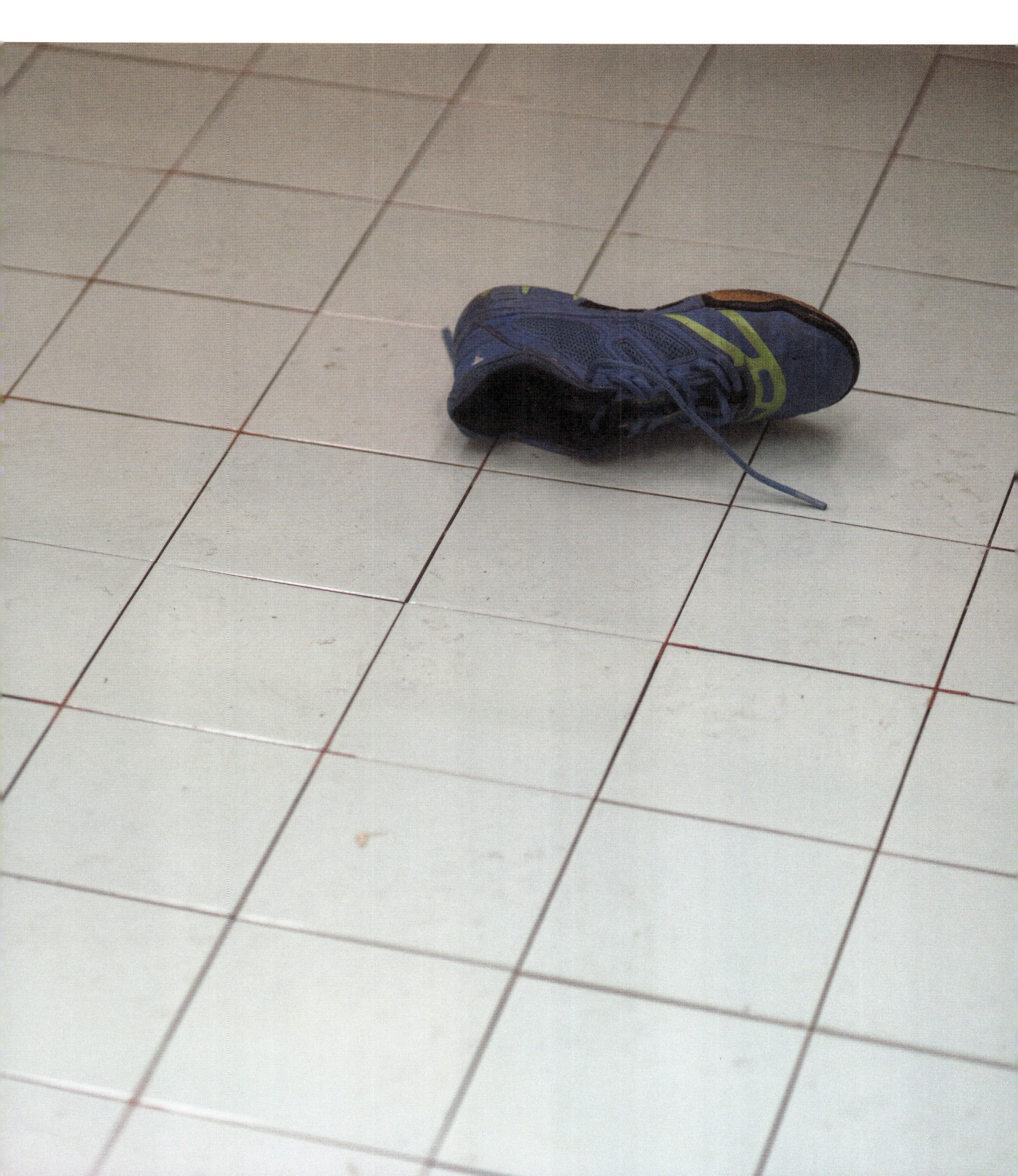

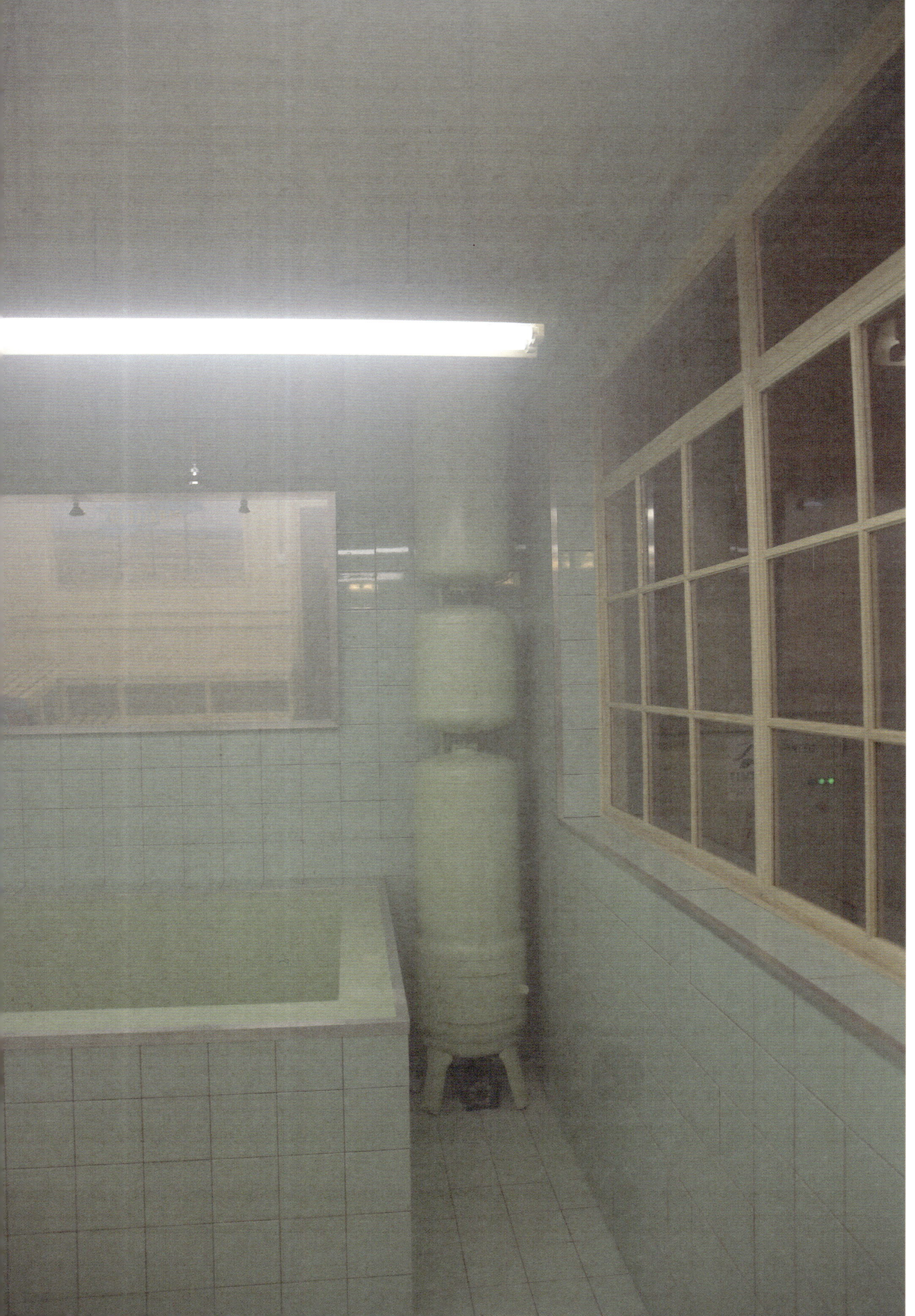

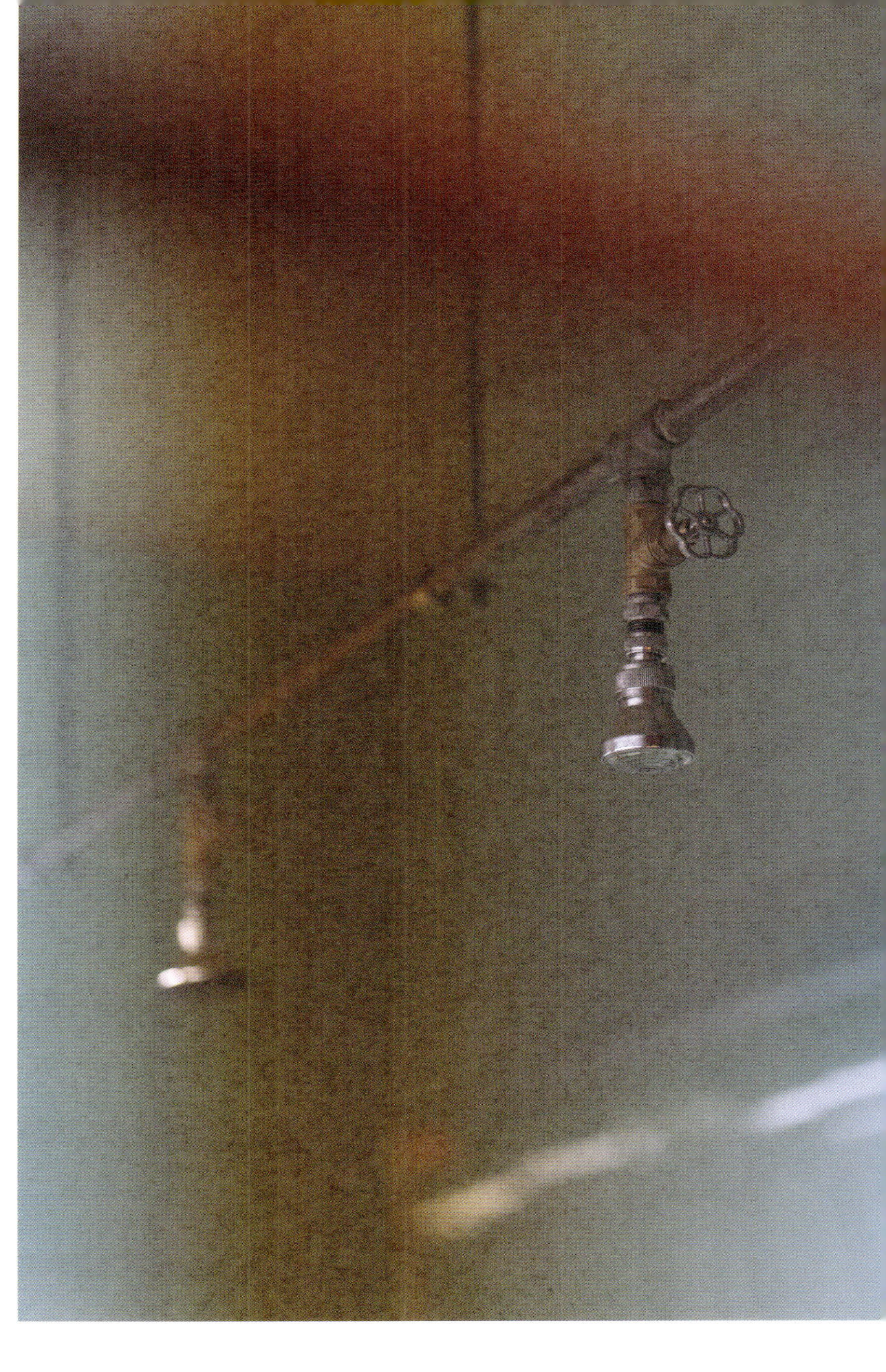

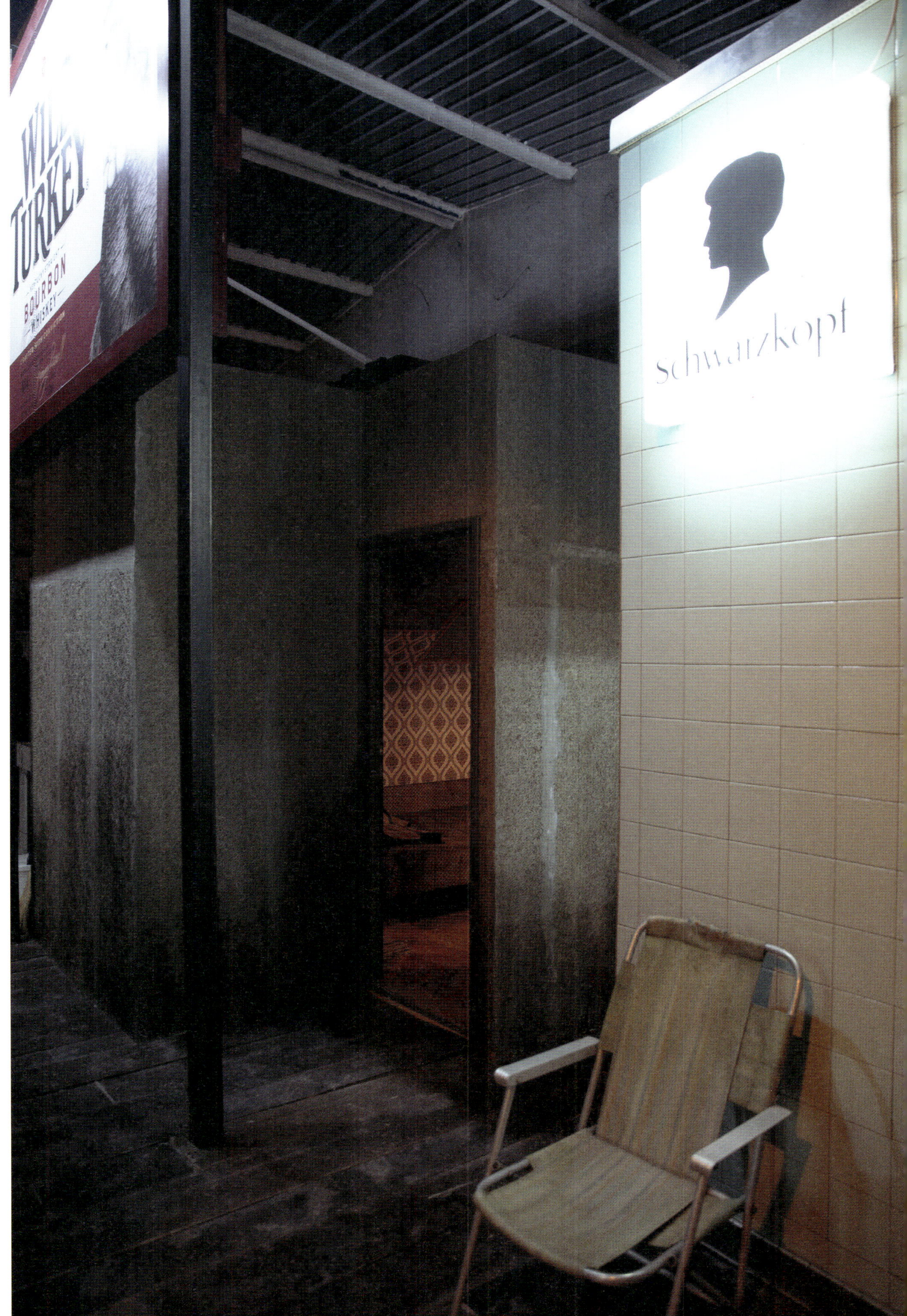

WILD
TURKEY
BOURBON
WHISKEY
schwarzkopf

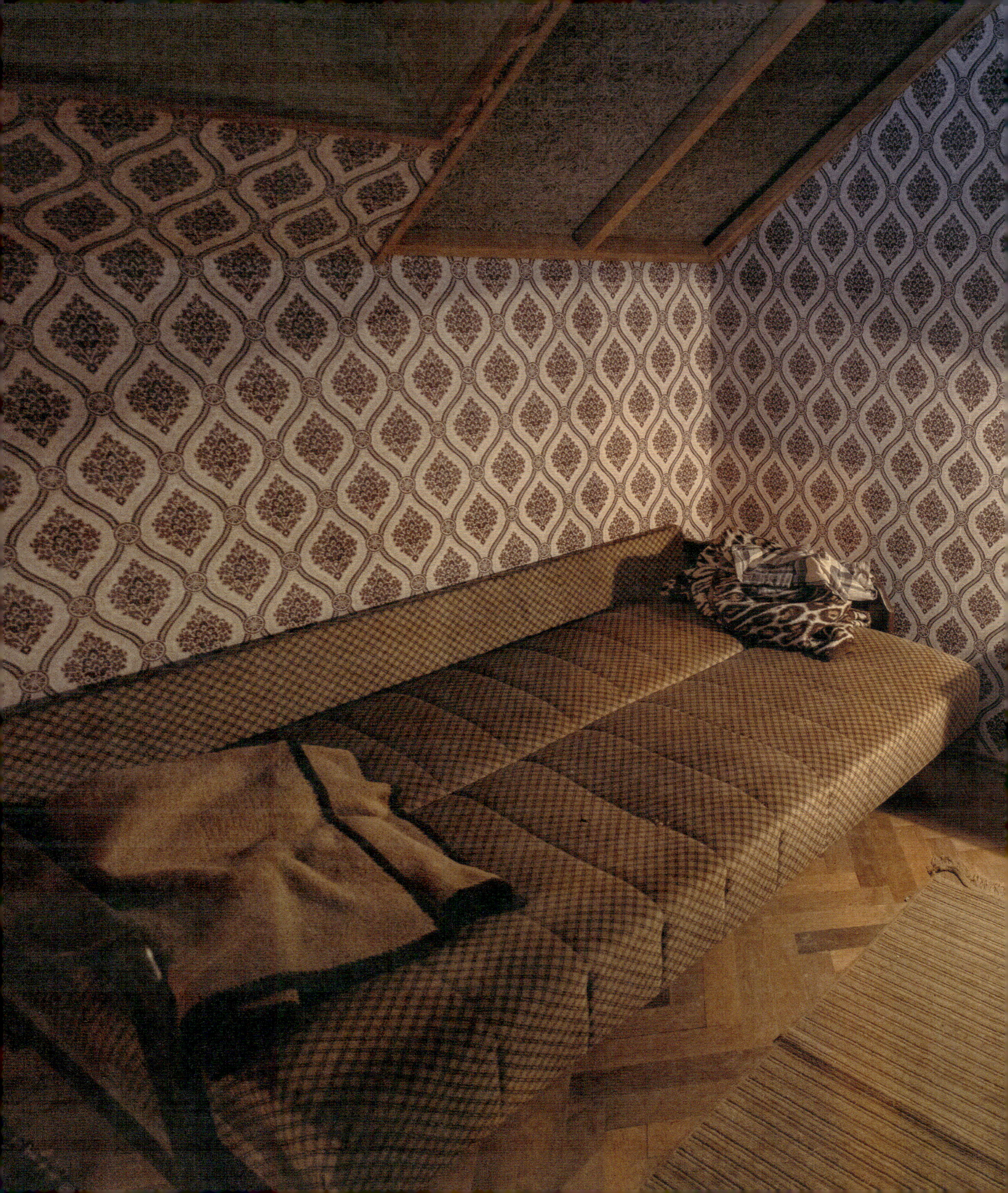

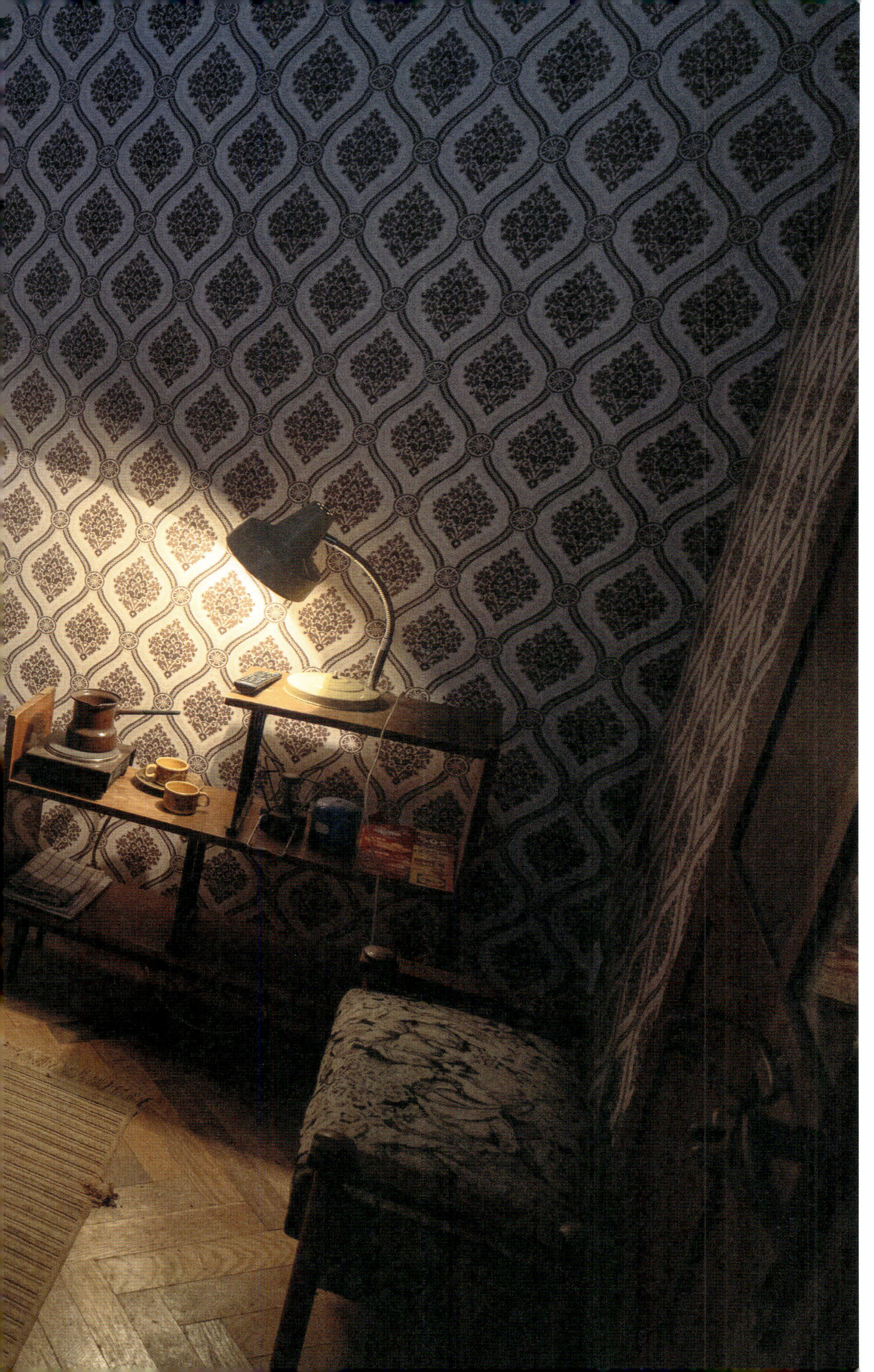

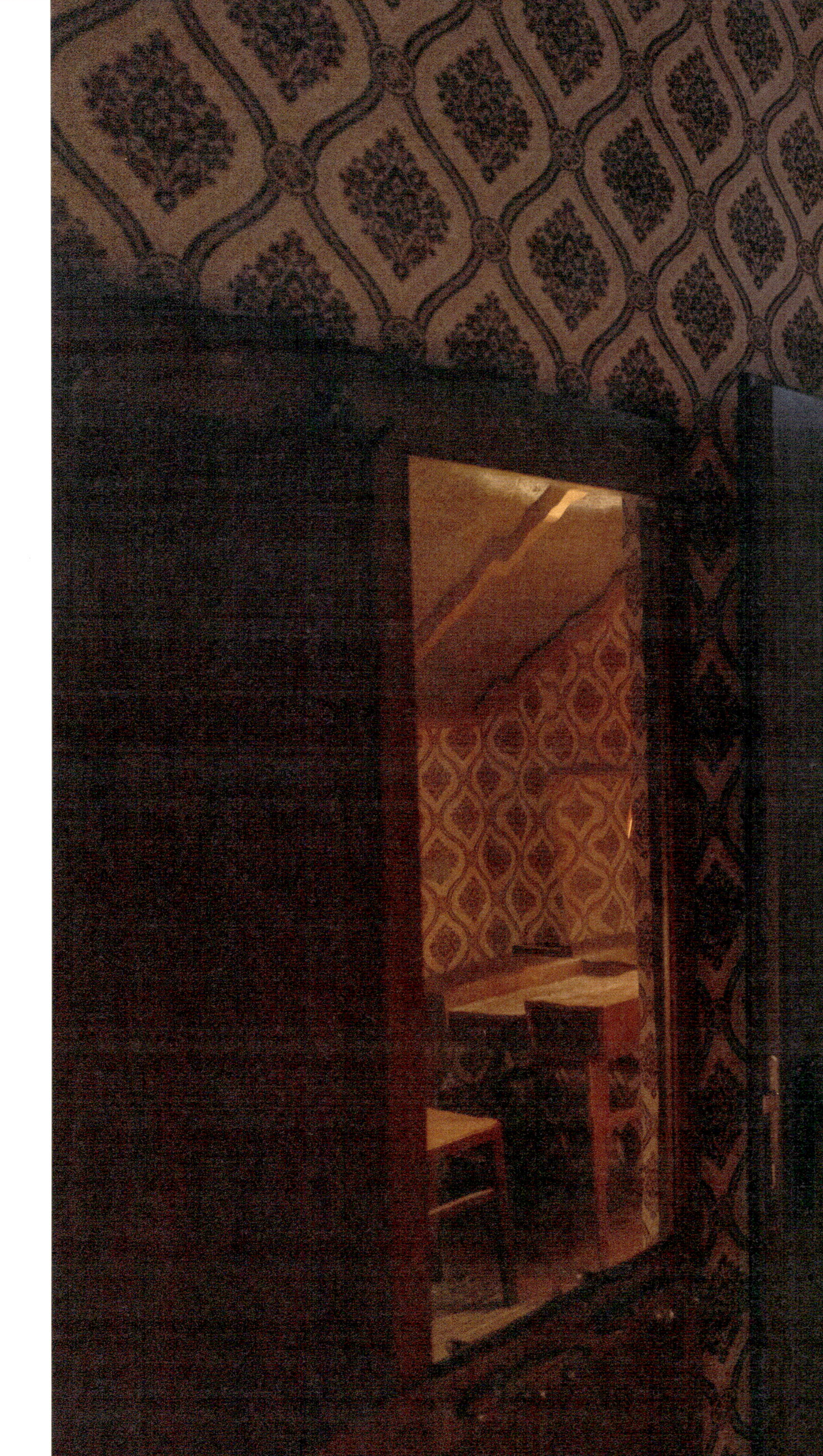

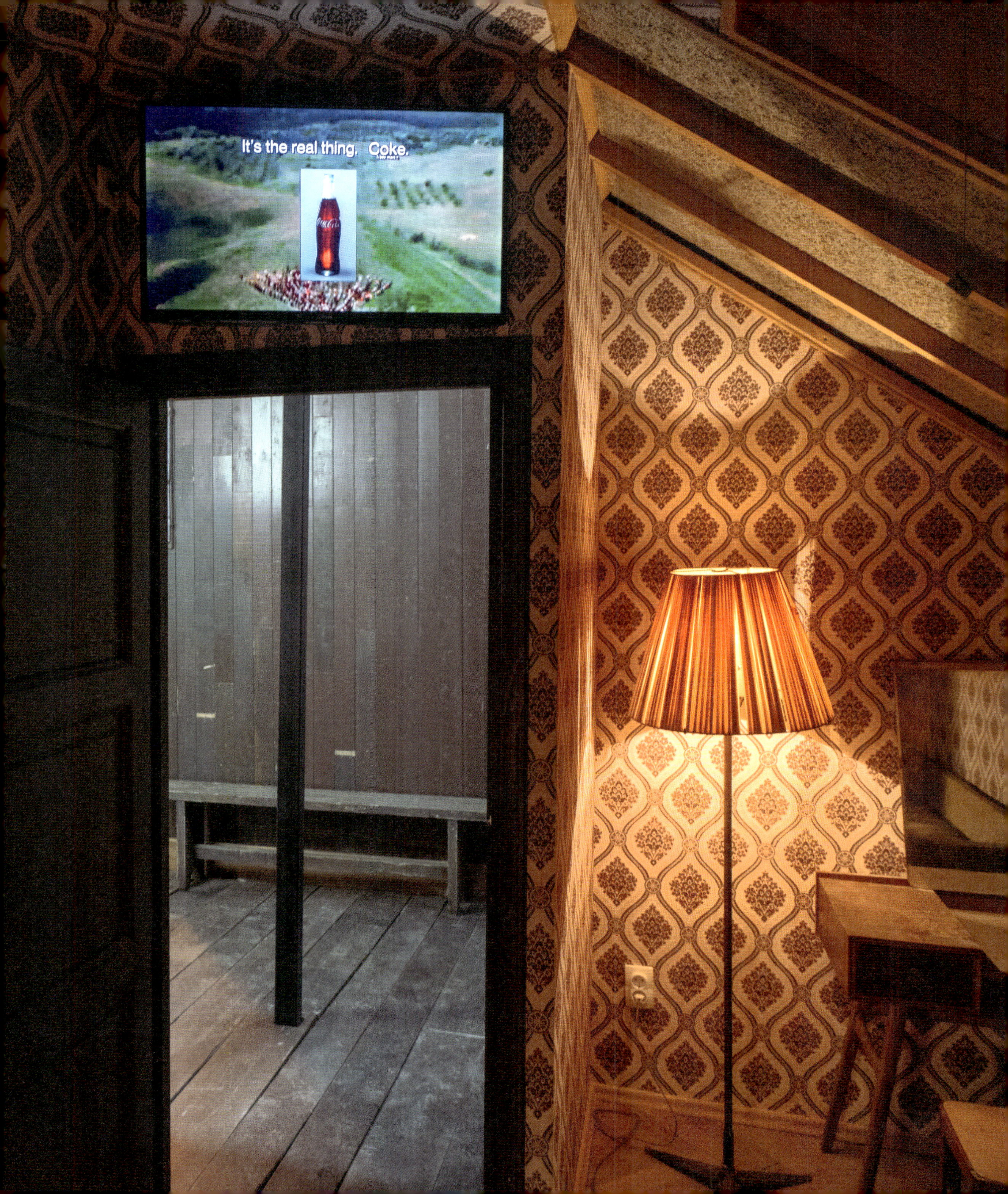

It's the real thing. Coke.

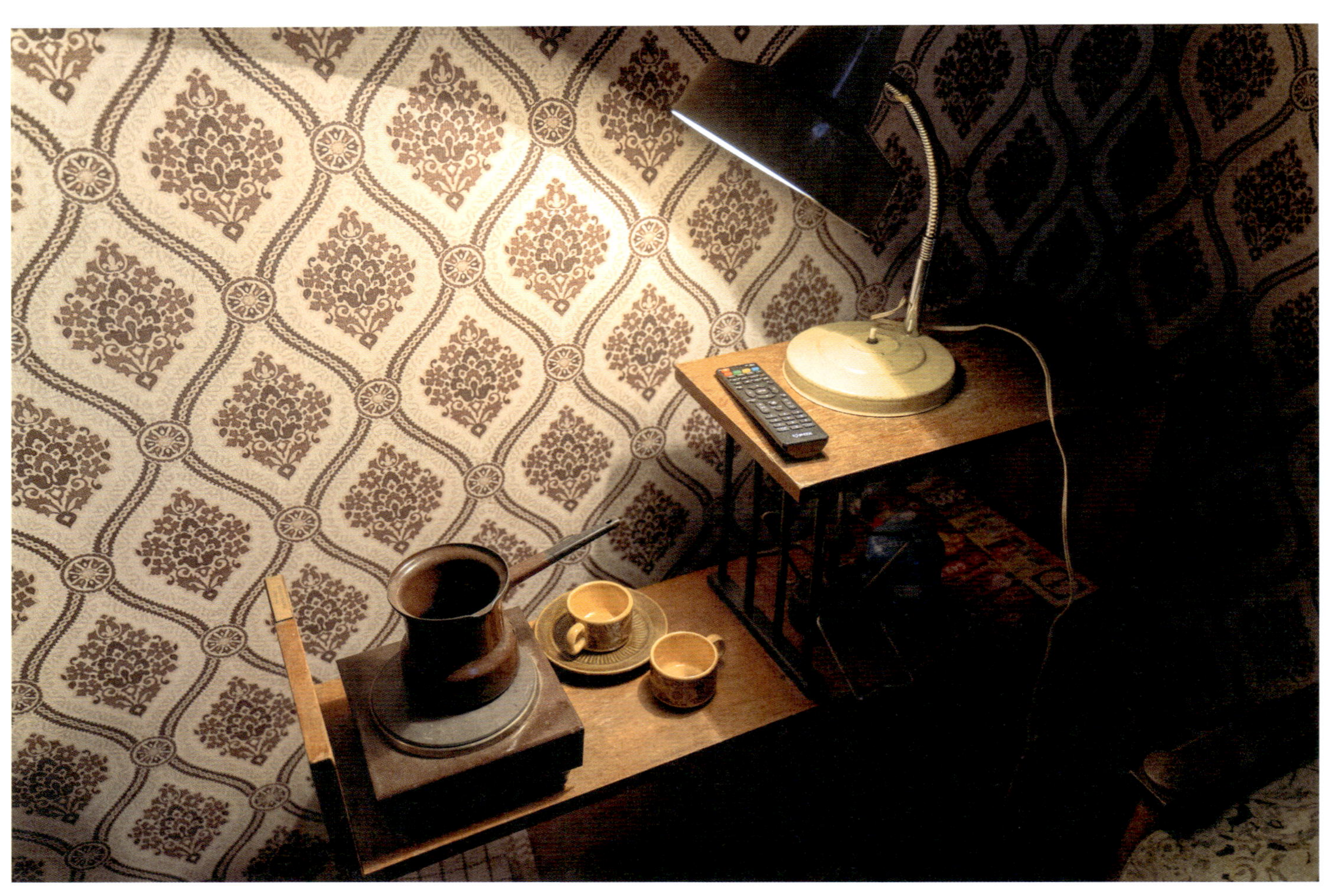

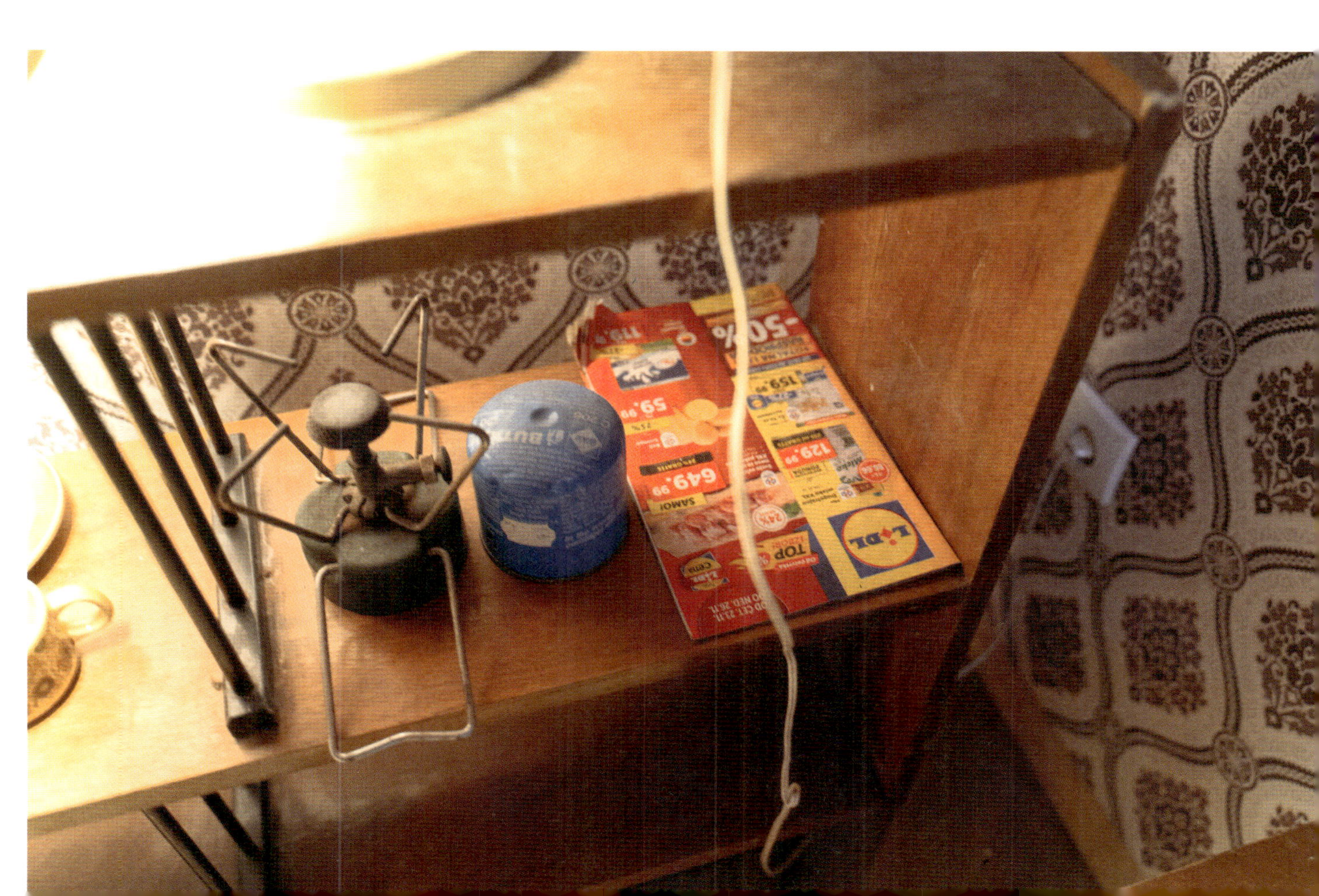

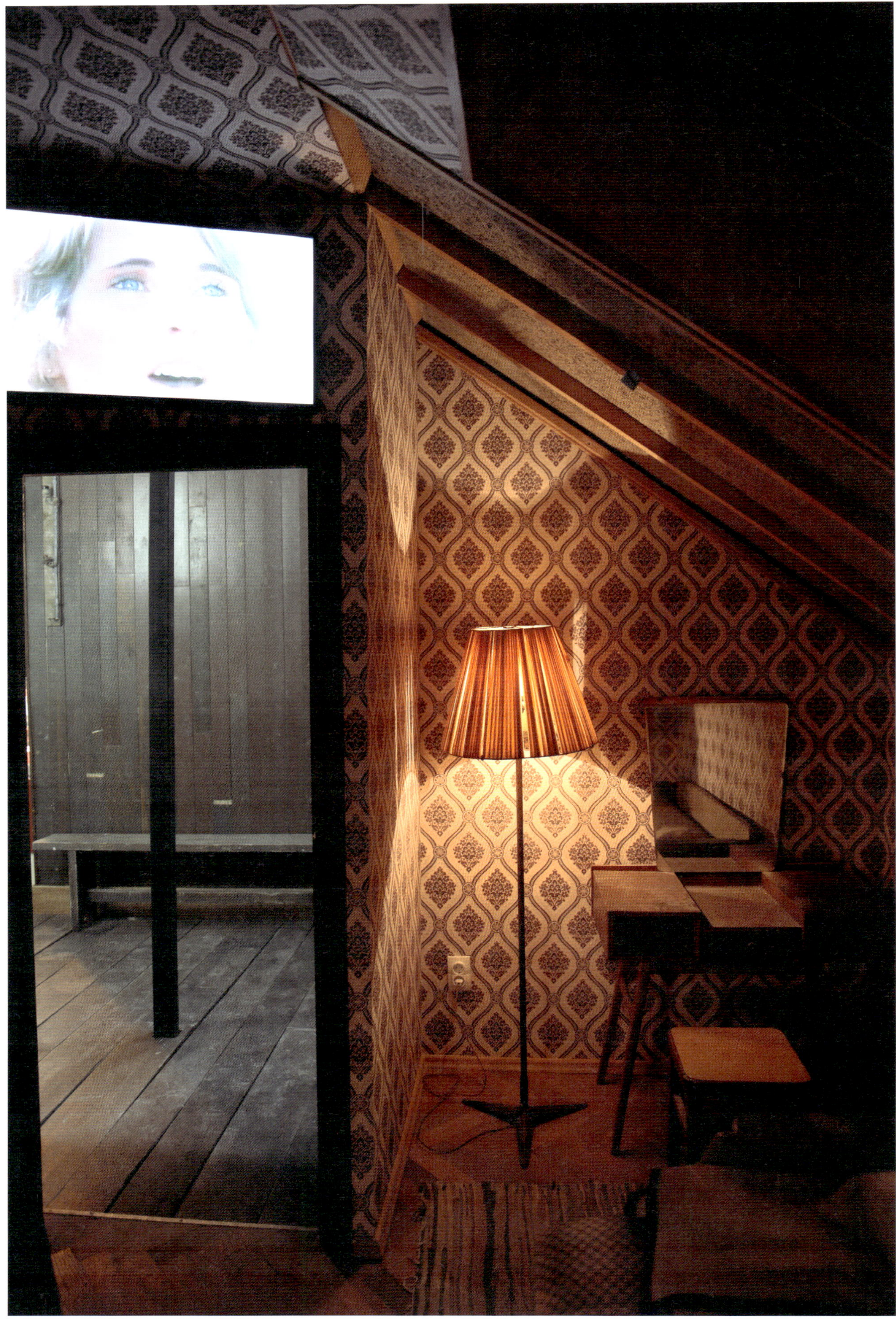

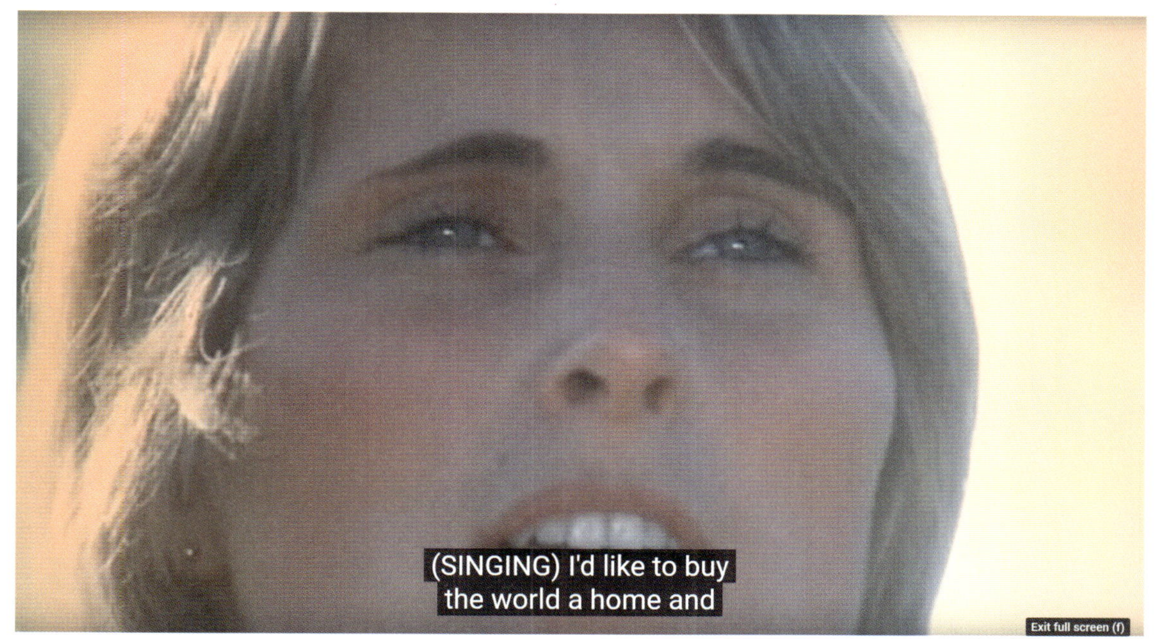
(SINGING) I'd like to buy
the world a home and
Exit full screen (f)

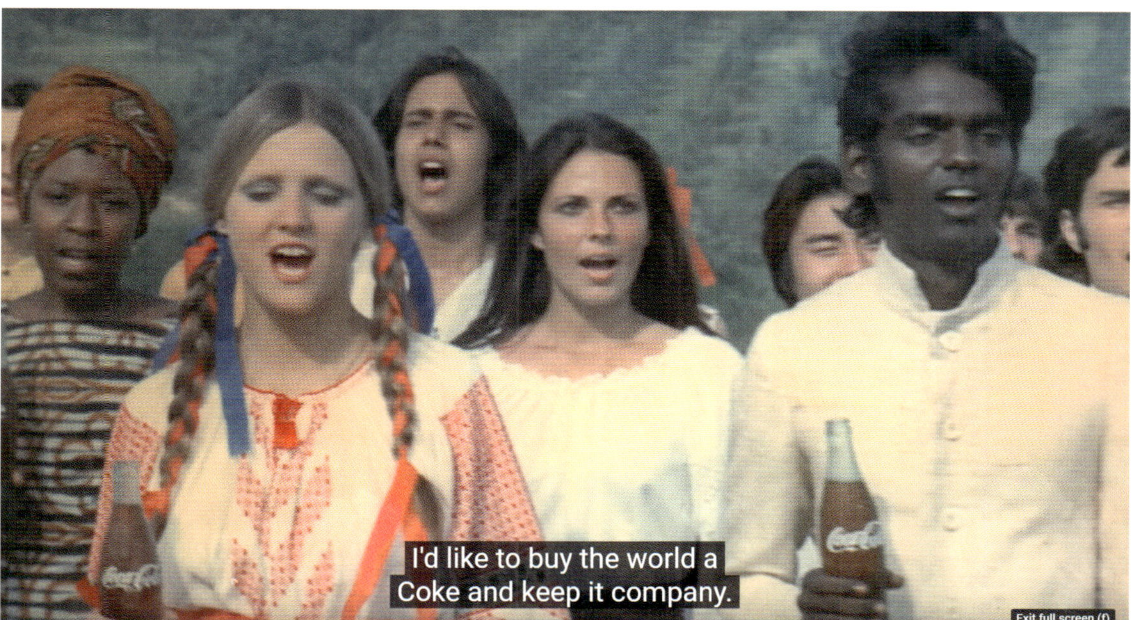
I'd like to buy the world a
Coke and keep it company.
Exit full screen (f)

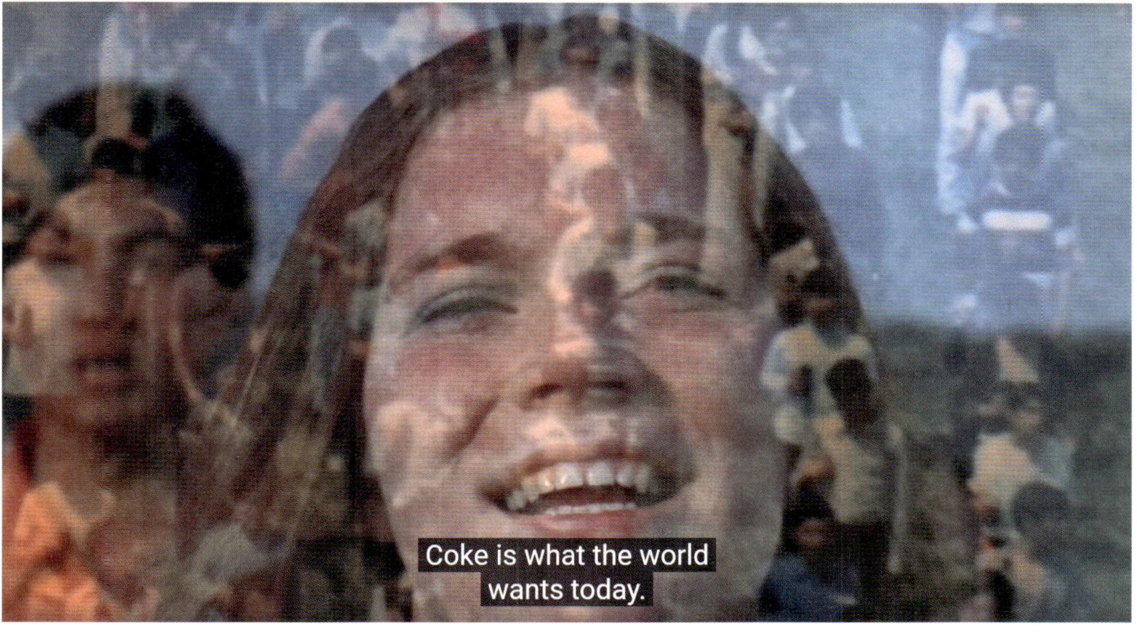
Coke is what the world
wants today.

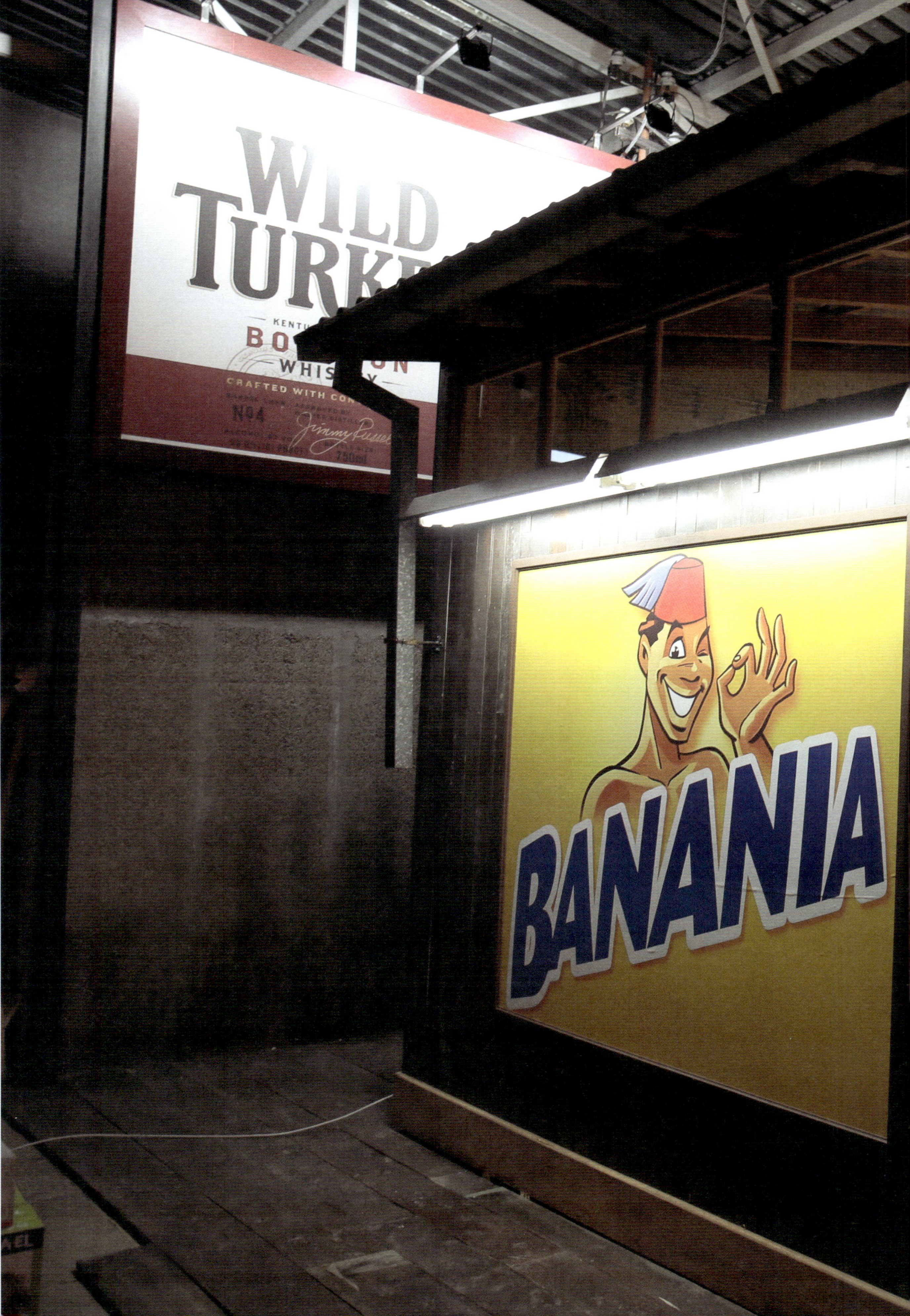
WILD
TURKEY
KENTU
BO
WHIS
CRAFTED WITH CO
N°4
Jimmy Russel
750ml
BANANIA

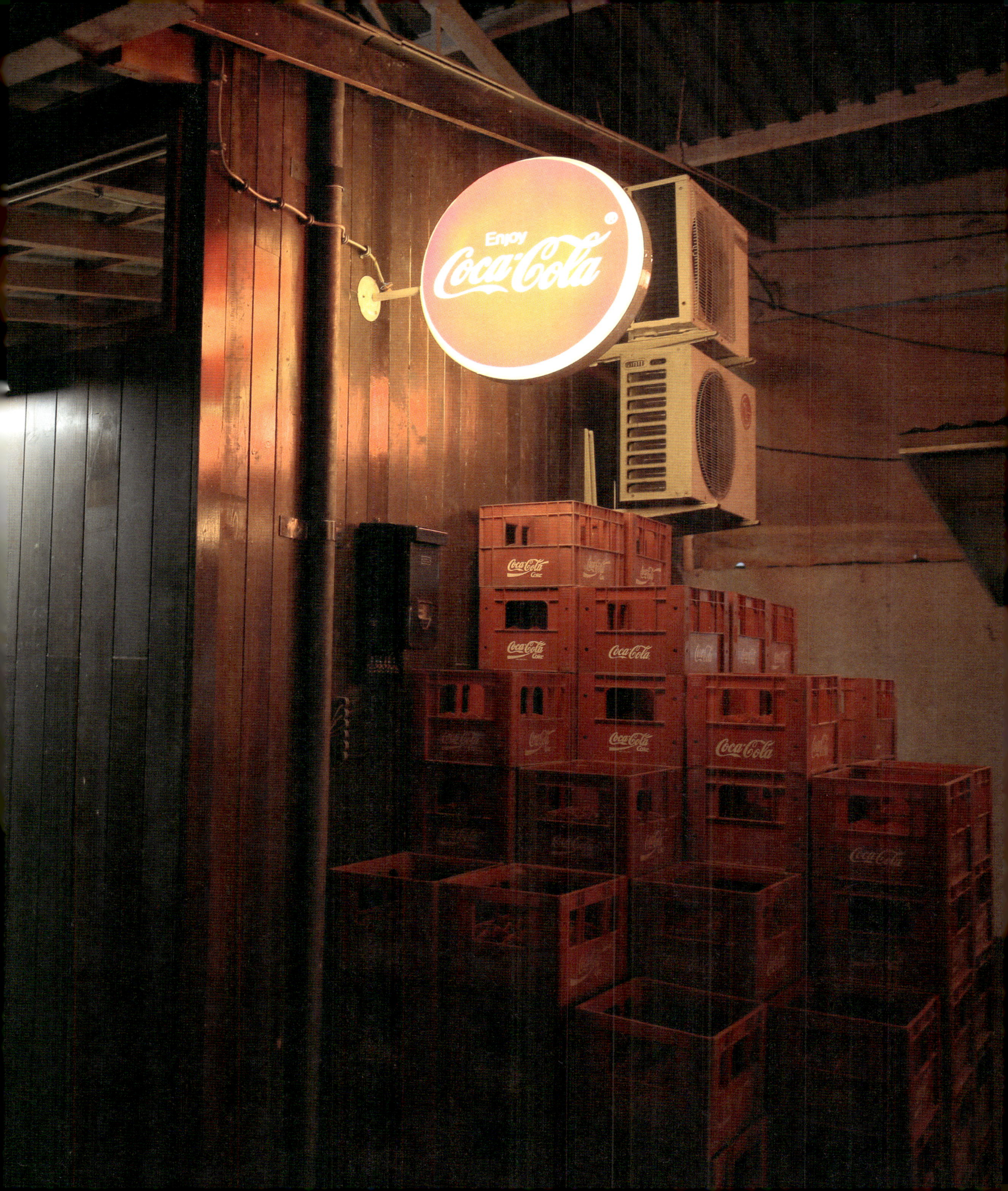

Enjoy
Coca-Cola
Coca-Cola
Coca-Cola
Coca-Cola
Coca-Cola
Coca-Cola

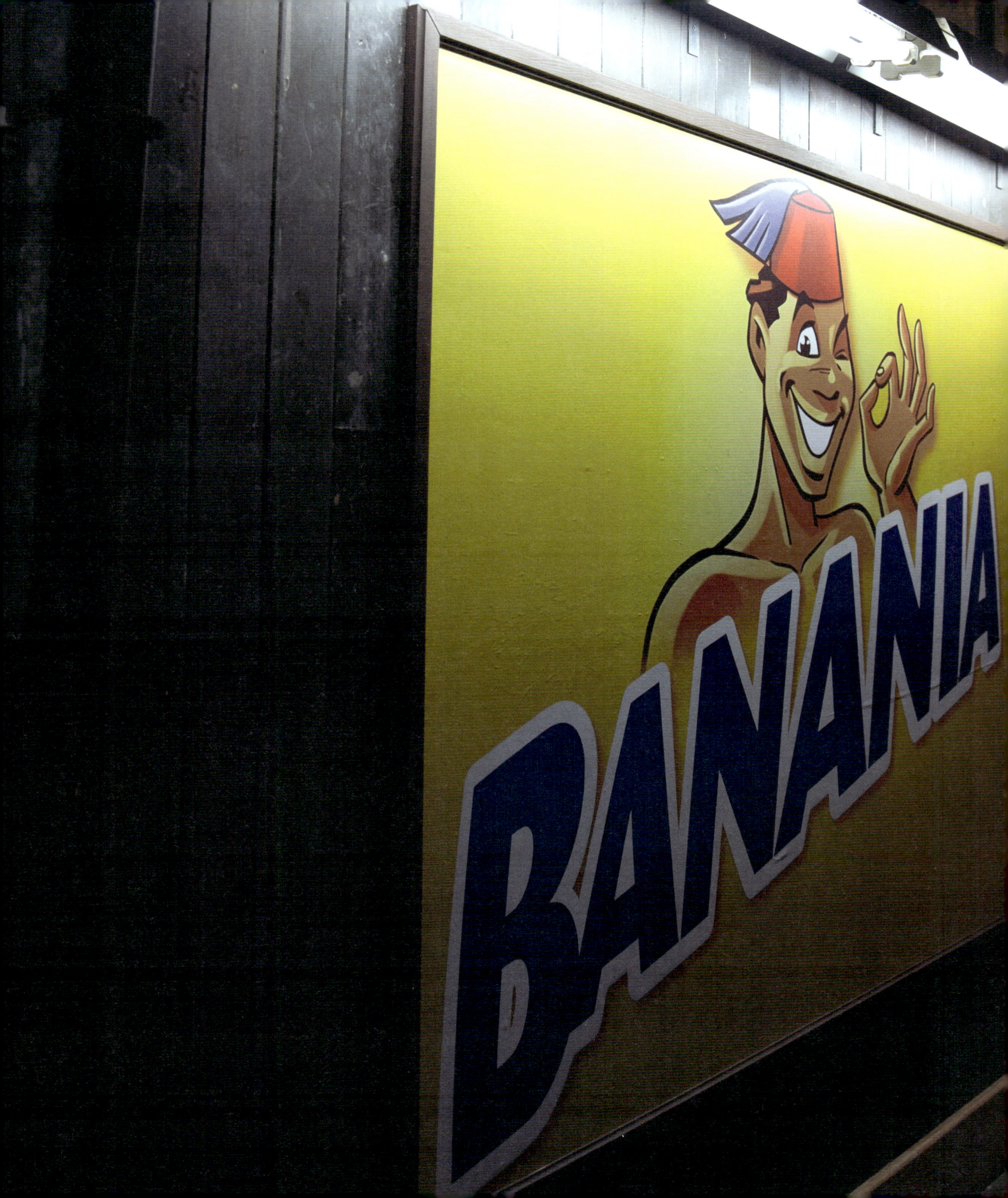
BANANIA

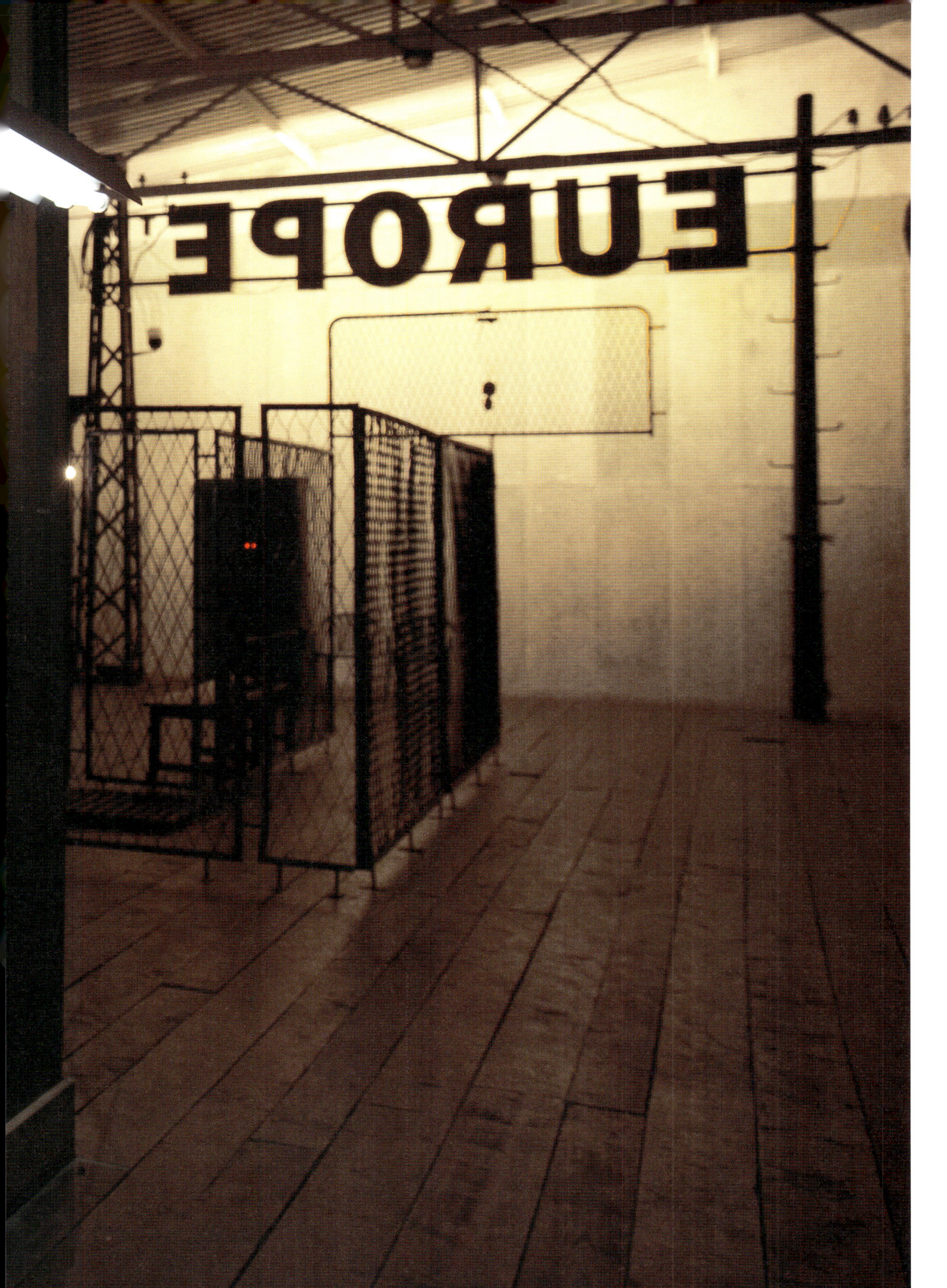

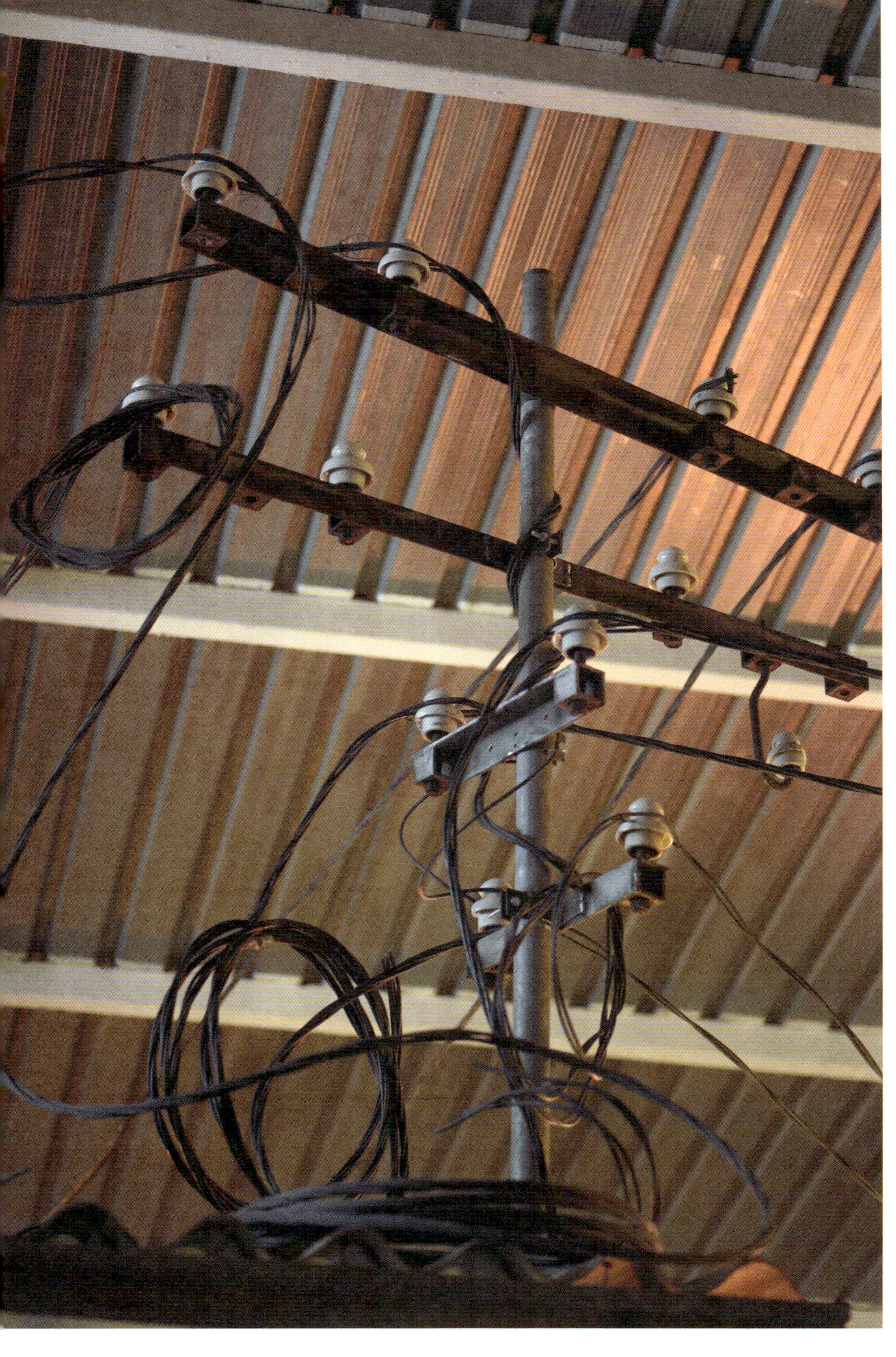

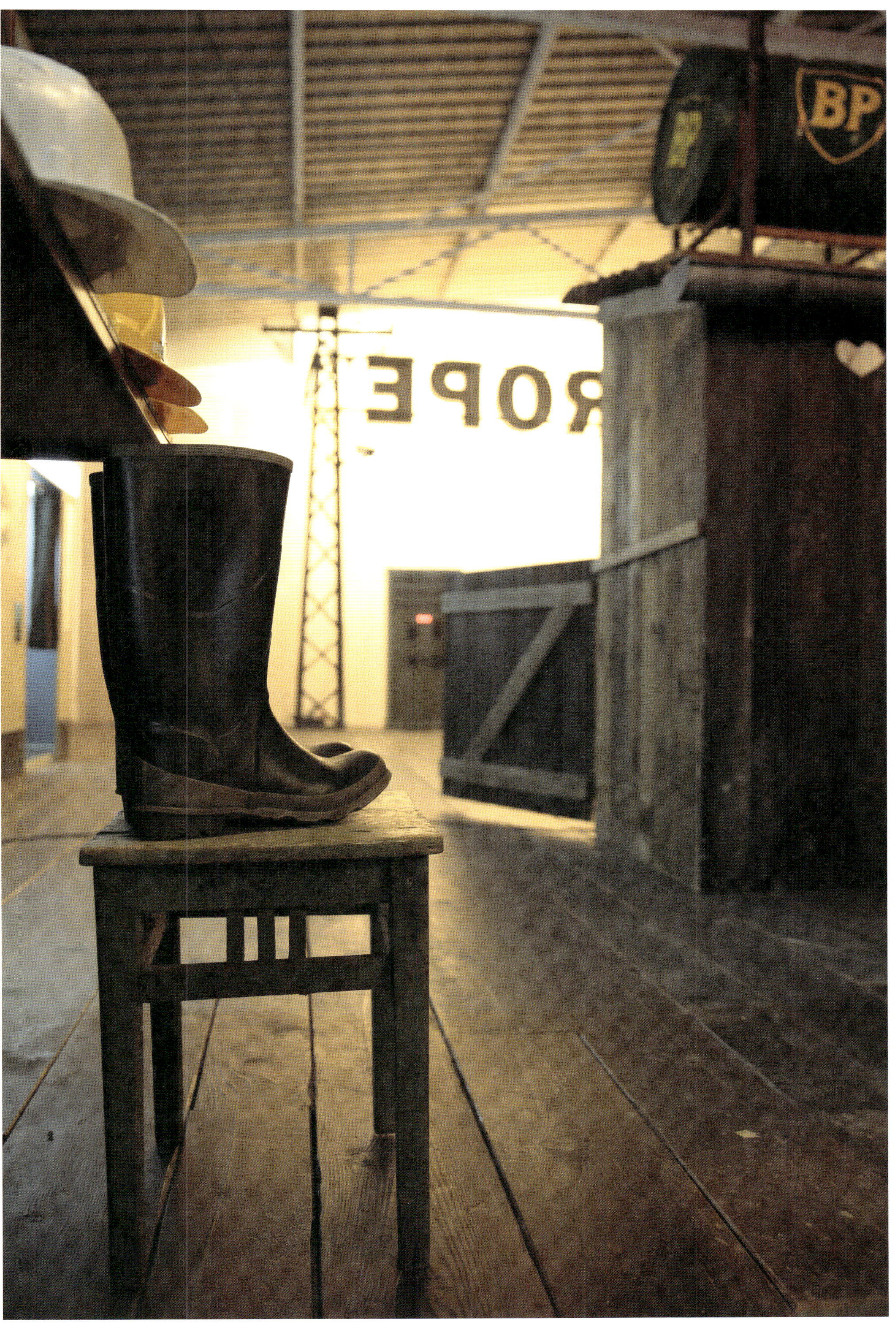

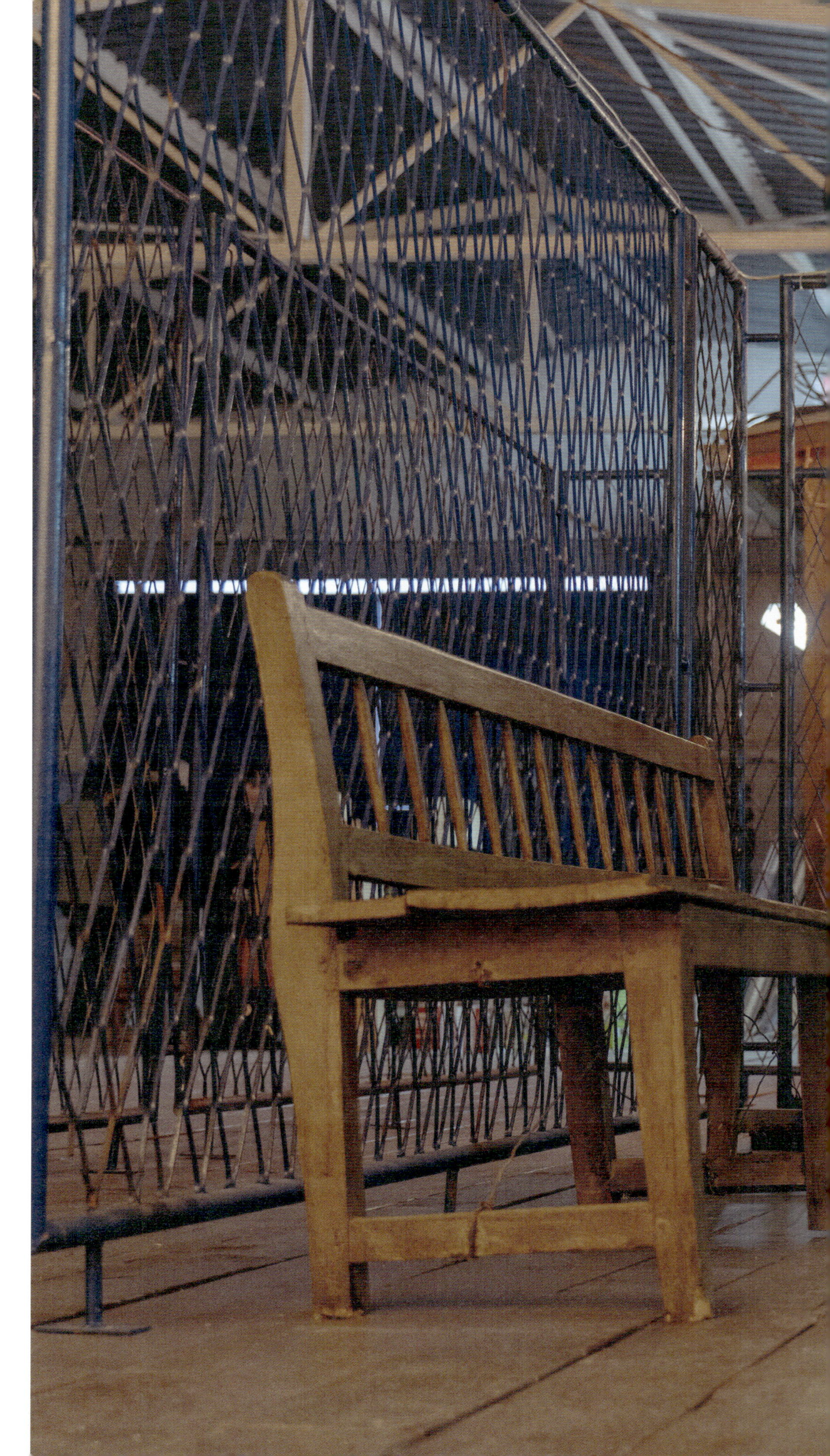

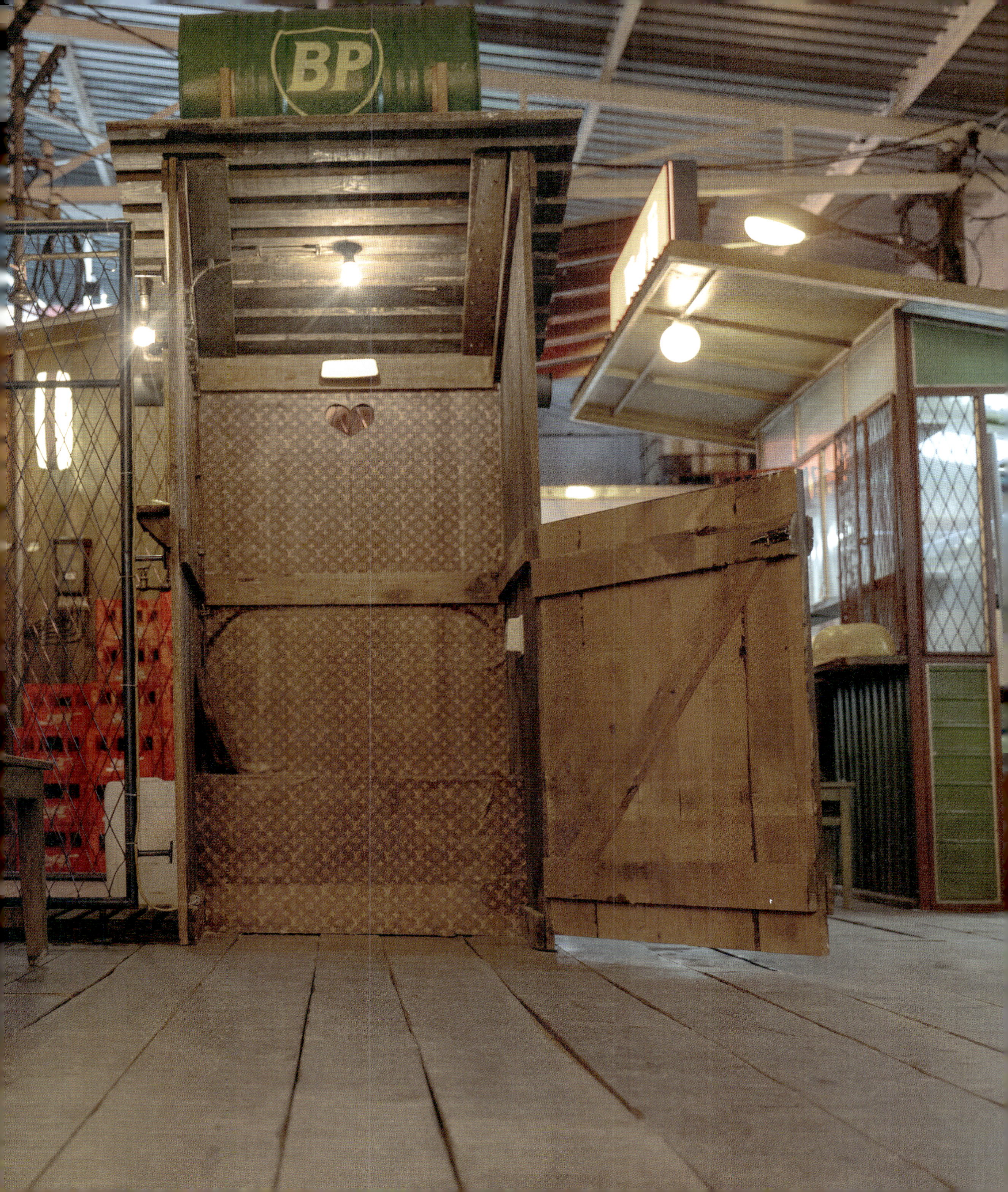
BP

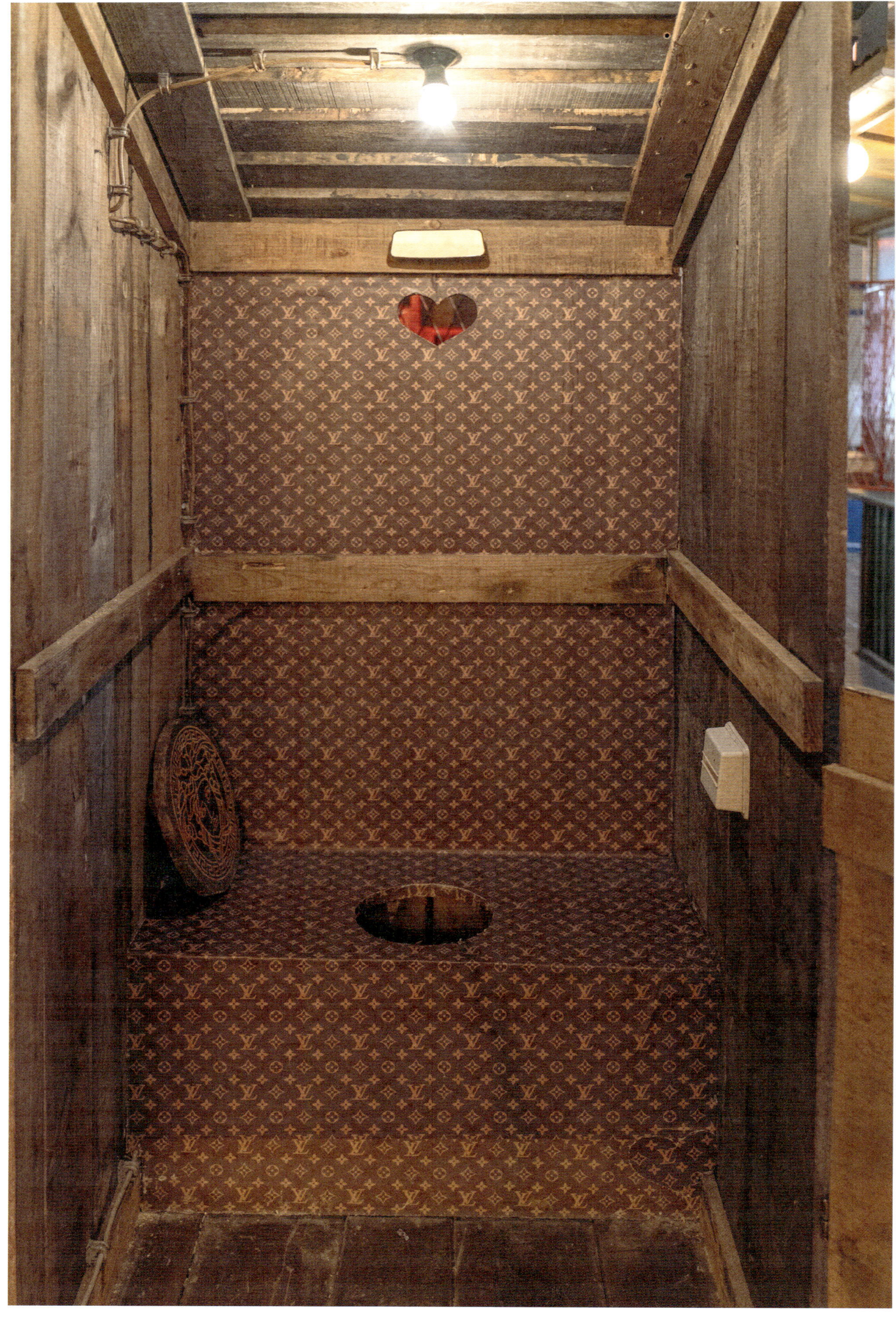

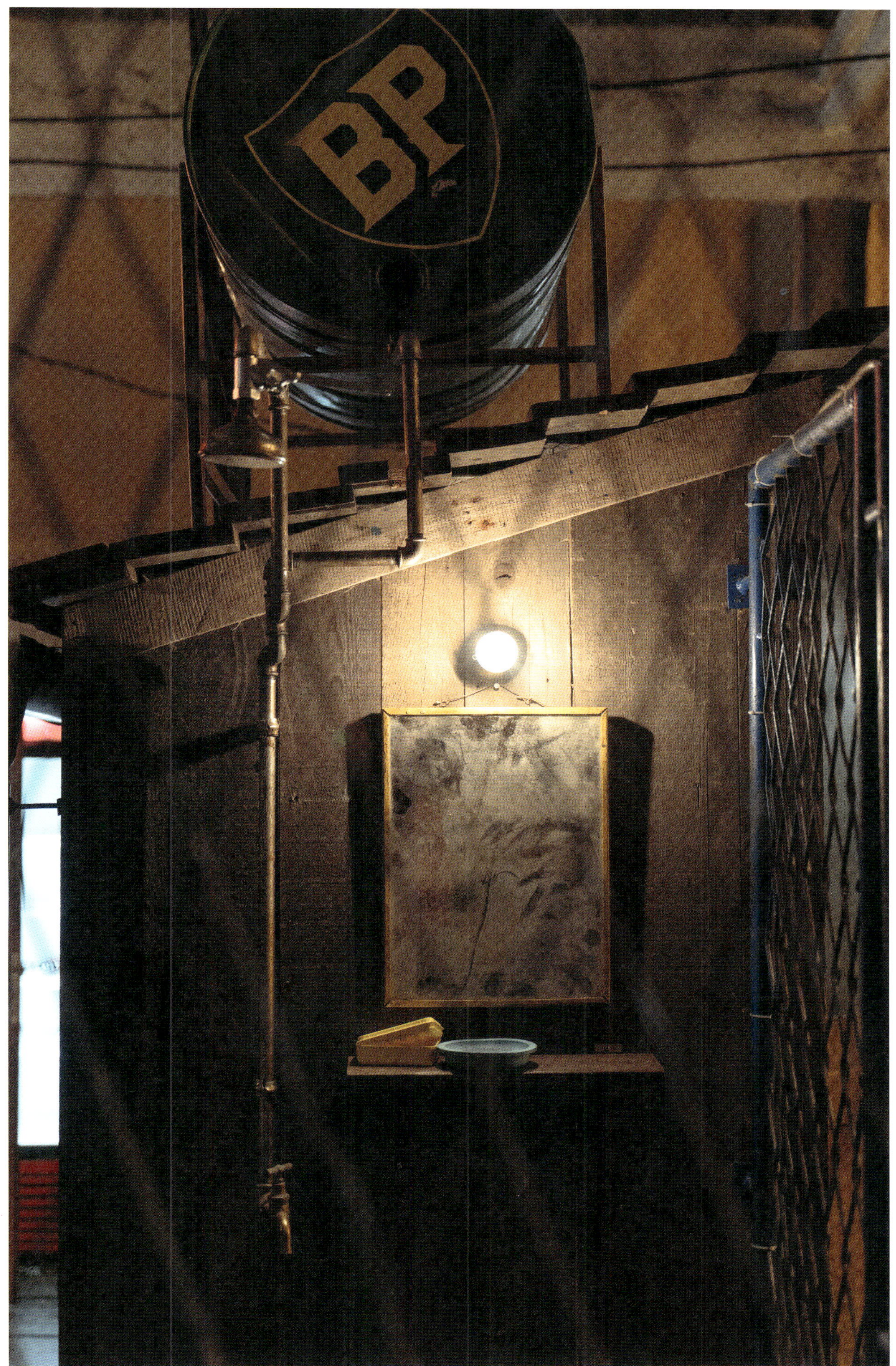

BP

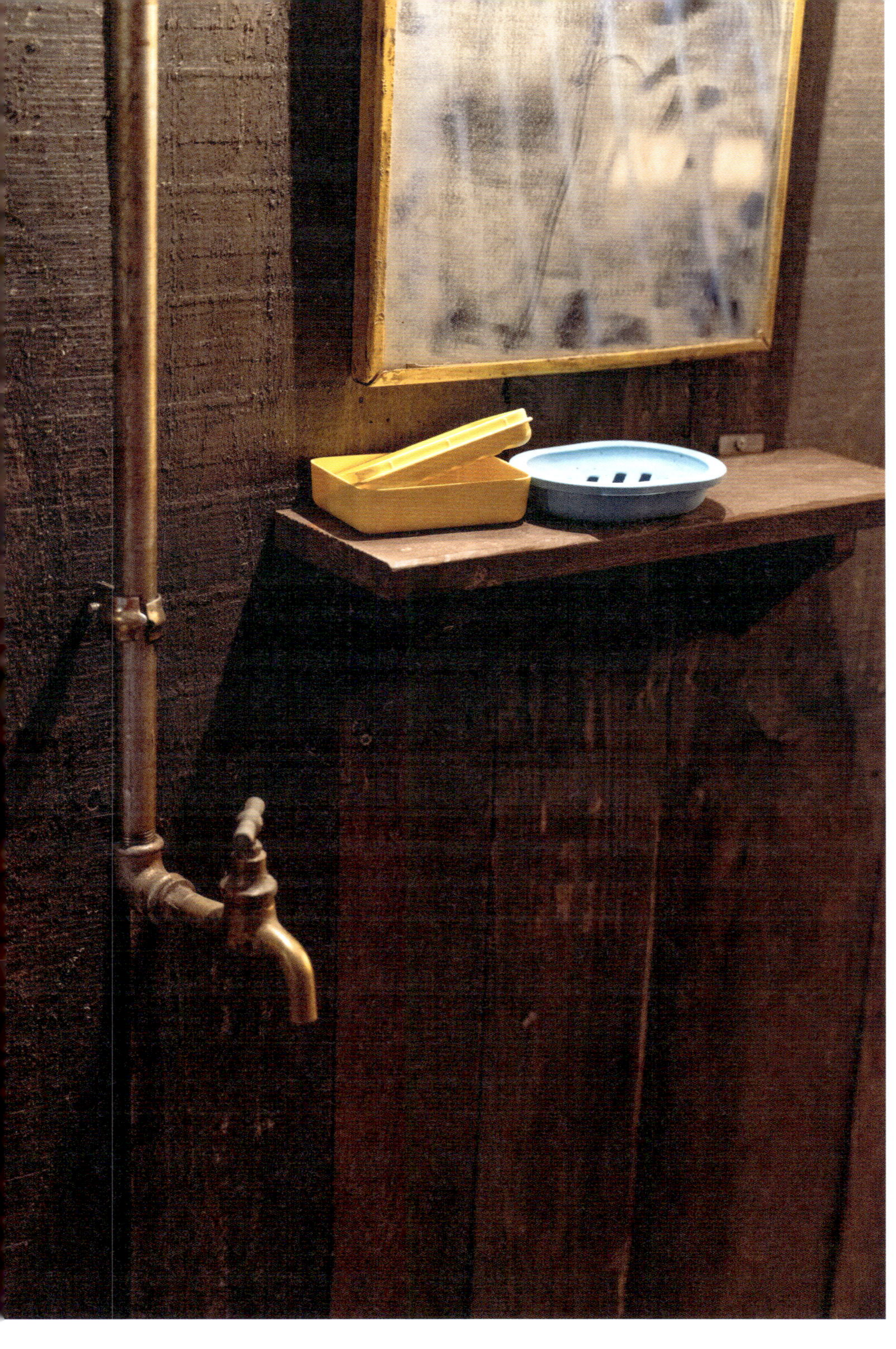

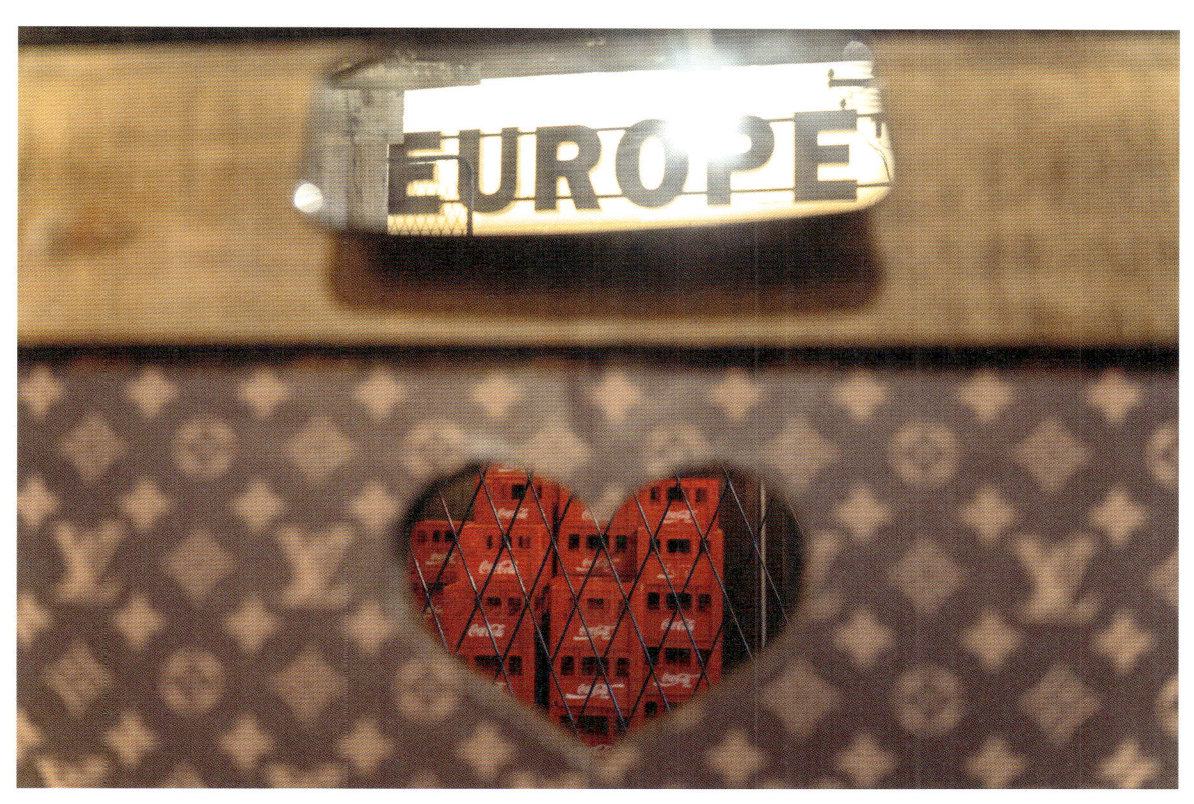
EUROPE

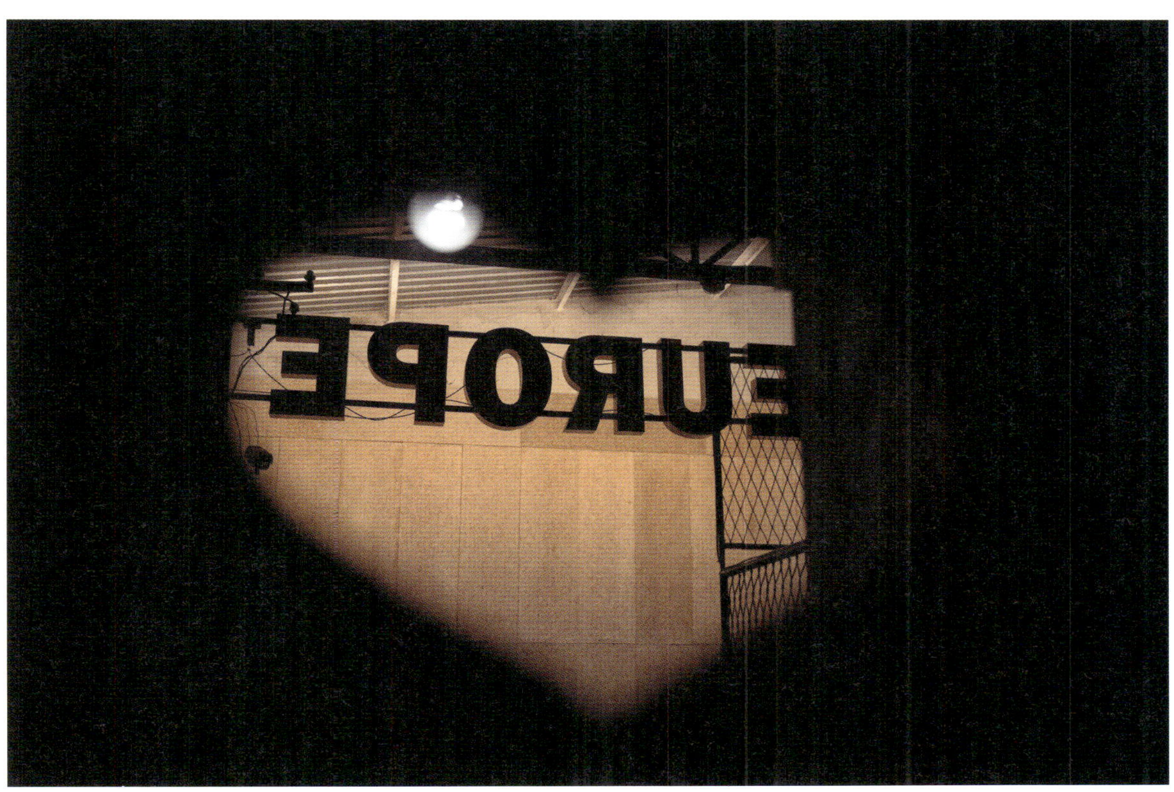
EUROPE

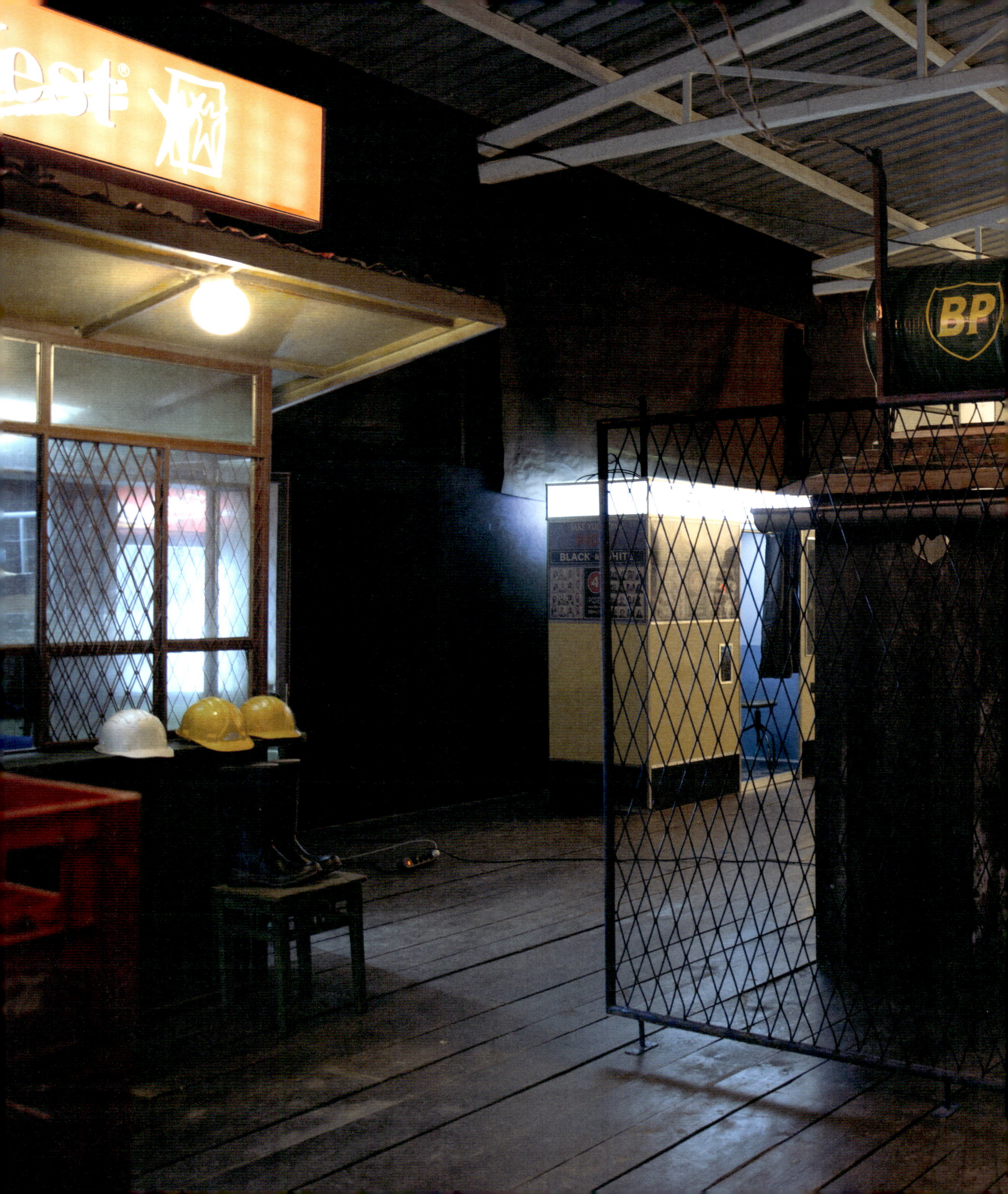
est
BP
BLACK & WHITE

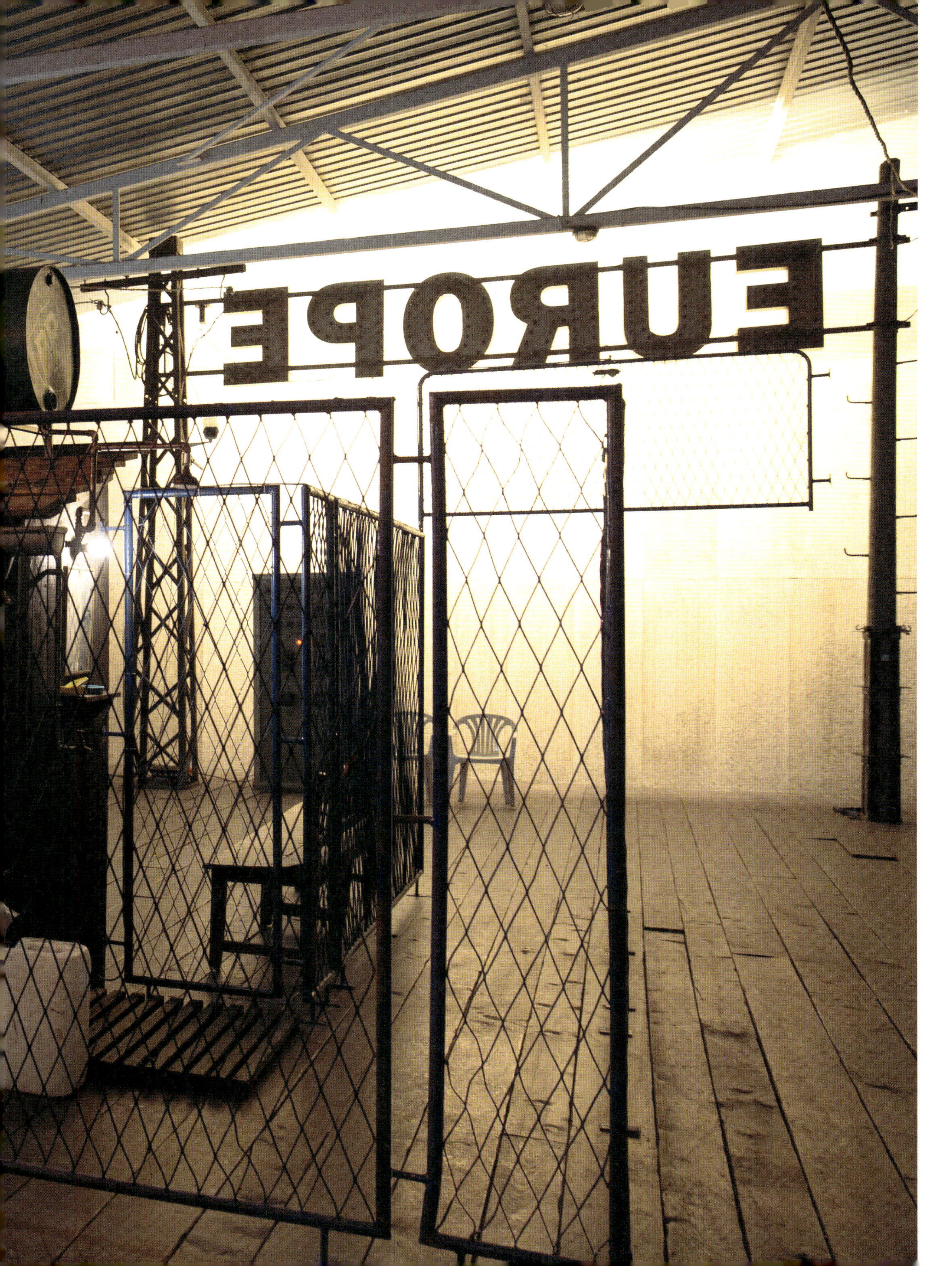

EUROPE

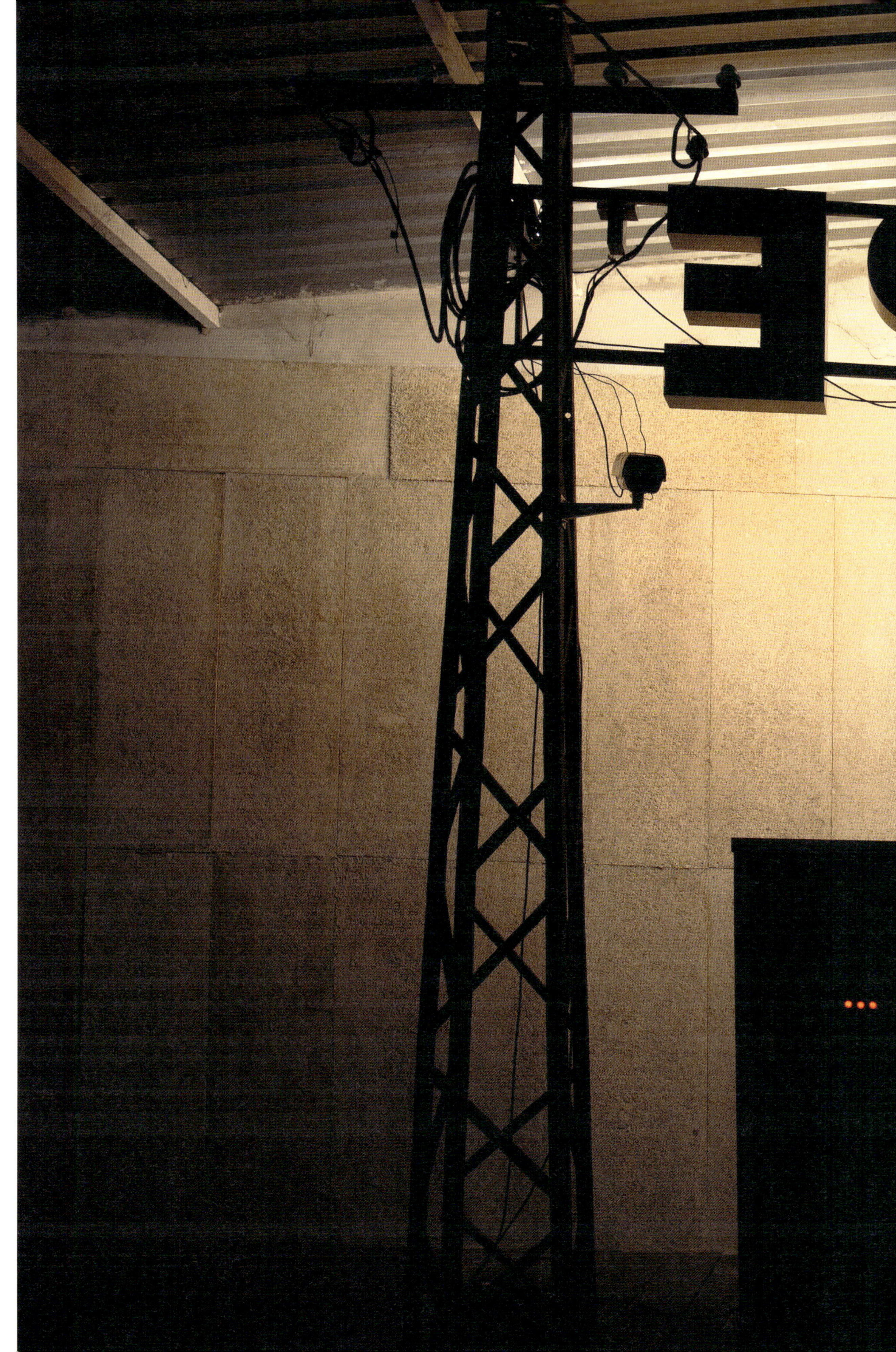

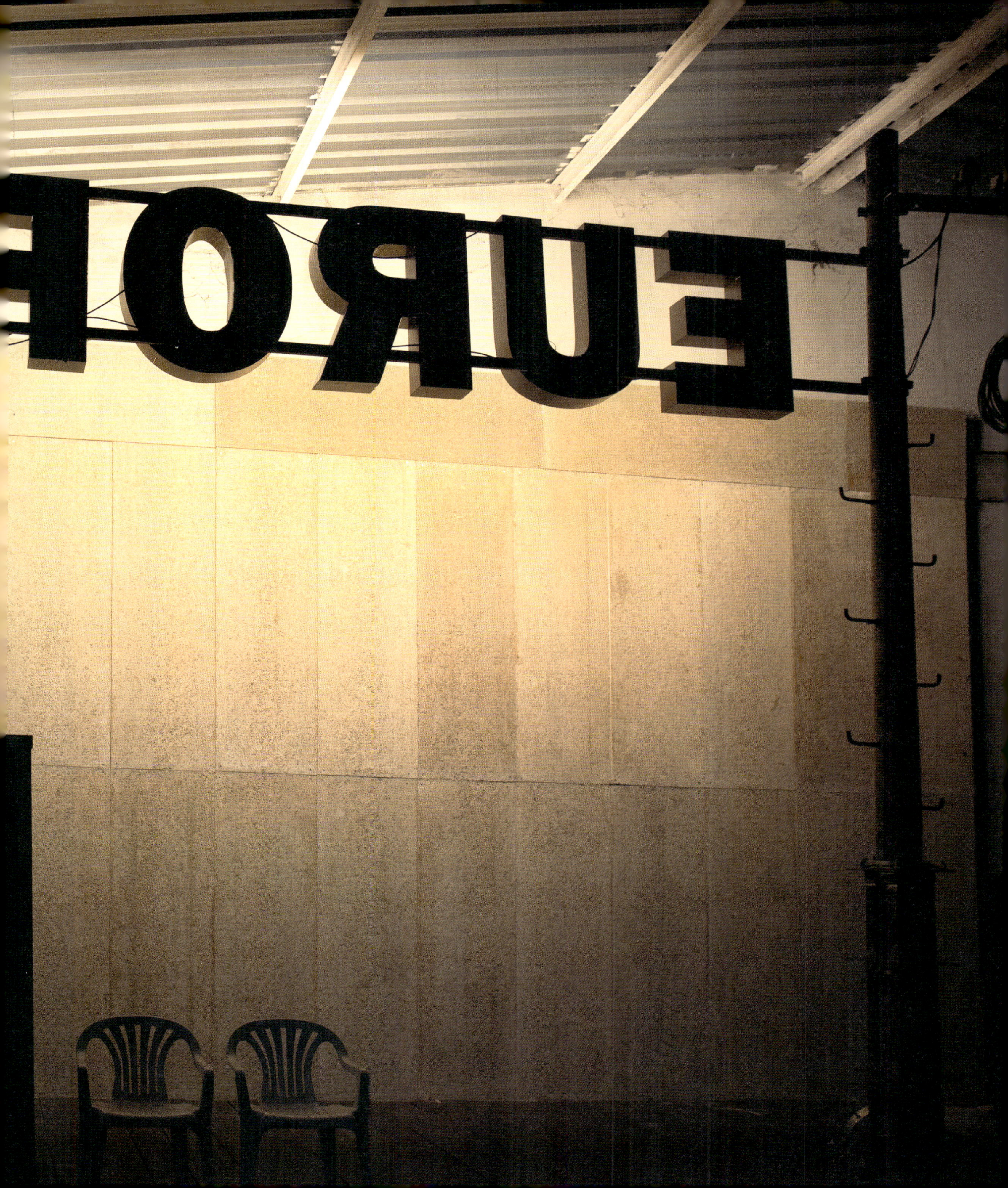

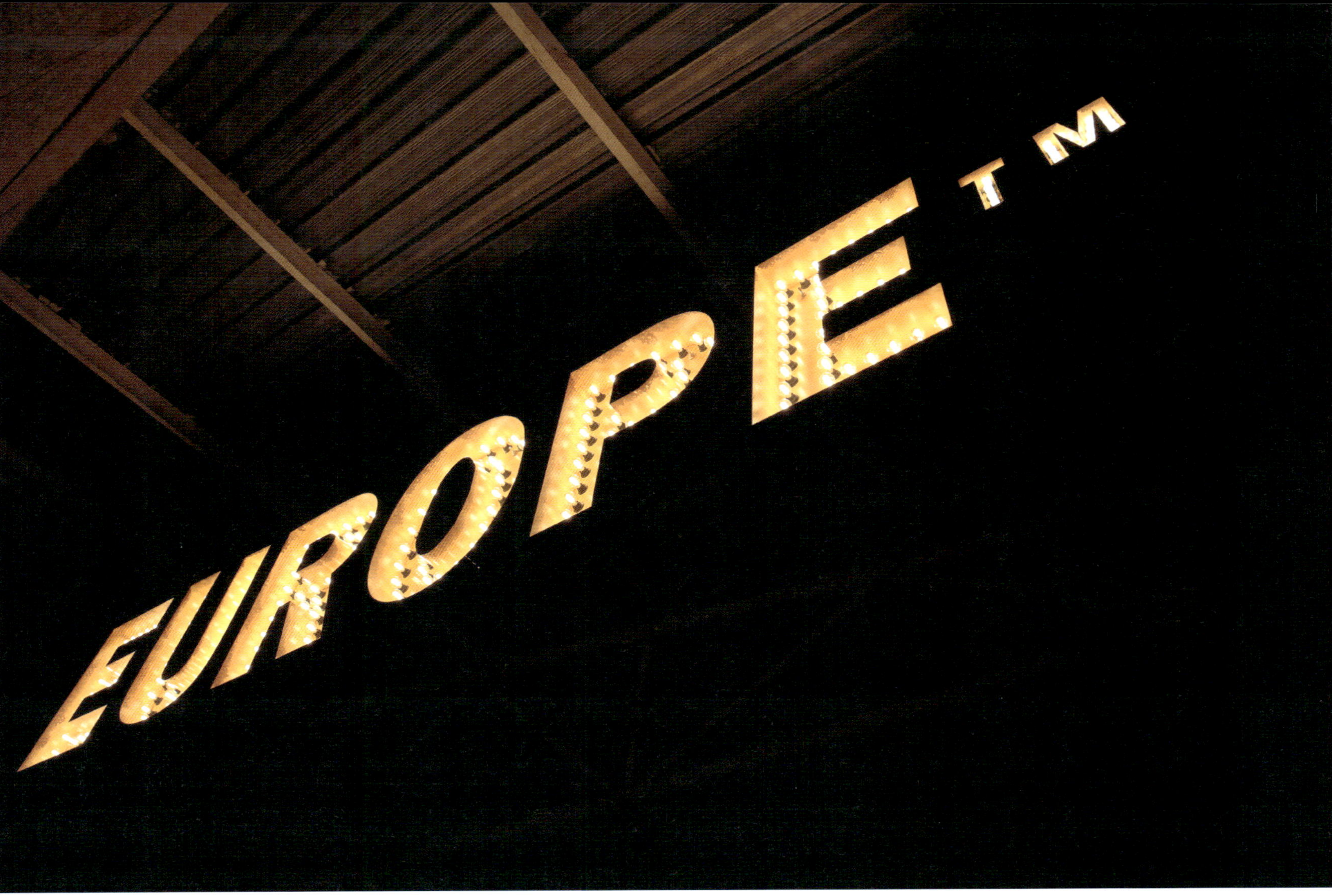

EUROPE ™

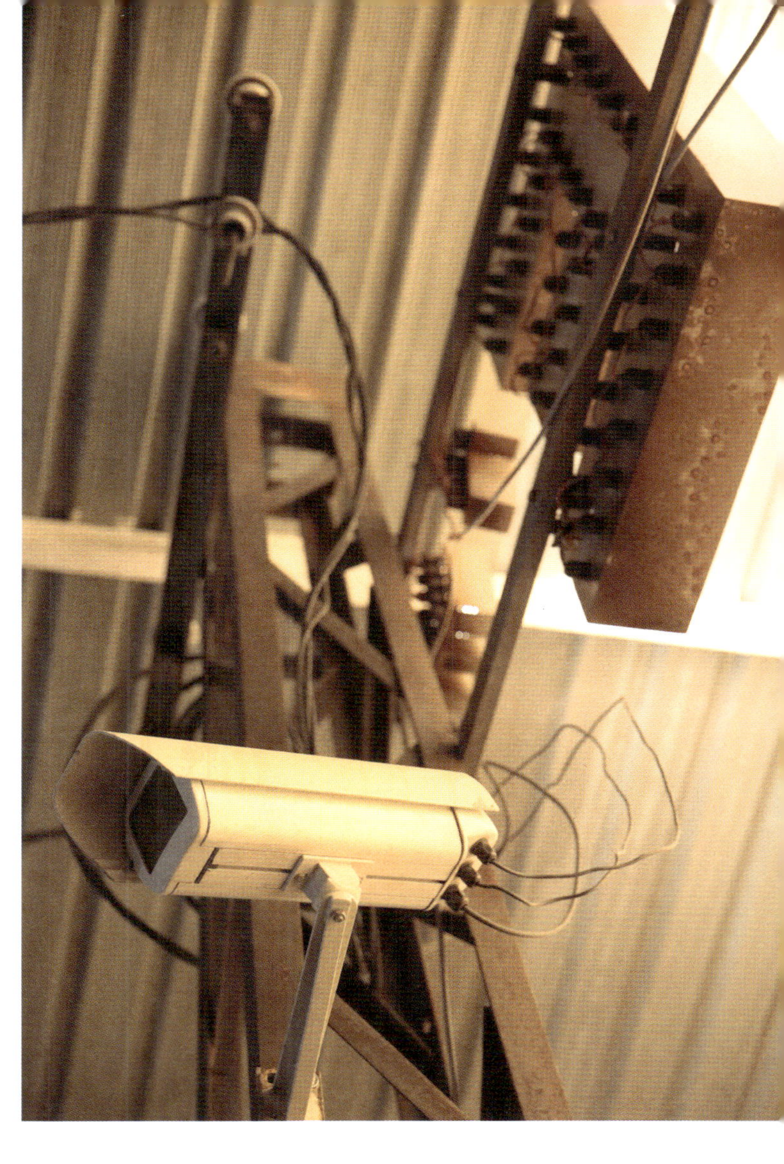

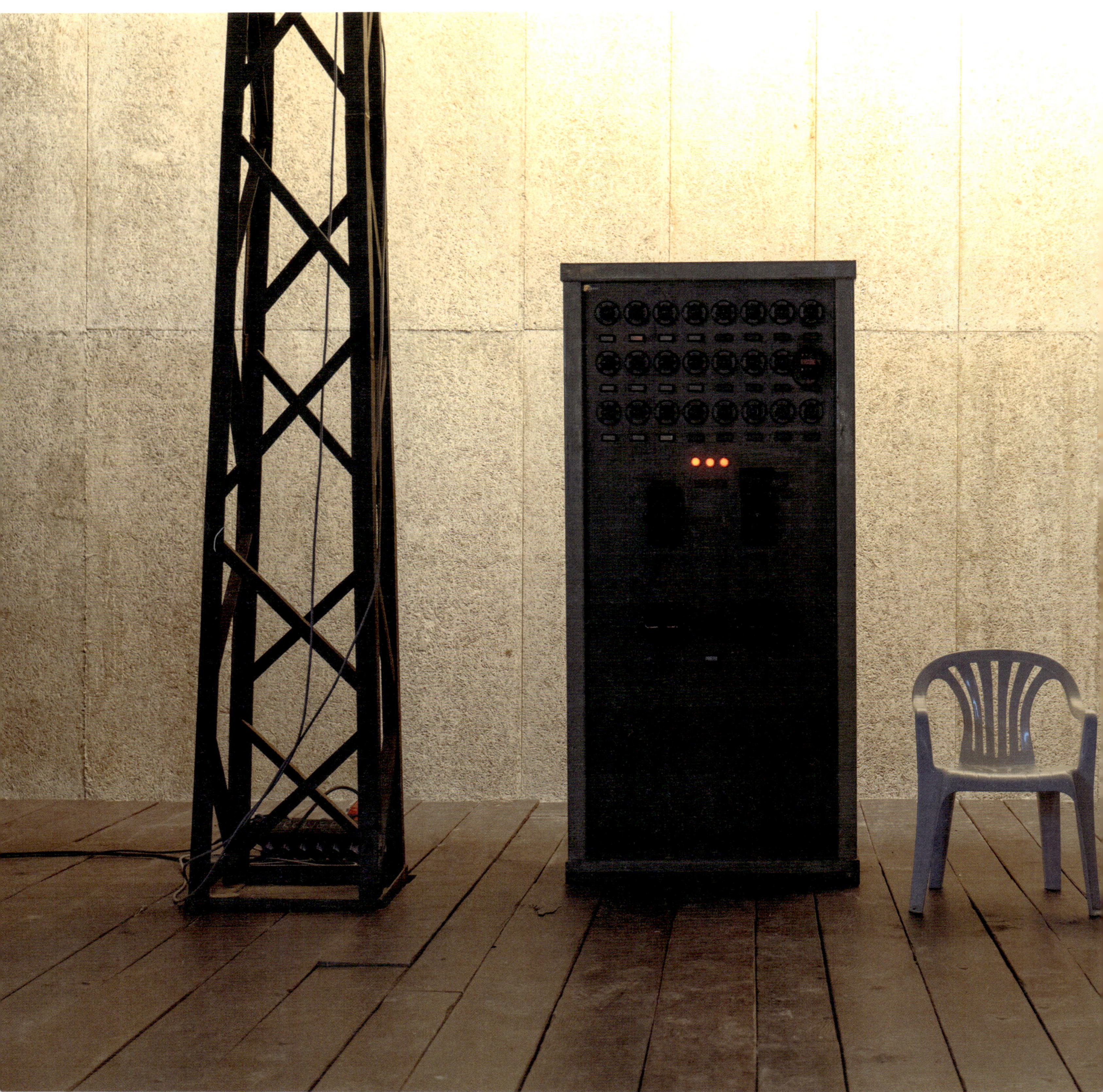

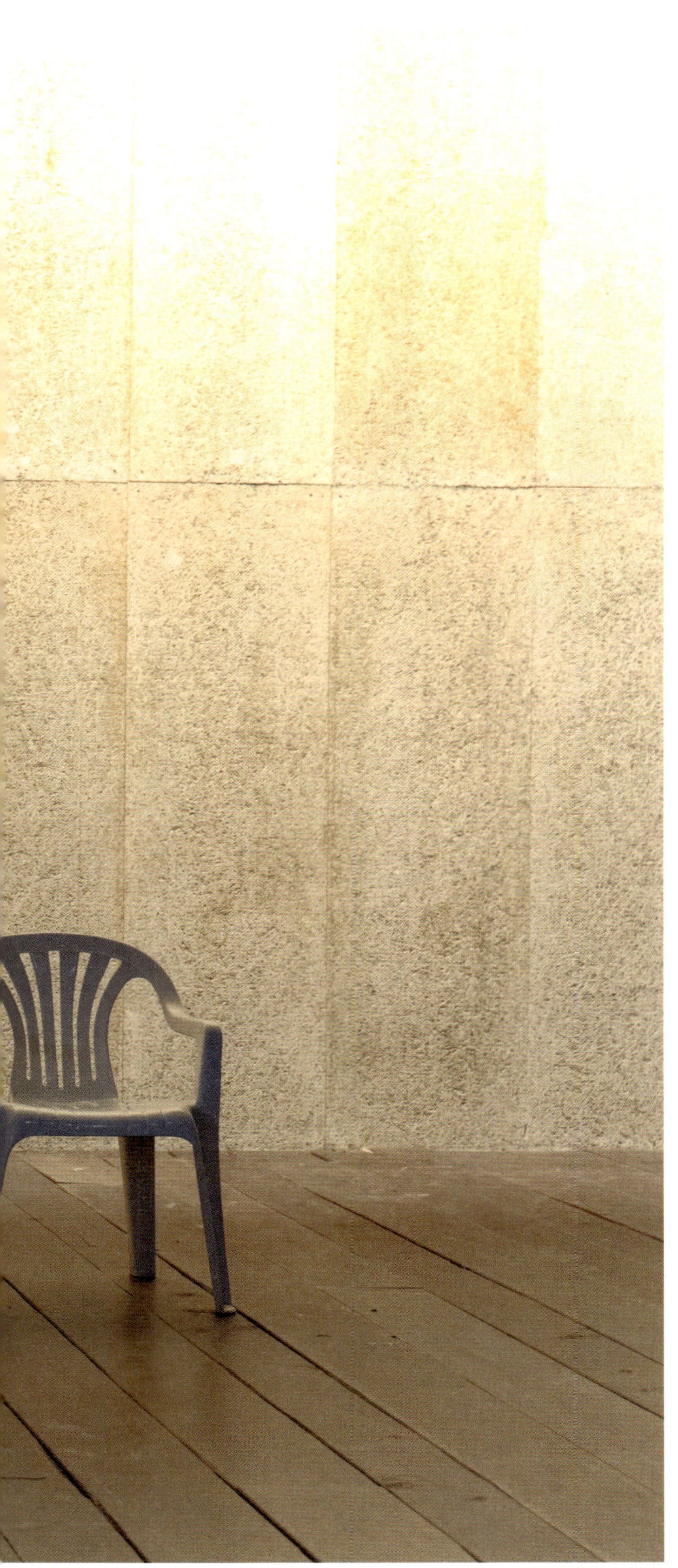

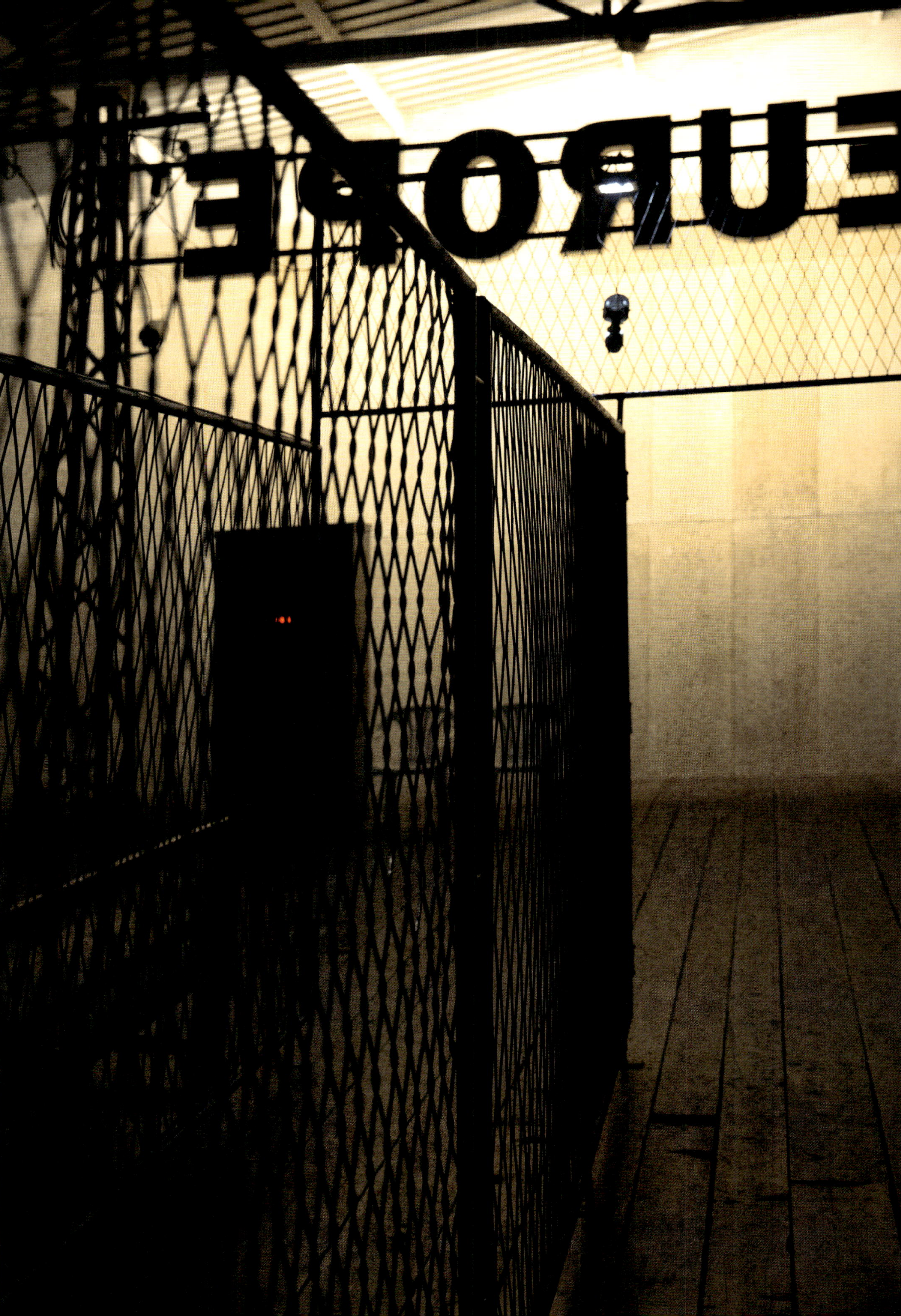

So also saßen wir im Belgrader Schauspielhaus
und freuten uns der Sonne und tranken den Sli-
wowitz und ich rauchte, obwohl ich mein Leben
lang Nichtraucher bin, voller Freude und wusste
RAUCHEN IST FREUDE, wenn es auch überall
in unseren freiheitsliebenden Demokratien etwas
suspekt ist.

Wie sagte schon unser anarchistischer Freund
Luis-August Blanqui 1852, Demokratie ist bubble
gum oder alles oder nichts oder „Was ist schon ein
Demokrat, ich bitte Sie? Dieser Begriff ist vage, banal ohne klare Bedeutung, ein ´Gummibegriff´“ –
wenn also die kleine Zigarette ein ziemlich garsti-
ger Dämon geworden zu sein scheint.

Jedenfalls ist es schön, so in der Sonne zu sitzen
und im 9. Höllengraben mit den Sündern, die
die Zwietracht säen und unsere Körper sind zur
Strafe zerschlitzt. Der Schnaps und die Zigarette
waren es und wir schauten uns in die Augen und
schön war es, da wir wussten man muss mutig
sein, wenn alles vorbei ist, man muss Titoist sein,
wenn Tito tot ist und wenn er die goldene Gürtel-
schnalle der serbischen Könige nicht mehr trägt
und der ostdeutsche und der Belgrader Künstler
am zerbombten Verteidigungsministerium vor-
beigehen und eine rote Rose am Grab von Gawrilo
Prinzip niederlegen. Dürfen wir das denn? Aleksandar Denić darf das. Und dann gehen wir tief in
Dantes Höllenkreise. Wunderbar kreuzt er in sei-
ner Phantasie und schafft für mich dem deutschen
Freund die Räume für unser ungebundenes Spiel
mit unseren mutigen Schauspielern, die Coura-
ge, Schönheit, Wahrheit und alles haben, was wir
brauchen für unser Inferno, für unser Fegefeuer
und unser Paradiso. So geschehen im Belgrader
Herbst des Jahres 2022. Und so reisen wir unver-
drossen durch so viele Städte und Länder. Und oh
Wunder sind noch immer voller Freude und sind
Freunde. Ohne Freundschaft keine Kunst. Und wir
denken an unseren großen und mutigen Genossen
Ossip Mandelstam, der uns den Kompass für die
„Comedia“ und für jede Art von Kunst hinterließ.
„Würden die Säle der Eremitage plötzlich verrückt,
würden sich die Bilder aller Schulen und Meister
von den Nägeln lösen und ineinander übergehen,
sich mischen und die Luft der Säle mit futuristi-
schem Gebrüll und tobender Erregung der Farben
füllen, bekämen wir etwas, was der Danteschen
„Kömödie“ vergleichbar wäre“. So, mein Freund,
jetzt gehen wir ins Trandafilović und trinken pivo
a la Jelen und essen ćevapčići und ich rauche eine
Zigarette.

So we are in Belgrade Drama Theatre, enjoying the sun, drinking schnapps, I am smoking, although I have been a non-smoker all my life, joyfully knowing SMOKING IS JOY, eventhough it is somewhat suspect everywhere in our freedom-loving democracies.

As our anarchist friend Luis-August Blanqui said in 1852, democracy is a bubble or, all or nothing, or "What is a democrat, please? This term is vague, banal, without clear meaning, a pliable term" – when the little cigarette seems to have become such a nasty demon.

Anyway, it's nice to sit like this in the sun, in the ninth pit of hell with the sinners who sow discord and our bodies are slashed for punishment. Schnapps and the cigarette, we are looking into each others eyes, it is nice, we know we have to be brave when it's all over, we have to be titoists when Tito is dead, eventhough he no longer wore the golden belt buckle of the Serbian kings, and the East German artist and Belgrade artist walk past the bombed Ministry of Defense and lay a red rose at Gavrilo Prinzip's grave. Are we allowed to do that? Aleksandar Denić is allowed to. And then we go deep into Dante's circles of hell. He is cruising wonderfully in his imagination and creating for me, his German friend, the spaces for our unbound play with our courageous actors, who have the bravery, beauty, truth and everything we need for our Inferno, our Purgatory and our Paradiso. This was the Belgrade autumn of 2022. And so we travel undaunted through so many cities and countries. What a wonder, we are still full of joy and still friends. There is no art without friendship. And we think of our great and courageous comrade Ossip Mandelstam, who left us the compass for the Commedia and for every kind of art. "If the halls of the Hermitage were suddenly to go mad, if the paintings of all schools and masters were to come loose from their nails and merge, mingle and fill the air of the halls with a futuristic roar and raging excitement of color, we would get something comparable to Dante's *Comedy*". So, my friend, let's go to Trandafilović for a Jelen beer and ćevapčići and I'll smoke a cigarette.

pismo Franka Kastorfa Aleksandru Deniću

I sedimo tako u Beogradskom dramskom pozorištu, radujemo se suncu, pijemo rakiju, ja pušim, iako sam nepušač celog života, radostan i svestan da je PUŠENJE RADOST, iako je ono pomalo sumnjivo svuda u našoj slobodoljubivoj demokratiji.

Kao što je naš prijatelj anarhista Luj-Ogist Blanki još 1852. godine rekao, demokratija je balon ili sve ili ništa, ili „A šta je demokrata, ma molim vas? Ovaj pojam je nejasan, banalan bez jasnog značenja, ´rastegljiv´ – kad je mala cigareta izgleda već postala toliko gadan demon.

Kako god, lepo je sedeti na suncu, u devetom krugu pakla sa grešnicima koji seju razdor, a tela su nam za kaznu razorena. Rakija i cigareta, gledamo smo se u oči, lepo je, znamo da čovek mora da bude hrabar kad sve prođe, da čovek mora da bude titoista kad Tito umre, iako on više na kaišu ne nosi zlatnu kopču srpskih kraljeva, a istočnonemački umetnik i beogradski umetnik prolaze pored bombardovanog Ministarstva odbrane i na grob Gavrila Principa spuštaju crvenu ružu. Da li smemo? Aleksandar Denić sme. I onda ulazimo duboko u Danteove krugove pakla. Divno krstari po mašti, i meni, njegovom nemačkom prijatelju, stvara prostore za našu slobodnu igru sa našim odvažnim glumcima koji poseduju hrabrost, lepotu, istinu i sve ono, što nam je potrebno za naš Pakao, za naše Čistilište i naš Raj. Bilo je to beogradske jeseni 2022 godine. I tako neumorno putujemo kroz mnoge zemlje i gradove. I, gle čuda, i dalje smo puni radosti i prijatelji smo. Nema umetnosti bez prijateljstva. I setimo se našeg velikog i hrabrog druga Osipa Mandeljštama koji nam je ostavio kompas za Komediju i svaku drugu vrstu umetnosti. „Kada bi dvorane Ermitaža najednom poludele, ako bi slike svih škola i majstora najednom pale sa eksera, ušle jedne u druge, smešale se i ispunile vazduh futurističkom rikom i pobesnelom kolorističkom uzrujanošću, dobilo bi se nešto nalik na Danteovu *Komediju*" Eto, prijatelju moj, a sad idemo do Trandafilovića na jelen-pivo i ćevape a ja ću da zapalim jednu.

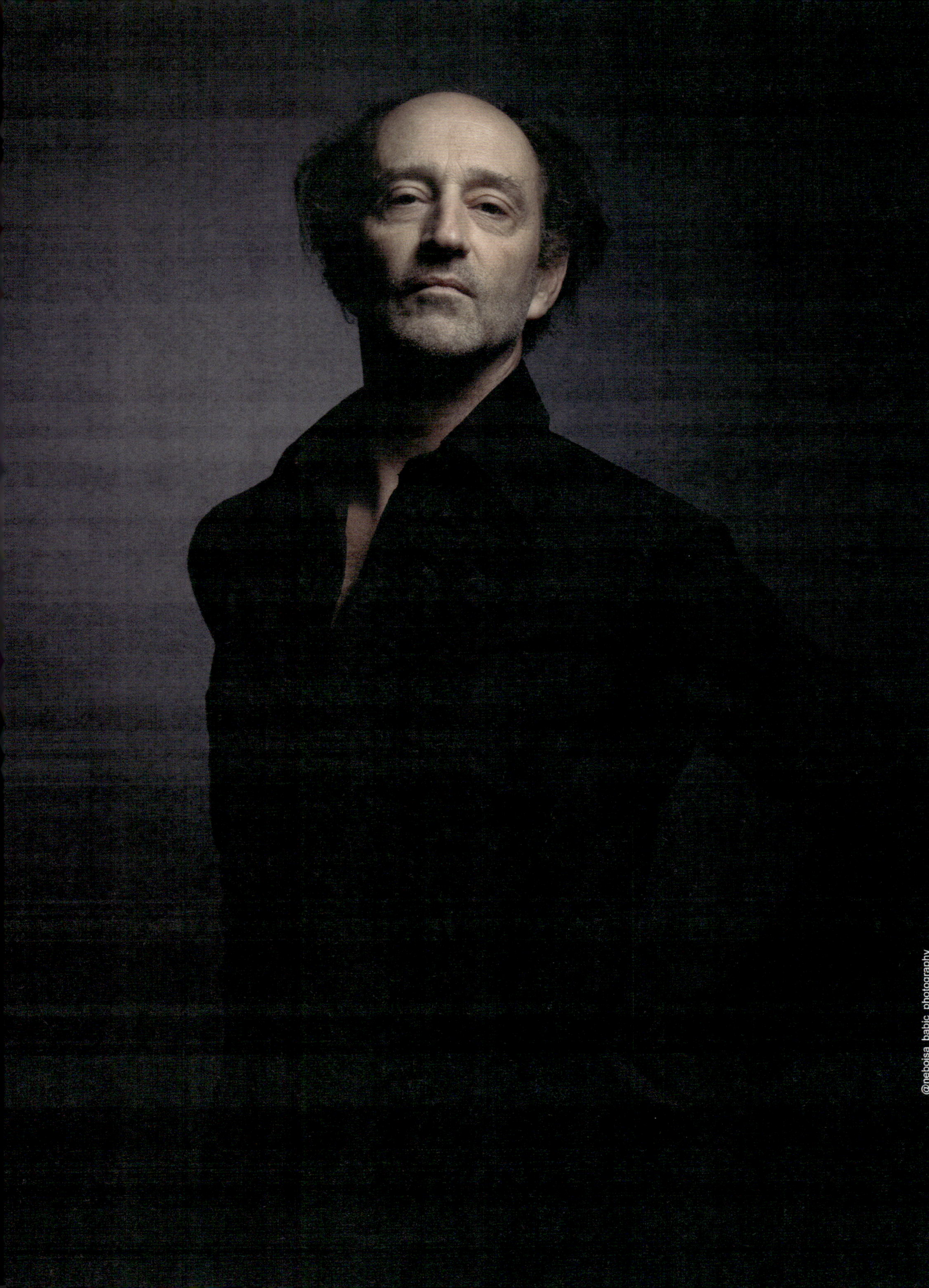
@nebojsa_babic_photography

Aleksandar Denić

Born n 1963 in Belgrade

1992 Graduated from the Faculty of Applied Arts and Design in Belgrade Graduated painter/scenographer

Since 2012, he has been actively participating in the academic community

2012–2015 Associate Professor of Scenography at the Faculty of Art and Design in Belgrade
2015–2016 Full-time professor of scenography at the Faculty of Art and Design in Belgrade
2021 Associate Professor at the Faculty of Dramatic Arts in Belgrade

Began his fruitful career in film as the designer of some of the Yugoslav and Serbian masterpieces of cinematography. He devoted the past decade almost exclusively to theater and opera scenography, the field in which he is recognized as one of the most prolific European creators.

From 1985 to 2021, he worked as the scenographer on the following films:

1985 Tajvanska Kanasta (assistant scenographer), directed by: Goran Marković, FRZ Beograd
1985 Jagode u grlu (assistant scenographer), directed by: Srdjan Karanović, Centar film
1988 Za sada bez dobrog naslova, directed by: Srdjan Karanović, Centar Film Production
1988 Jednog lepog dana, directed by: Boža Nikolić,TV Belgrade Production
1992 Mi nismo andjeli, directed by: Srdjan Dragojević, Avala Film Production
1993 Heidi (assistant scenographer) directed by: Michael Rhodes, Walt Disney TV, Harmony Gold Ltd.
1993 Vizantijsko plavo, directed by: Dragan Marinković,Vans Production
1995 Underground (set designer/ props scenographer), directed by: Emir Kusturica, CIBY 2000
1996 Rasputin (set designer/props scenographer), directed by: Uli Edel, HBO
1997 Tempête dans un verre d'eau, directed by: Aronld Barkus, Double A Productions
1998 Rane, directed by: Srdjan Dragojević, COBRA Production
2001 Super 8 Stories, directed by: Emir Kusturica, Fandango, Pandora, Rasta Film
2001 Boumerang, directed by: Dragan Marinković, Film Link Inc., Vans, Zillion production
2002 Deathwatch, directed by: Michael Basset, FAME Production
2004 Pad u raj, directed by: Miloš Radović, MACT Productions, Neue Impuls Film, Rocketta Film
2006 Guča, directed by: Dušan Milić, RASTA FILM, Pandora, Deluxe film
2007 Agi & Ema, directed by: Milutin Petrović, MONTAGE, ART & POPCORN
2008 Die rote Zora, directed by: Peter Kahane, STUDIO HAMBURG FILM PRODUKTION
2009 Zone of the Death, directed by: Milan Konjević, Milan Todorović, TALKING WOLF PRO
2010 Neke druge priče, directed by: Ana Marija Rosi, BALKAN FILM
2011 Cat Run, directed by: John Stockwell, WORK IN PROGRESS, Lleju Production
2012 Chernobyl Diaries, directed by Bradley Parker, Alcon entertainment
2014 Mala istorija Srbije, (TV series) directed by Jug Radivojević
2014 Travelator, directed by Dušan Milić, Film DELUX international
2015 Darknes, directed by Jug Radivojević, Inat entertainment
2016 Das Rheingold (TV film), directed by Frank Castorf, Festspiele Bayreuth
2016 Die Walküre (TV film) directed by Frank Castorf, Festspiele Bayreuth
2016 Siegfried (TV film) directed by Frank Castorf, Festspiele Bayreuth
2016 Götterdämmerung (TV film) directed by Frank Castorf, Festspiele Bayreuth
2017 Zona Zamfirova 2, directed by Jug Radivojević, RTV Pink
2018 From the House of the Death (TV film) directed by Frank Castorf, Andy Somer, Bayerische Staatsoper
2021 Faust (TV film) directed by Frank Castorf, Jakob Pitzer,ORF, Staatsoper Wien

From 1988 to 2011, he worked on scenography for theater, opera and ballet in Yugoslavia:

1988 Žlivotni venac i drug Slovenjac Aca Popović, directed by Puriša Djordjević, SKC Beograd
1989 Draga Jelena Sergejevna Lj. Razumovska, directed by Gorčin Stojanović, Jugoslovensko dramsko pozorište
1990 Hajde da se igramo, collectively directed by, Jugoslovensko dramsko pozorište
1991 Staza Divljači Franz Xaver Kroetz, directed by Alisa Stojanović, Atelje 212
1991 Žabar Rainer Werner Fassbinder, directed by Gorčin Stojanović, Atelje 212
1992 Nega Mrtvaca Aca Popović, directed by Radmila Vojvodić, Srpsko Narodno pozorište, Novi Sad
1992 Sveti Nik - Nikolas Edvard Kejv život i veze Gorčin Stojanović, directed by Gorčin Stojanović, Bitef teatar
2001 Čovek slučajnosti Jasmina Reza, directed by Tanja Mandić Rigonat, Narodno pozorište
1999 Rodoljupci Jovan Sterija Popović, directed by Dejan Mijač, Jugoslovensko dramsko pozorište
2004 Terasa Jovan Hristić, directed by Tanja Mandić Rigonat, Jugoslovensko dramsko pozorište
2005 Ledeni svitac Vladan Radoman, directed by Tanja Mandić Rigonat, Madlenijanum
2005 Kiseonik Ivan Viripajev, directed by Tanja Mandić Rigonat, Belef festival-Jugoslovensko dramsko pozorište,
2004 Sumnjivo lice Branislav Nušić, directed by Stefan Sablić, Kruševačko Pozorište
2006 Spusti se na zemlju Gordana Goncić, directed by Jug Radivojević, Pozorište na Terazijama
2008 Sudija V. Moberg, directed by Tanja Mandić Rigonat, Narodno Pozorište
2006 Heroji Predrag Perišić, directed by Slavenko Saletović, Pozorište na Terazijama
2009 La Strada F. Felini, directed by Slavenko Saletović, Pozorište na Terazijama
2006 Poseta stare dame Fridrih Direnmat, directed by Stefan Sablić, Bitef teatar
2007 La Kapinera balet directed by Mikele Merola, Pozorište na Terazijama
2007 Hitler i Hitler K.Kostjenko, directed by Tanja Mandić Rigonat, Atelje 212
2007 Krčmarica Mirandolina K.Goldoni, directed by Jug Radivojević, Pozorište Bosko Buha
2008 Talenti i obožavaoci J.Ostrovski, directed by Slavenko Saletović, Narodno Pozorište
2008 Instant seksualno obrazovanje Djordje Milosavljević, directed by Jug Radivojević, Pozorište B. Buha
2008 Seksualne neuroze naših roditelja Lucas Barfus, directed by Tanja Mandić,Narodno Pozorište
2012 Dabogda te majka rodila Vedrana Rudan, directed by Tanja Mandić Rigonat, Pl.Ivan Zajc Rijeka
2008 Bog Pakla Sam Shepard, directed by Svetlana Dimčević, Atelje 212
2009 Dečko koji obećava Nebojša Pajkić,directed by Žanko Tomić, Pozorište Boško Buha
2009 Protuve piju čaj Dragoslav Mihailović,directed by Jug Radivojević, Šabačko pozorište,
2011 Producent Mell Brooks, directed by Jug Radivojević, Pozorište na Terazijama
2011 Heda Gabler Henrik Ibsen, directed by Snežana Trišić, Narodno pozorište u Beogradu
2010 Put oko sveta Branislav Nušić, directed by Jug Radivojević, Kruševacko Pozorište
2010 Igra u Tami Djordje Milosavljević, directed by Jug Radivojević Pozorište Boško Buha
2010 Anželika Jacques Ibert, directed by Stefan Sablić, Opera Madlenijanum
2010 Rita Gaetano Donizetti, directed by Stefan Sablić, Opera Madlenijanum
2010 Na slovo na slovo Duško Radović, directed by Darijan Mihailović Pozorište na Terazijama
2009 Moć sudbine G.Verdi, directed by Darijan Mihailović Opera Narodno Pozorište Beograd
2009 Svici Tena Štivičić, directed by Tanja Mandić Rigonat, Atelje 212
2011 Zli dusi Fjodor M. Dostojevski, directed by Tanja Mandić Rigonat, Narodno pozorište u Beogradu
2011 Jovča Borisav Stanković, directed by Jug Radivojević, Šabačko pozorište

From 2012 he worked on scenography for theater, opera and ballet on the international stage:

2012 Adio Kauboju Olja Savičević Ivančević, directed by Ivica Buljan, Splitski ljetni festival
2013 Konstantin Dejan Stojiljković, directed by Jug Radivojević, Narodno pozorište u Beogradu
2013 Še vedno vihar Peter Handke, directed by Ivica Buljan, SNG Ljubljana
2014 Ana Karenjina Lav Tolstoj, directed by Jug Radivojević, Madlenijanum
2014 Naši sinovi Vojislav Jovanović Marambo, directed by Tanja Mandić Rigonat, Narodno pozorište u Beogradu
2014 Striček Vanja Anton Čehov, directed by Ivica Buljan, SSG Trieste
2014 Vučjak Miroslav Krleža, directed by Ivica Buljan, Hrvatsko narodno kazalište Zagreb
2015 Mamma Mia Benny Andersson Björn Ulvaeus, directed by Jug Radivojević, Pozorište na Terazijama
2015 Elementarne čestice Michel Houellebecq, directed by Ivica Buljan, Dubrovačke ljetne igre
2015 Jugoslavija moja dežela Goran Vojnović, directed by Ivica Buljan, SNG Ljubljana
2016 Pijani Ivan Viripaev, directed by Boris Liješević, Atelje 212
2016 Hotel Slobodan promet George Feydeau, directed by Bori Liješević, Jugoslovensko dramsko pozorište
2016 Tri zime Tena Štivičić, directed by Ivica Buljan, Hrvatsko narodno kazalište, Zagreb
2017 Ljudožerci Gregor Strniša, directed by Ivica Buljan, SNG Maribor
2017 Fantom iz opere Andrew Lloyd Webber, directed by Jug Radivojević, Pozorište na Terazijama

2017 Kos David Harrower, directed by Miki Manojlović, Radionica integracije, Beograd
2017 Ciganin ali najljepši Kristian Novak, directed by Ivica Buljan, Hrvatsko narodno kazalište Zagreb
2018 Svetozar Milovan Vitezović, directed by Jug Radivojević, Srpsko Narodno pozorište, Novi Sad
2018 Brilijantin Warren Casey, Jim Jacobs, directed by Jug Radivojević, Ljubljana Slovenija
2018 Zašto je poludeo gospodin R.? Rainer Werner Fassbinder, directed by Bobo Jelčić, Jugoslovensko dramsko pozorište
2019 Tri sestre A. Čehov, directed by Bobo Jelčić, Hrvatsko narodno kazalište
2019 Knjeginja od Foli Beržera George Feydeau, directed by Jug Radivojević, Narodno pozorište Niš
2020 Sa druge strane jastuka directed by Jug Radivojević, Pozorište na Terazijama
2021 Tiho teče Misisipi Vladimir Tabašević, directed by, Ivica Buljan Beogradsko dramsko pozorište
2021 U čeljusti medveda David Crook, directed by Svetlana Dimčević, Bitef teatar
2021 Gospodjica Julija Avgust Strindberg, directed by Haris Pašović, Madlenijanum
2022 My name is Goran Stefanovski Goran Stefanovski, directed by Branislav Mićunović, Drama Theatre Skopje
2022 Shakespeare in love Marc Norman and Tom Stoppard,directed by Ana Tomović
2023 Idiot Fjodor Dostojevski, directed by Ivica Buljan,BDP,Beograd
2023 (PRA)Faust, Johan Volfgang Gete directed by Boris Liješević,BDP,Beograd

In 2008, he directed the stage cantata Atlas by Anja Djordjević at the Yugoslav Drama Theatre

Numerous critical and scholarly reviews have been devoted to Denić's theater scenographies. His scenes
are characterized by monumentality, architectural and scenographic constructions that, with bold innovation,
examine the boundaries between art and applied art, reality and fantasy. His stage design is often characterized
by disparity between scenographic details and the environments described in dramatic works that are staged.
This artistic Freedom is recognized as Denić's unique vision of drama texts and a kind of author's signature. An
abundance of stage elements that have independence in relation to the written original, represents a consciously developed system of visual communication. Engaged messages are communicated through the semioticization
of certain stage elements, guided by the author's intention to create a fictitious dramatic space, which sets a new
theme for the piece, a visual way of recontextualizing the dramatic text.

From 2012, he collaborated with the most important European theaters and cultural institutions, from the Viennese
Burgtheater and Berlin Volksbühne, to the Paris Odeon, working on stage sets for plays, operas and ballets:

2012 La Dame aux Camélias Alexandre Dumas, directed by Frank Castorf, Théâtre de l'Odéon, Paris
2012 Amerika Franc Kafka, directed by Frank Castorf, Schauspielehaus Zürich
2013 Das Duell Anton Čehov, directed by Frank Castorf, Volksbühne Berlin
2013 Das Rheingold – Der Ring des Nibelungen Richard Wagner, conductor Kiril Petrenko directed by Frank
Castorf, Bayreuther Festspiele
2013 Die Walküre – Der Ring des Nibelungen Richard Wagner, conductor Kiril Petrenko directed by Frank
Castorf, Bayreuther Festspiele
2013 Siegfried – Der Ring des Nibelungen Richard Wagner, conductor Kiril Petrenko directed by Frank
Castorf, Bayreuther Festspiele
2013 Götterdämmerung – Der Ring des Nibelungen Richard Wagner, conductor Kiril Petrenko directed by
Frank Castorf, Bayreuther Festspiele
2013 Reise ans Ende der Nacht Louis-Ferdinand Céline, directed by Frank Castorf, Residenztheater München
2014 Faust J.W.Goethe, directed by Martin Kušej, Burgtheater Wien
2015 Gemetzel Albert Ostermaier directed by Thomas Schadt, Nibelungenfestspiele Worms
2015 Pastor Ephraim Magnus Hans Henny Jahnn, directed by Frank Castorf, Deutsches SchauSpielHaus
Hamburg
2015 Baal Bertolt Brecht, directed by Frank Castorf, Residenztheater München
2015 Tschewengur Andrej Platonov, directed by Frank Castorf, Staatstheater Stuttgart
2016 Die Abenteuer des guten Soldaten Švejk im Weltkrieg Jaroslav Hašek, directed by Frank Castorf,
Residenztheater München
2016 Der Schweinestall Pier Paolo Pasolini, directed by Ivica Buljan, Residenztheater München
2016 Die Kabale der Scheinheiligen. Das Leben des Herrn de Molière Mihail Bulgakov, directed by Frank
Castorf, Volksbühne Berlin
2016 Faust Charles Gounod, conductor Bertrand de Billy, directed by Frank Castorf, Wiener Staatsoper
2017 Faust J.W.Goethe, directed by Frank Castorf, Volksbühne Berlin
2017 Die fremde Frau und der Mann unter dem Bet Fjodor Dostojevski, directed by Frank Castorf, Schauspielehaus Zürich

2017 Eines langen Tages Reise in die Nacht Eugene O'Neill Schauspiel Stuttgart, directed by Armin Petras
2017 Les Misérables Victor Hugo, directed by Frank Castorf, Berliner Ensemble
2018 Der haarige Affe Eugene O'Neill, directed by Frank Castorf, Deutsches SchauSpielHaus Hamburg
2018 Der Balkon Jean Genet, directed by Ivica Buljan, Residenztheater München
2018 Aus einem Totenhaus Leoš Janáček, conductor Simone Young,directed by Frank Castorf, Bayerische Staatsoper München
2018 Don Juan Molière, directed by Frank Castorf, Residenztheater München
2018 Hunger Knut Hamsun, directed by Frank Castorf, Salzburger Festspiele
2018 Ein grüner Junge Fjodor Dostojevski, directed by Frank Castorf, Schauspiele Koeln
2019 Galileo Galilei–Das Theater und die Pest Bertolt Brecht, directed by Frank Castorf, Berliner Ensemble
2019 Bajazet Racine/Artaud, directed by Frank Castorf, Théâtre Vidy-Lausanne
2019 Justiz Friedrich Dürrenmatt, directed by Frank Castorf, Schauspiele Zürich
2019 La forza del destino Giuseppe Verdi, directed by Frank Castorf, Deutsche Oper Berlin
2019 Faust J.W.Goethe, directed by Martin Kušej, Burgtheater Wien
2020 Bestialitetens historie Jens Bjørneboe, directed by Ivica Buljan, Det Norske Teatret Oslo
2020 Molto Agitato György Ligeti/Johannes Brahms/Georg Friedrich Händel/Kurt Weill, conductor Kent Nagano, directed by Frank Castorf, Staatsoper Hamburg
2020 Die Vögel Walter Braunfels, conductor Ingo Metzmacher, directed by Frank Castorf, Bayerische Staatsoper München
2021 Fabian Erich Kästner, directed by Frank Castorf, Berliner Ensemble
2021 Vsi ptice Wajdi Mouawad, directed by Ivica Buljan, Mini teatar Ljubljana
2021 Faust Charles Gounod, conductor Bertrand de Billy, directed by Frank Castorf, Wiener Staatsoper
2021 Lärm. Blindes Sehen. Blinde sehen! Elfride Jelinek, Directed by Frank Castorf, Akdemietheater Wien
2021 Zdenek Adamec Peter Handke, directed by Frank Castorf, Burgtheater Wien
2021 Der Geheimagent Joseph Conrad, directed by Frank Castorf, Deutsches SchauSpielHaus Hamburg
2022 Molière – Ich bin ein Dämon, Fleisch geworden und als Mensch verkleidet, directed by Frank Castorf, Schauspiele Koeln
2022 Schwarzes Meer, directed by Frank Castorf, Landestheater St. Pölten
2022 Wallenstein, directed by Frank Castorf, Staatsschauspiel Dresden
2022 Kdo se boji Virginie Woolf? Edward Albee, directed by Ivica Buljan, Mini Teater Ljubljana
2022 Božanstvena komedija Dante Aligijeri, directed by Frank Castorf, BDP Beograd
2023 Boris Godunow Modest P. Mussorgsky, directed by Frank Castorf, Hamburgische Staatsoper
2023 Medea, directed by Frank Castorf, Epidauros Festival
2023 Angeli v Ameriki Tony Kushner, directed by Ivica Buljan, Mini Teater Ljubljana
2023 Jutranja zvezda Karl Ove Knausgård,directed by Ivica Buljan,SNG Drama Ljubljana
2023 Red Water Jurica Pavičić directed by Ivica Buljan HNK Split
2023 Roberto Zucco Bernard-Marie Koltès,directed by Ivica Buljan, Det Norske Teatret, Oslo
2024 Heldenplatz Thomas Bernhard directed by Frank Castorf, Burgtheater Wien

2020 "Vererben der Wut" Oder John Heartfield erfindet das epische Theater Rückblick und Nachwirkungen
Online-Projekt der Sektion Darstellende Kunst/Akademie der Künste, Berlin

Selected exhibiting activities:

1987 Exhibition To Frizure, SKC, Belgrade
1990 Exhibition Iz života veverica, SKC, Belgrade
2004 Exhibition True Lies, Ludwig Museum, Budapest
2019 Exhibition Aleksandar Denić, the world builder: photos of his stage sets, Deutsche Oper Berlin
2022 Exhibition Poetics of the Real. German avant-garde stage design 1989-2019, Madrid

In the past decade, he became one of the busiest European scenographers. In his visual interpretations of dramatic texts, the scene becomes a peculiar and elaborate semiotic system that considers postmodernism through artistic means everyday life, history, identity, the relationship between the theatrical and the media spectacle, as well as social tasks and opportunities of art itself. It is for this reason that Denić's stage designs represent some of the most successful and critically acclaimed European and global visual dramaturgies that self-consciously explore their own communication potentials. He is the recipient of numerous awards.

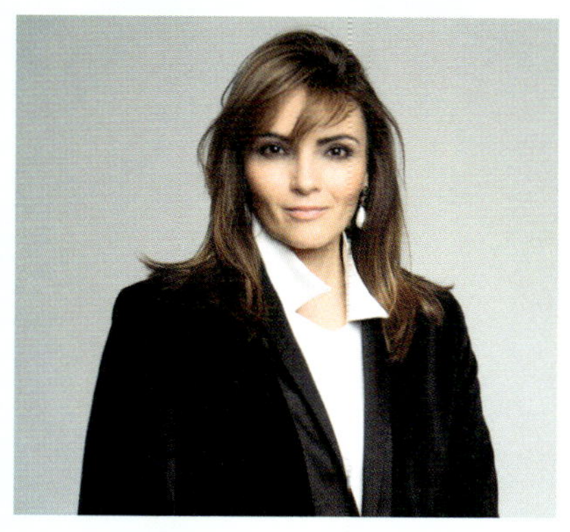

Ksenija Samardžija, after completing her degree in Art History at the Faculty of Philosophy in Belgrade and passing the curatorial exam at the National Museum in Belgrade, took the initiative to establish the artistic association PODR.UM in 2013. Through this endeavor, she has played a vital role in coordinating a wide range of exhibitions, art residency programs, presentations, and other events that aim to build meaningful connections between artists and the public. Additionally, her involvement in international projects has had a significant impact on promoting contemporary artists and creating opportunities for the showcasing of new artwork. Her experience at the Heritage House (Belgrade) has further honed her expertise in curatorial work, collection management, and understanding market conditions.

Since 2019, Samardžija has been serving as the director of the Foundation Saša Marčeta, which is committed to supporting contemporary art and operates within the 19th-century hictoric palace, Bioskop Balkan.

Ksenija Samardžija, nakon završetka studija istorije umetnosti na Filozofskom fakultetu u Beogradu i položenog kuratorskog ispita u Narodnom muzeju u Beogradu, osniva umetničko udruženje PODR.UM 2013. godine. Kroz ovu inicijativu, odigrala je ključnu ulogu u koordinaciji različitih izložbi, programa umetničkih rezidencija, prezentacija i drugih događaja čiji je cilj uspostavljanje značajnih veza između umetnika i publike. Takođe, njen angažman u međunarodnim projektima imao je uticaj na promovisanje savremenih umetnika i stvaranje prilika za predstavljanje njihovog rada. Iskustvo u Kući legata (Beograd) dodatno je usavršilo njeno primenjeno znanje u kustoskom radu i upravljanju zbirkama.

Od 2019. godine, Samardžija obavlja dužnost direktora Fondacije Saša Marčeta, koja se obavezuje da podržava savremenu umetnost i deluje unutar istorijskog zdanja Bioskopa Balkan.

Stevan Vuković is a curator, art historian and theoretician by profession. He graduated in philosophy at the Faculty of Philosophy of the University of Belgrade, and attended doctoral studies at the same department, as well as post-graduate studies in art theory at the Jan van Eyck Aakademie in Maastricht and art studies in public space at the Bauhaus Dessau. He has been publishing texts on contemporary art, theory and philosophy of art continuously since 1992. He won the Lazar Trifunović award for the best text on art in Serbia in 1998. Since 1996, he has been working as an independent curator. He designed and realized a large number of author's and co-author's exhibitions, among which stand out: "Second Yugoslav Youth Biennale", Konkordija, Vršac (1996), "Balkan Consulate: Mission Belgrade", Rotor Galerija, Graz (2002), "Urban Fog of Belgrade" *Urban Drift*, Berlin, (2003), "Belgrade Art Inc." Secession, Vienna (2004), "When I open my eyes I see a film," Modern Gallery, Ljubljana, (2010/11), "The Last Youth in Yugoslavia", Museum of the History of Yugoslavia, Belgrade (2011/12), "Before the Court", Gallery Nadežda Petrović, Čačak (2016), "The death of art! Long live art!", 19th Biennale of Arts in Pancevo, 2020.

Stevan Vuković je po vokaciji kustos, istoričar i teoretičar umetnosti. Diplomirao je filozofiju na Filozofskom fakultetu Univerziteta u Beogradu, i pohađao doktorske studije na istom odeljenju, kao i postdiplomske studije teorije umetnosti u na Jan van Eyck Aakademie u Mastrihtu i studije umetnosti u javnom prostoru na Bauhaus Dessau. Objavljuje tekstove o savremenoj likovnoj umetnosti, teoriji i filozofiji umetnosti u kontinuitetu od 1992. Dobitnik je nagrade Lazar Trifunović, za najbolji tekst o umetnosti u Srbiji 1998. Od 1996. radi kao samostalni kustos. Osmislio je i realizovao je veći broj autorskih i koautorskih izložbi, među kojima se izdvajaju: "Drugo jugoslovensko bijenale mladih", Konkordija, Vršac (1996) , "Balkan Konzulat: Misija Beograd", Rotor Galerija, Grac (2002), „Urban Fog of Belgrade" *Urban Drift*, Berlin, (2003.), "Belgrade Art Inc." Secession, Beč (2004),„Kada otvorim oči vidim film," Moderna galerija, Ljubljana, (2010/11), „Poslednja mladost u Jugoslaviji", Muzej istorije Jugoslavije, Beograd (2011/12), „Pred sudom", Galerija Nadežda Petrović, Čačak (2016), "Smrt umetnosti! Živela umetnost!", 19. Bijenale umetnosti u Pančevu, 2020.

Exposition Coloniale

The Pavilion of the Republic of Serbia at the 60th International Art Exhibition – La Biennale di Venezia
April 20th – November 24th, 2024
Paviljon Republike Srbije na 60. Međunarodnoj izložbi savrmene umetnosi u Veneciji
20. april – 24. novembar 2024.

EXHITION | IZLOŽBA
Aleksandar Denić
Exhibition Coloniale

CURATOR | KUSTOS
Ksenija Samardžija

COMMISSIONER | KOMESAR
Jelena Medaković

CONSTRUCTION MENAGEMENT | IZRADA EKSPONATA
CDPC doo Belgrade, Arch. Rade Mihajlović

PROJECT ART DEPARTEMENT ASSISTANT | ASISTENT IZRADE EKSPONATA
Danilo Mladjenović

ARTIST ASSISTANT | ASISTENT UMETNIKA
Nebojsa Antešević

CURATOR ASSISTANT | ASISTENT KUSTOSA
Ljubica Milovanović

VISUAL IDENTITY | VIZUELNI IDENTITET
Isidora M. Nikolić

PRESS OFFICE | ODNOSI SA JAVNOŠĆU
Lightbox srl

PROGRAMSKI SAVET | ADVISORY BOARD
**Radoš Antonijević, Nikola Šuica, Dragan Zdravković,
Ivana Bašičević Antić, Mileta Poštić**

PRODUCTION AND ORGANIZATION | PRODUKCIJA I ORGANIZACIJA
**Muzej grada Beograda
Fondacija muzeja grada Beograda
CDPC doo Belgrade**

TECHNICAL INSTALATION AND SUPORT | TEHNIČKA POSTAVKA I REALIZACIJA
**CDPC doo Belgrade
KAI Arhitecture Interiors**

SPECIAL PROJECT ADVISER | SAVETNIK PROJEKTA
Christopher Yggdre

The Pavilion of Republic of Serbia is realized under the patronage of the Ministry of Culture of Republic of Serbia and organized by City Museum Belgrade, in collabortaion with CDPC doo.

Paviljon Republike Srbije se realizuje pod pokroviteljstvom Ministarva kulture u ogranizaciji Muzeja grada Beograda u saradnji sa CDPC doo.

I thank Grafo lit and special thanks go to Saša Marčeta Fondation for the support.

Zahvaljujem se Grafo litu, a posebno se zahvalujem Saša Marčeta Fondaciji na podršci.

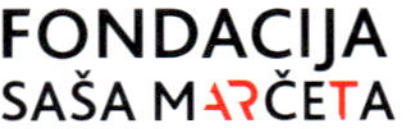

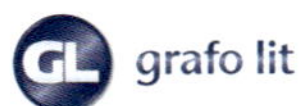

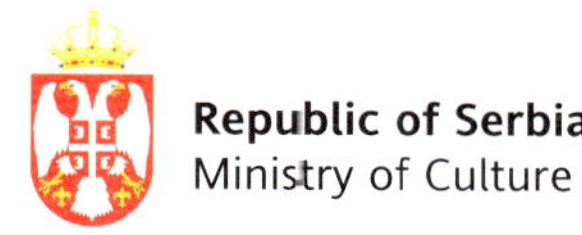 Republic of Serbia
Ministry of Culture

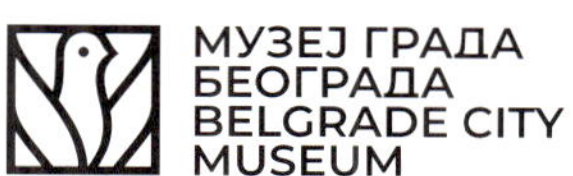 МУЗЕЈ ГРАДА БЕОГРАДА
BELGRADE CITY MUSEUM

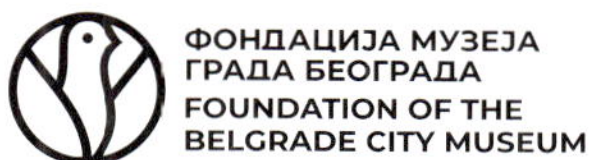 ФОНДАЦИЈА МУЗЕЈА ГРАДА БЕОГРАДА
FOUNDATION OF THE BELGRADE CITY MUSEUM

PUBLISHER | IZDAVAČ
Muzej grada Beograda | Belgrade City Museum
Mousse Publishing

FOR PUBLISHER | ZA IZDAVAČA
Jelena Medaković

AUTORI TEKSTOVA | TEXTS AUTORS
Ksenija Samardžija
Stevan Vuković
Christopher Yggdre
Frank Castorf

TRANSLATION | PREVOD
Mark Brogan, Siniša Vlajković, Bojana Denić

DESIGN | DIZAJN
Isidora M. Nikolić

PHOTOGRAPHY | FOTOGRAFIJA
Vladimir Miladinović, Aleksandar Denić

PORTRAIT PHOTOGRAPHY | FOTOGRAFIJA PORTRETA
Nebojša Babić

ENGLISH PROOFREADING | LEKTURA ENGLESKOG TEKSTA
Mark Brogan, Dr Paul Leonard Murray

SERBIAN PROOFREADING | LEKTURA SRPSKOG TEKSTA
Milena Klačanin, Sonja Ocić

PRINT | ŠTAMPA
Birograf

CIRCULATION | TIRAŽ
1000

ISBN Belgrade City Museum 978-86-6433-068-8
ISBN Mousse Publishing 978-88-6749-625-9

€ 25 / $ 27

CIP - Каталогизација у публикацији
Народна библиотека Србије, Београд
792.071.1:929 Денић А.(083.824)
7.038.53(497.11)"20"(083.824)
DENIĆ, Aleksandar, 1963-
    Aleksandar Denić : Exposition Coloniale : [The Pavilion of the Republic of Serbia at the 60th International Art Exhibition – La Bienale di Venezia, April 23th – November 24th, 2024] / [autori tekstova, texts autors Ksenija Samardžija ... [et al.]] ; [translation, prevod Mark Brogan, Siniša Vlajković, Bojana Denić] ; [photography, fotografija Vladimir Miladinović, Aleksandar Denić]. - Beograd = Belgrade : Muzej grada Beograca, 2024 ([Beograd] : Birograf). - 157 str. : fotogr. ; 27 cm
Deo teksta uporedo na engl. i srp. jeziku. - Umetnikova slika. - Biographes: str. 153-157. - Bibliografija uz tekst.
ISBN 978-86-6433-068-8
a) Денић, Александар (1963-) - Изложбени каталози
COBISS.SR-ID 138579465

Distributed by
Mousse Publishing
Contrappunto s.r.l.
Via Pier Candido Decembrio 28,
20137, Milan–Italy

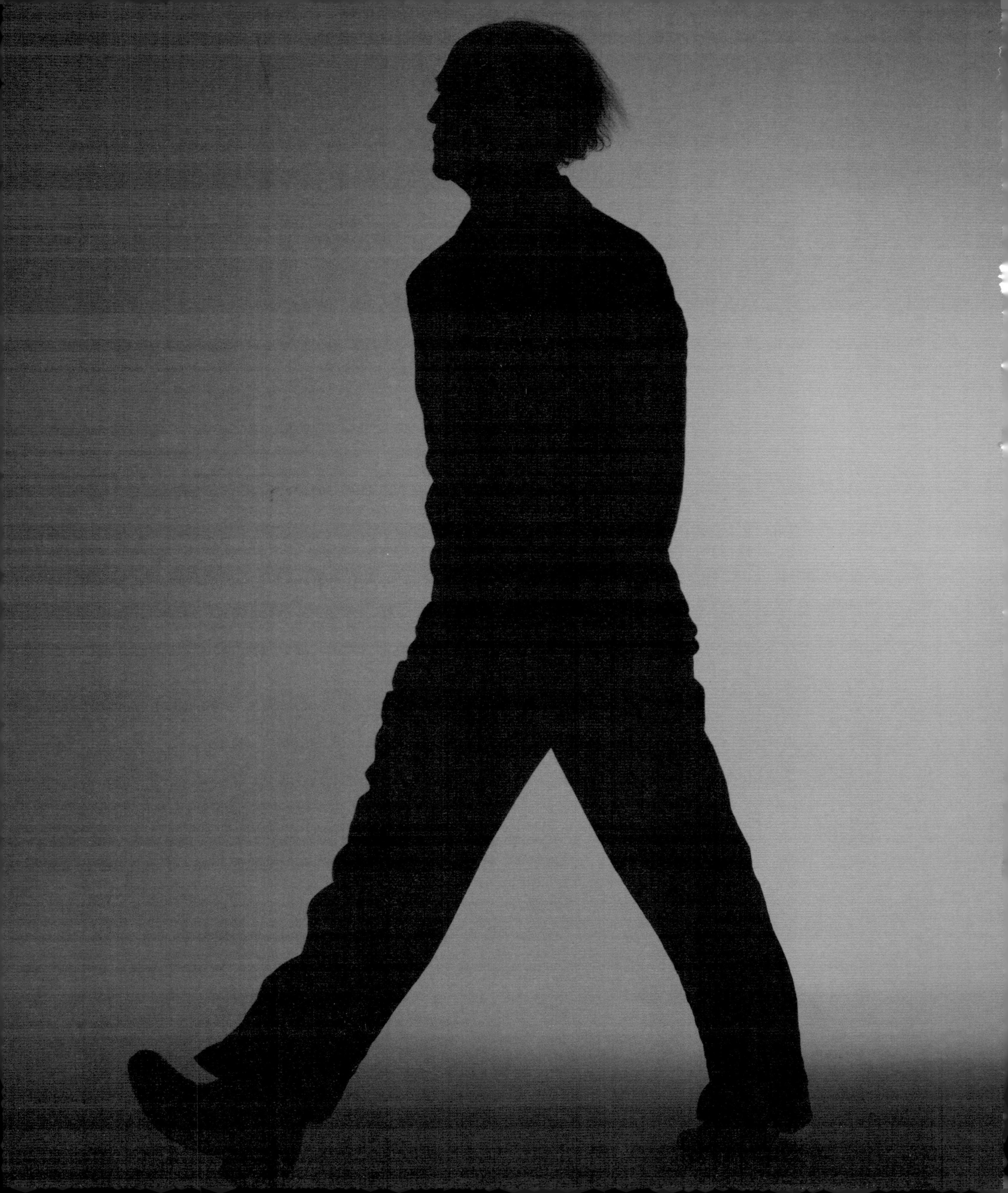